HAL LINDSEY

&

THE RESTORATION OF THE JEWS

Other titles from Still Waters Revival Books

Christ's Second Coming: Will it be Premillennial?
David Brown (Introduction by Ken Gentry)

The Five Points of Christian Reconstruction from the Lips of Our Lord
Mark Duncan

Calvinism, Hyper-Calvinism and Arminianism
Ken Talbot & Gary Crampton
(Introduction by Dr. D. James Kennedy)

Messiah the Prince or The Mediatorial Dominion of Jesus Christ
William Symington

A Display of Arminianism
John Owen

Calvinism in History
N.S. McFetridge

A Defense of Liberty Against Tyrants
Junius Brutus

Forthcoming:

Television and Dominion
Steve Schlissel

Spurgeon's Sovereign Grace Sermons
Charles Spurgeon

Light for the World: Studies in Reformed Thought
Ken Gentry

For This Reason: An Introduction to Biblical Apologetics
Ken Talbot & Gary Crampton

The Education of a Covenant Child
Ken Talbot & Gary Crampton
(Introduction by Samuel Blumenfeld)

The Family: A Biblical View
Fred DiLella

The Marrow of Modern Divinity
by Edward Fisher with Thomas Boston's notes.

What is Calvinism? or the Confession of Faith in Harmony With the Bible and Common Sense
William D. Smith

HAL LINDSEY
&
THE RESTORATION OF THE JEWS

Steve Schlissel

David Brown

Still Waters Revival Books
"PUBLISHING THE TRUE PEACE"
12810-126 St. Edmonton, AB Canada T5L OY1

First printing, August 1990

Special thanks to Messiah's Christian Reformed Church, 2662 East 24th Street, Brooklyn, New York 11235 for their encouragement and support of the republication of *The Restoration of the Jews*.

Published by **Still Waters Revival Books**
12810-126 St. Edmonton AB Canada T5L 0Y1

Other Scripture from the King James Version or the authors own translation.

Much of the original spelling and format of the 1861 edition of *The Restoration of the Jews* has been retained.

Printed in the United States of America

ISBN 0-921148-11-9

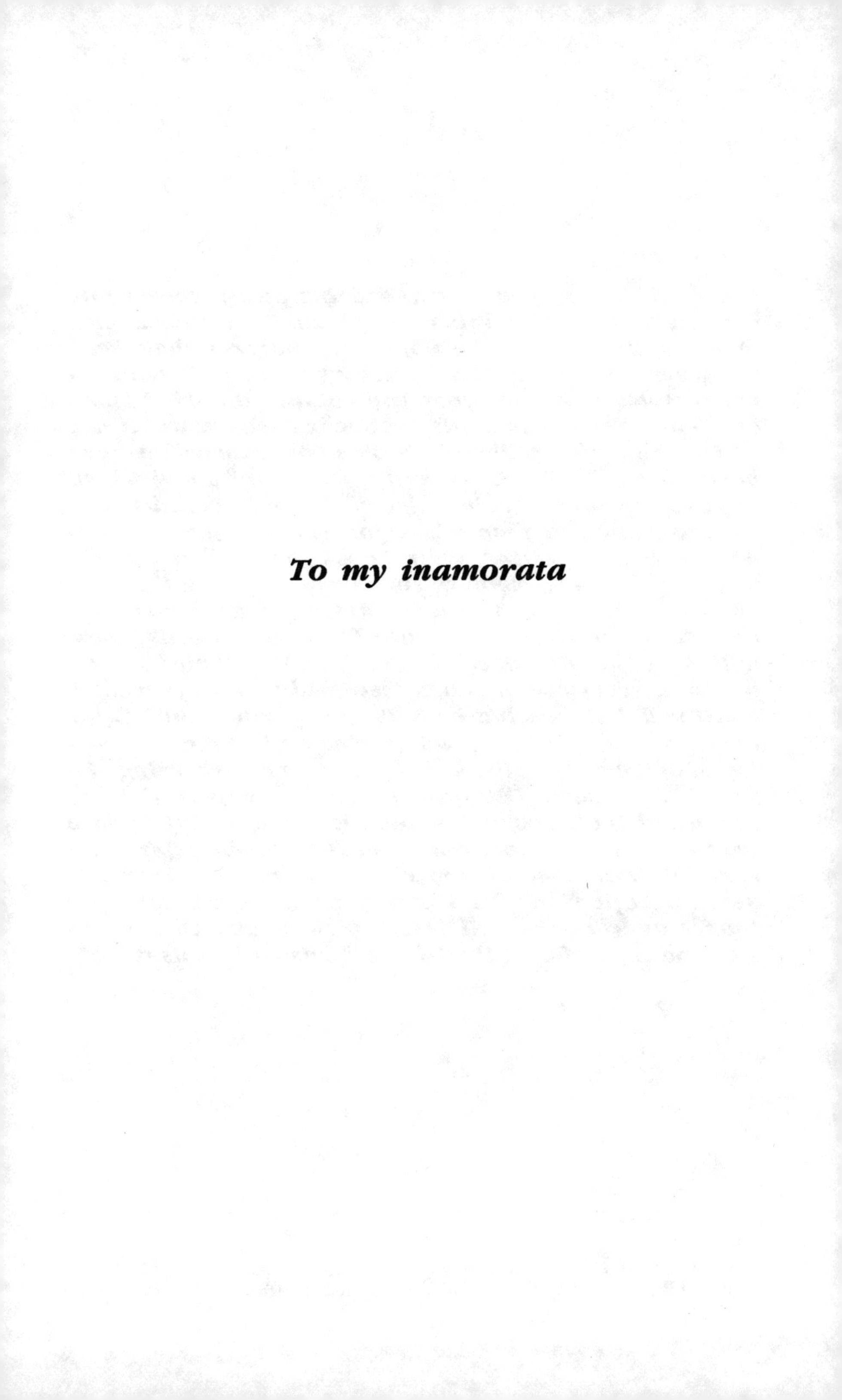

To my inamorata

Once he came to his own, and his own received him not. But "at the second *time Joseph shall be made known to his brethren; and the house of Pharaoh shall hear the weeping" as one has touchingly said. O what an unexampled mourning that will be!...But the most glorious feature of it will be its* evangelical character. *It will be the fruit of a believing "*look *upon Him whom they have pierced."...And O, when they see that blood which as a nation they have murderously shed, turned into a fountain open to themselves for sin and for uncleanness—when they find their robes washed and made white in that very blood of the Lamb—how will they water a free pardon with their tears, how generously will they detest forgiven sin (to use Dr. Owen's words), how will they be disposed to exclaim to their Gentile brethren everywhere, "Come hear, all ye that fear God, and I will declare what he hath done for my soul!" O for the apostle's spirit of great sorrow and continual heaviness of heart for them, "of whom as concerning the flesh, Christ came," and for his glowing expectations of the benefit ourselves as Gentiles would experience from their conversion! And the drops of that spirit are certainly falling upon the churches. But showers are needed. "Upon* the land of my people *shall come up thorns and briars*—UNTIL the Spirit be poured upon us from on high!" *But "I the Lord will hasten it in its time."**

---

*David Brown, *Christ's Second Coming: Will it be Premillennial?* (Edmonton, AB: Still Waters Revival Books, [1882, 7th edition] 1990), pp. 408, 409.

TABLE OF CONTENTS

Now, whatever any individual Christian reconstructionist might say, either from ignorance or honest disagreement, it can hardly be maintained that reconstructionism itself is anti-semitic. Calvin's position (as excerpted above) is mine, and I am a "reconstructionist." I can testify that while not every reconstructionist would agree with my position, my views on this issue are not only accepted *within the reconstructionist world as being perfectly consistent with the system, but sought out.*

This being the case, I think it would be best to bury the charge of anti-semitism in the sea of disproved contentions. If you should meet or read a reconstructionist who is, in fact, anti-semitic, please put him in touch with me. And as for me, if I should meet a dispensationalist who really believes that the church's efforts to reach the Jews with the Gospel will be successful, I'll be sure to send him to you so that you can convince him of the futility of his optimism!

*Steve Schlissel (1988)**

---

*Cited from *Appendix C: To Those Who Wonder if Reconstructionism Is Anti-Semitic* in *The Debate Over Christian Reconstruction* (Ft. Worth, TX: Dominion Press/Atlanta, GA: American Vision Press, 1988), p. 260.

Publisher's Preface

by Reg Barrow

And so all Israel shall be saved: as it is written, There shall come out of Sion the Deliverer, and shall turn away ungodliness from Jacob: For this is my covenant unto them, when I shall take away their sins. As concerning the gospel, they are enemies for your sakes: but as touching the election, they are beloved for the fathers' sakes. For the gifts and calling of God are without repentance (Romans 11:26-29).

It is no secret that many Christian Reconstructionists consider themselves heirs to the Reformers of the sixteenth century, as well as the Puritans and Covenanters who followed in their tracks. Iain Murray points out these same "earlier Reconstructionists" (my term) were predominantly postmillennial and propagated the message of a future (pre second advent) Gospel prosperity for the Jews—long before dispensationalism was invented in the 1830's.[1] One example cited in Murray's excellent work reads:

> From the first quarter of the seventeenth century, belief in a future conversion of the Jews became commonplace among the English Puritans. In the late 1630's, and in the national upheavals of the 1640's—the period of the Civil Wars—the subject not infrequently was mentioned by Puritan leaders. As ground for hopefulness in regard to the prospects of Christ's kingdom it was introduced in sermons before Parliament or on other public occasions by William Strong, William Bridge, George Gillespie, and Robert Baillie, to name but a few. The fact that the two last-named were commissioners from the General Assembly of the Church of Scotland at the Westminster Assembly, which was convened by the English Parliament in 1643, is indicative of the agreement on this point between English and Scottish

---

[1]Cf. Gary DeMar, *The Debate Over Christian Reconstruction* (Ft. Worth, Texas: Dominion Press, 1988), p. 102.

divines. Some of the rich doctrinal formularies which that Assembly produced, bear the same witness.[1]

Puritan and Reformed

My personal respect for the Puritan, Reformed and Covenanter writings and theology should be evident from previous and forthcoming publications of Still Waters Revival Books—which I own and operate. This can be demonstrated by the following two quotes taken from our recent publications:

> The keen student might well ask if there are any real differences in either principle or practice between what has been tagged as "theonomy" and "reconstruction" by some, and the historic Covenanter Testimony exposited by Symington, "For Christ's Crown and Covenant." Unquestionably, some profess to discover significant disparities between them. But, on careful examination, perceived differences between the "theonomic" and "historic Covenanter" positions, prove to be matters of semantics and not substance. The basic similarities between them seem clear enough.[2]

> Incredibly, one of the objections to Christian Reconstructionism from both the dispensational and the semi-reformed camps is the charge that reconstructionism is a "new" theology. Christian Reconstruction is not new, it is simply a return to classic Reformed theology that characterized the writings of Calvin, the Puritans, and Presbyterian theologians of the nineteenth century. The consistent application of this theology transformed Calvin's Geneva and Puritan New England into truly Christian cultures. ***Christian Reconstruction is nothing more than the application of the whole of the Bible to the whole of life***. Rather than being a new theology, it is actually an attempt to go back to the "old" theology believed, taught, and practiced in the Southern Presbyterian Church as recently as the late 1800's by men such as Major Robert L. Dabney. Reconstructionism only seems new because of the theological shift caused by the rise of dispensational ideas that has taken place this century.[3]

Taking into account that there will always be those who claim these statements are an oversimplification; it can not be disputed that the clear connection of theological convictions with historic Reformed (Covenantal) Christianity—rooted in *sola Scriptura* and and the system of doctrine taught in the *Westminster Confession of Faith* (1647)—is synonymous with what, in our contemporary setting, has

---

[1]Iain Murray, *The Puritan Hope: Revival and the Interpretation of Prophecy* (Edinburgh, Scotland: The Banner of Truth Trust, [1971] 1984), p. 43, 44.

[2]Raymond Joseph from the Introduction to *Messiah the Prince or the Mediatorial Dominion of Jesus Christ* by William Symington (Edmonton, Alberta: Still Waters Revival Books, [1884 edition] 1990).

[3]Mark Duncan, *The Five Points of Christian Reconstruction From the Lips of our Lord* (Edmonton, Alberta: Still Waters Revival Books, 1990), p. 2.

been denominated "Christian Reconstruction". In as far as these writings (of which the *Westminster Confession and Catechism's* are probably the greatest) teach scriptural truth and are imbibed by "Reconstructionists," I am content to bear the name "Reconstructionist" to the glory of God. Moreover, the present controversies—especially regarding eschatology—between Reconstructionist's and Dispensationalist's—can be viewed in a most positive light. A.A. Hodge stated,

> The Church has always advanced toward clearer conceptions and more accurate definitions of divine truth through a process of active controversy. And it has pleased Providence that several great departments of the system revealed in the inspired Scriptures should have been most thoroughly discussed, and clearly defined in different ages, and in the bosom of different nations.[1]

Another area where this is especially apparent is in the move away from the empirical (Thomistic) apologetical method. This method has hampered the Reformed church's defense of the faith by attempting to lay a foundation in the sand of humanistic philosophy rather than upon the rock of Truth, God's self-attesting Word. The Westminster divines were clearly presuppositional when wearing their theological hat (WCF 1:4); but had not yet "experienced" the philosophical reformation that we are witnessing in the late 20th Century—a yet *more refined* expression of *sola Scriptura!*[2] Notwithstanding, there were surely those from early days who could be said to have held to what is today called "axiomatic presuppositionalism". James Walker states,

> The Bible is its own evidence. The Spirit who miraculously gave it of old to prophets and apostles, now unveils it supernaturally to God's elect, and brings home the conviction of its divinity...from this point of view you find the old divines even disposed, one might say, to look askance upon what we call the external evidences...Reference is then made to the Confession of Faith, where the only proofs of the divinity of Scriptures are drawn from the scriptures themselves. You have the same view strongly put by Rutherford, and still more strongly by Halyburton...[3]

Though they surely had their differences the works of Gordon Clark and Cornelius Van Til have broken a lot of ground (and a lot

---

[1]A.A. Hodge, *Outlines of Theology* (Edinburgh, Scotland: The Banner of Truth Trust, 1972), p. 95.

[2]Cf. Talbot and Crampton, *For This Reason: An Introduction to Biblical Apologetics* (Edmonton, Alberta: Still Waters Revival Books, forthcoming).

[3]James Walker, *The Theology and Theologians of Scotland 1560-1750* (Edinburgh, Scotland: Knox Press, (1888) 1982), p. 40, 41.

of autonomous and false presuppositions) regarding the veracity of scripture. Clark sites another example of how Hodges' principle can be seen to have been developing concerning apologetics,

> It was in 1840 that Louis Gaussen published his famous little book *Theopneustia*. Gaussen was a Swiss theologian who, like J. Gresham Machen in this century, was deposed from the ministry and driven out of the church because of his adherence to the truth of the Scriptures. And his book *Theopneustia* is a defense of inspiration. In it Gaussen amasses the astounding amount of material that the Scriptures have to say about themselves. And although that was a century ago, no one should approach the question of inspiration without a good knowledge of Gaussen's work, or at least without a good knowledge of what the Bible has to say about itself.[1]

With the amount of books, newsletters, cassettes, video's etc. available, it should now be clear that Christian Reconstruction is not new. It should also be clear that it is not stagnant. At this point it would probably be best characterized as a movement from the classics to the cutting edge—a stirring of the waters—God's Spirit producing a revival of *sound doctrine* coupled with the *practical application* of the whole Bible (Old and New Testament) to contemporary society. In a word, ***a full-orbed Reformation brought about by the Spirit and Word of God!***

Anti-Semitism and the Westminster Confession of Faith

Regarding anti-Semitism (while remaining cognizant that Christian Reconstruction is a return to the historic standards along with some fine tuning à la Hodge above) it is interesting to note that the Westminster Assembly also produced the Directory for the Publick Worship of God (1645). As Steve Schlissel has perceptively pointed out, this document contains the following words (in the section on 'Publick Prayer before the Sermon'): "To pray for the propagation of the gospel and kingdom of Christ to all nations; ***for the conversion of the Jews***, the fullness of the Gentiles, etc." (emphasis added). It is very hard, yea well nigh impossible, to image hating someone while you are praying for their conversion. Therefore, this statement alone should serve as an indication that anyone holding to the Reformed/Reconstructionist faith, while remaining consistent with the historic confessions, could not be labeled as holding views leading in any way to another holocaust. Consistency here logically precludes anti-semitism.

---

[1]Gordon Clark, *God's Hammer: The Bible and Its Critics* (Jefferson, Maryland: The Trinity Foundation, 1987), pp. 39, 40.

Providence and Publishing

Ironically, in the providence of our great God and Saviour Jesus Christ, I have been granted the privilege of publishing Steve Schlissel's and David Brown's answer to Hal Lindsey latest book *The Road To Holocaust*. This irony can be illustrated in the following two considerations.

A Diet from Dallas

First, it was in my late teens that I first became acquainted with the writings of Hal Lindsey. As an unbeliever, I was given some Christian books (by my younger brother Greg) which included Hal Lindsey's *Liberation of Planet Earth*.[1] Combined with the Bible this title of Lindsey's and another Christian book, "helped" lead me to a knowledge of Jesus Christ. (Being a Calvinist, I recognize that the Spirit of God regenerates the sinner, who is dead in trespasses and sins, ordinarily using the ordained means such as the preaching [or writing] of the Word of God [James 1:18]).[2]

After becoming a Christian I regularly frequented Christian bookstores devouring all manner of spiritual "food." In this theologically naive state I enthusiastically imbibed Dispensational thought via the Ryrie study Bible and the writings of the likes of Hal Lindsey, John Walvoord *et al.* In my youthful zeal, not aware at this time that other schools of thought existed regarding prophetic interpretation, I purchased and distributed—free of charge—many (hundreds) of Mr. Lindsey's books, passing them on to whoever would read them. The bookstore saw me so often, buying multiple copies to give away (a strategy I still suggest, only pass out good Reformed books) that they volunteered to give me a discount on everything I purchased. This continued for some time as I slowly retreated from my social and ethical responsibilities (not to mention the law of God as a rule of life [John 14:15]) while I awaited the rapture; which I was

---

[1]Though I am grateful for the guidance afforded, as a young Christian, through Lindsey's *Liberation of Planet Earth,* it has become clear the Mr. Lindsey is probably just about as confused concerning his soteriology as he is concerning eschatology. In other words, I think that many of our modern "Gospel" presentations, bearing the leaven of Arminianism and/or Pelagianism, are used of God in spite of there weak theology (for many of them at least quote scripture). Cf. Ken Talbot and Gary Crampton, *Calvinism, Hyper Calvinism and Arminianism* (Edmonton, Alberta: Still Waters Revival Books, 1990) or John Owen, *A Display of Arminianism* (Edmonton, Alberta: Still Waters Revival Books, 1989).

[2]For an excellent explanation of the scriptural doctrine of salvation see the *Westminster Confession of Faith* (1647), especially the sections concerning Effectual Calling (X), Justification (XI) and Saving Faith.(XIV).

convinced would take place at any moment. Seeing that God was daily delaying the "great snatch" (the rapture) I continued on a course of Biblical study. Being an inquisitive individual I began to read books by amillennialist's and postmillennialist's. This break with my *dispensational diet from Dallas* forced me to deal with the arguments of proponent's of what were at that time rival systems; not just the straw men that many of their premillennial opponents customarily executed. After numerous times through the scriptures and many books representing the various eschatological positions I was left with no conclusion but to reject my earlier dispensational premillennialism. Some time later I embraced postmillennialism as the system that best represents the teaching of the Bible and as the eschatological teaching most consistent with a Reformed hermeneutic (see the Further Study list at the back of this book for some of the books that helped bring me to this conclusion). Recently I've come across many who now testify of postmillennial convictions who were also "raised" on the Lindsey, Ryrie, Walvoord brand of premillennialism promulgated by their many writings. This return to the eschatology of victory is a sign of hope and revival. Thus, I consider it a great privilege, in light of the fact that I at one time zealously and voluntarily spread dispensational literature, to be granted this publishing opportunity to demonstrate the reformational (reconstructionistic) love of God for the Jews from a postmillennial perspective.

Israel Josiah

The second consideration (and one even more astounding to me) is that long before I had heard that Hal Lindsey was attacking Christian Reconstructionists as implicit anti-semites, my wife and I had named our first born son ***Israel Josiah!*** Now does this sound like a name that a Reformed/Reconstructionist publisher would name his son if he were an anti-Semite? Given Hal Lindsey's scenario you would think a Reconstructionist would favor such names as Haman (Ester 3:1-15) or maybe Sanballat or Tobiah (Neh. 2:10,19; 4:1-8; 6:14), but certainly not ***Israel Josiah!*** *Brethren, my heart's desire and prayer to God for Israel is, that they might be saved (Rom. 10:1).*

Reconstruction and Restoration

It is my hope that this book will begin to clear up the misunderstandings among Christian brothers that have been fostered by *The Road to Holocaust*. Futhermore I believe that Christian Reconstruction (as defined earlier) offers the most consistent view of Biblical truth yet formulated. As opposed to Lindsey's thesis (in TRTH) my own "Reconstructionist" view regarding the Jews is summed up in our recent republication of *Christ's Second Coming: Will it be Premillennial?* also by David Brown. Commenting on Romans 11:26-29 he writes:

> In this chapter the apostle teaches that the rejection of God's ancient people under the gospel is to be taken with two limitations: first, that "even at this present time (the period of rejection) there is a remnant according to the election of grace;" and next, that *the people at large*—the bulk and body of the nation—as *contradistinguished from this elect remnant*, shall yet be brought in.[1]

As will be clearly established by *Hal Lindsey and the Restoration of the Jews*, Lindsey's claim that Christian Reconstructionism employs "a system of prophetic interpretation that historically furnished the philosophical basis for anti-Semitism,"[2] would more accurately read that Christian Reconstructionism employs the ***"system of prophetic interpretation that historically furnished the Biblical basis for the most glorious future imaginable for the Jews!"***

---

[1]David Brown, *Christ's Second Coming: Will it be Premillennial?* (Edmonton, Alberta: Still Waters Revival Books, [1882, 7th edition] 1990), p. 406.

[2]Hal Lindsey, *The Road to Holocaust* (New York, NY: Bantam Books, 1989), back cover and p. 25.

How odd
Of God
To choose
The Jews

—William Norman Ewer

But not so odd
As those who choose
A Jewish God
But spurn the Jews

—Cecil Browne

I speak the truth in Christ — I am not lying, my conscience confirms it in the Holy Spirit — I have great sorrow and unceasing anguish in my heart. For I could wish that I myself were cursed and cut off from Christ for the sake of my brothers, those of my own race, the people of Israel. Theirs is the adoption as sons; theirs the divine glory, the covenants, the receiving of the law, the temple worship and the promises. Theirs are the patriarchs, and from them is traced the human ancestry of Christ, who is God over all, forever praised! Amen.

—St. Paul

The Reformed Faith and the Jews

Foreword by Steve Schlissel

A few words are in order which may help the reader appreciate the significance of the republication of Dr. David Brown's *Restoration of the Jews.* Too many Reformed folk are ignorant of the prominent place afforded to the future of the Jews in their own Reformed history and confessions. Too widespread among Dispensationalists is the idea that a Reformed view of the Jews is anti-Semitic. It is hoped that a careful reading of Dr. Brown's treatise, will bury the false notions of both Christian groups. The following thoughts are offered toward the same end.

The Road to Confusion

This reprinting has been made all the more befitting by the recent appearance of yet another book by Hal Lindsey, *The Road to Holocaust.* Mr. Lindsey's goal in writing the book was to associate a particular current of Reformed theology with the persecution of the Jews, to encourage Christians to suspect as latent or patent anti-Semites all who demur from his portrayal of the future. He suggests that "Dominion theology" is "creating the kind of philosophical atmosphere that can lead to another period of anti-Semitism."[1] He insinuates that "Dominion theology" may "give a theological framework from which unscrupulous men can promote another holocaust for the children of Israel."[2] Moreover, the definite impression is given to the reader that the war against the Jews, 1933-1945, can be attributed to what he calls a "false interpretation of prophecy," *by which he seems to mean, any other than his own.* He has written "this book...to seek to prevent Christians from once again contributing to this same kind of tragedy."[3] The school of thought most likely to so

---

[1]Hal Lindsey, *The Road to Holocaust* (New York, NY: Bantam Books, 1989) pp. 282-3.

[2]*Ibid*, p. 283.

[3]*Ibid*, p. 25.

contribute, according to Mr. Lindsey, is Christian Reconstructionism. I hope to demonstrate that, while Mr. Lindsey raises legitimate concerns, he has laid the causes on the wrong theological doorstep.

To characterize Mr. Lindsey's treatment of Reconstructionists[4] as somewhat sensationalistic is probably fair. However, it seems to me that some Reconstructionists may have asked for this sort of abuse by their own employment of similar tactics. When truth begins to be treated like a commodity, things can get ugly. But provoked or not, Mr. Lindsey's response is confused and inaccurate. I find that he has oversimplified many truths, overstated what Reconstructionists believe, and frequently overstepped the bounds of responsible Christian scholarship. I will provide you with just three examples.[5]

Befuddlement #1: Law and Grace

Under the subheading, "The Dominionists' View of the Law,"[6] Mr. Lindsey quotes R.J. Rushdoony, "the patriarch of modern Reconstructionism," as follows: "So central is the Law to God, that the demands of the law are fulfilled as the necessary condition of grace." Lindsey immediately adds, "In other words, we earn grace by keeping the Law. Talk about putting the cart before the horse! Any attempt to earn grace destroys its very meaning."

Now if Rev. Rushdoony actually believed what is predicated of him by Mr. Lindsey, that would be grim indeed, a very definite return to medieval Romanism. However, after reading Rushdoony's original source several times, it appears that he was deliberately and seriously misrepresented. This is what Rev. Rushdoony wrote: "So central is the law to God, that the demands of the law are fulfilled as

---

[4]I use the term "Reconstructionist" to refer to those who hold to a Positive Future Orientation in eschatology (most are unabashedly Postmillennial), *and* who believe in the continuing validity and principal applicability of the Law of God in this and every period of human history, *and* who hold to the principle of presumptive continuity between the testaments (covenant theology). Generally speaking, there are many Reformed Christians who may hold to one of these distinctives without regarding themselves as Reconstructionists, but most who hold to all would not object to the name. I fear that force of habit, and my own decided preference for being referred to as simply "Reformed," may result in my using these terms somewhat interchangeably.

[5]Several errors in Lindsey's arguments, particularly those in which appeal is made to the early Church Fathers as supporting the Dispensational view of the future, will be put to rest by Dr. Brown in his first chapter. Dr. Brown's treatment of the Fathers' testimony on this question is courageously honest. It will be seen at once that here is a man who really believes in *sola Scriptura*.

[6]Lindsey, *op. cit.*, p. 156.

the necessary condition of grace, and God fulfills the demands of the law on Jesus Christ. Jesus Christ, as the new Adam, head of the new humanity, kept the law perfectly, *to set forth the obedience of the new race or humanity*, and died on the cross as the sinless Lamb of God, *to fulfill the requirement of the law against sinners*."[7] Note well that the emphases are Rushdoony's. Thus, it is Mr. Lindsey who has "destroyed the meaning" of Rev. Rushdoony's words, for, while Rev. Rushdoony sets forth Christ as the One who has set us free from the curses of the Law, Mr. Lindsey makes him out to say that *we must earn grace*.[8] To make matters worse, a little later in the same chapter, Mr. Lindsey, as if he were setting forth the true, Biblical position as over against Reconstructionists, says, "We owed God perfect obedience to His Law. We couldn't pay, so Jesus died in our place."[9] Lindsey concludes, "The Reconstructionists' failure to correctly interpret an issue as clearly revealed in the New Testament as Law and Grace is a major doctrinal error...The Apostle Paul declared this error serious enough to call those who taught it 'accursed.'"[10] Mr. Lindsey would do well to remember that the Apostle also called accursed those who misrepresented his teachings (Romans 3:8).

For, unfortunately, this sort of misrepresentation is not untypical. Equally disturbing is Mr. Lindsey's apparent inability, or unwillingness, to understand the nature of the issues raised by Reconstructionists in regard to the Law. Their doctrine of the place of the Law in the life of the Christian is not distinctive. It is the teaching of all Reformed and Presbyterian confessions. When the proper place of God's Law was being rediscovered during the Reformation, it was noted that it could be viewed as having three "uses." The first use of the Law is as a revelation of the righteousness and holiness of God, judging the sinner, even provoking sin in him as a sinner. By showing the sinner to be a rebel against a holy God, the first use is conviction of sin, leading him to repentance and faith in Christ as his Substitute and Savior.

---

[7]R.J. Rushdoony, *Institutes of Biblical Law* (Phillipsburg, NJ: Presbyterian and Reformed, 1973), p. 75.

[8]This misquote has also been noted and critiqued by Greg Bahnsen and Ken Gentry in their *House Divided* (Tyler, TX: Institute of Christian Economics, 1989), p. 378. They also note that Lindsey "cannot—he does not even try!—(to) cite *one* sentence from Reconstructionist literature that even remotely appears anti-Semitic (p.378)."

[9]Lindsey, *op. cit.*, p. 160.

[10]Lindsey, *op. cit.*, p. 164.

The second use of the Law is in the restraint of sin, particularly operative in the field of "common grace," or, the civil realm.

The third use, as the perfect model for the justified, the way of life in which he should walk, was, according to Calvinism, a principle use. It was this use that divided the Lutherans (who rejected it) from the Reformed (who embraced it).

It is what might be called a fourth use,[11] as *the* foundation for a political and social philosophy, that is being discussed in Christian circles today. But seeing that Mr. Lindsey says that, "(it) is correct to say that Biblical Law should serve as a *pattern* for civil law as John Calvin taught",[12] one wonders why he is so ardently opposed to the advocacy of its employment as such. Perhaps he had in mind only its second use. Even then, one wonders what Mr. Lindsey's reasons are for affirming that the Law is a proper pattern. Is it because he recognizes the fact that since it is from God, it is therefore perfect? Authoritative? Desirable? The necessary condition for social peace and prosperity? If so, he may be more Reformed than he realizes!

The simple and indisputable fact is this: Man, Christian or non-Christian, cannot live without law. While it can be readily understood why non-Christians would reject God's Law as the standard under which they would choose to live, it is perplexing and inconsistent for a *Christian* to do so.

Befuddlement #2: Interpretation

Moving on to another example which illustrates the difficulty in critiquing *The Road to Holocaust*, in dealing with a question which he says is "of utmost importance," Mr. Lindsey asks, "Who are the people Jesus calls 'these brothers of mine.'?" (Matthew 25:40). He answers, "All the evidences of the context and parallel passages demand that the group the LORD Jesus calls 'His brothers' are believing Israelites. No doubt this will be especially applicable to the 144,000 Israelites who will be the LORD's main evangelists during the seven-year Tribulation that immediately precedes His Return."

How this conclusion can be gotten from the context and parallel passages is nothing short of amazing! May we not allow Jesus Christ to define for us who He intends by the word "brothers"? He has done

---

[11]According to Rev. Roger Wagner in his taped lecture, "What is a Theonomist", available from Mount Olive Tape Library, Box 422, Mt. Olive, MS 39119. $2.50. Catalog $7. (Bound $11). Include tape number, RW100A1, when ordering.

[12]Lindsey, *op. cit.*, p. 157

just that in Matthew 12:50: "*Whoever does the will of My Father in heaven is my brother...*" One interpretation, therefore, tries to understand the words from our Lord's mouth by other words from His mouth (and found within the same book, a significant hermeneutical principle).[13] The other interpretation *puts words* in His mouth, and that in accordance with the demands of an artificially contrived system that has itself been imposed on Scripture, namely, Dispensationalism.[14]

Befuddlement #3: What A-'s and Post-'s Have In Common

We complete our illustrations with this third example. Mr. Lindsey (on p. 30) writes, "In summary, the most important doctrines the Amils and Postmils hold in common are: (1) that the Church has been given all the covenants and promises made to Israel; (2) that the Church has forever taken Israel's place in God's plan, and therefore Israel has no future as a believing Nation; (3) that Christ's coming for the Church is *not* an any-moment possibility or expectancy, but something that can only occur after the Church has purified herself and established the Kingdom of God." This assessment is in dire need of repair (reconstruction?), more than I can provide in this space. Allow the following to suffice, point for point:

The Promises of God

(1) *The Bible* says "*All* the promises of God in Him (Christ) are Yea, and in Him Amen, unto the glory of God by us (Christians, believers, whether Jewish or Gentile)." (2 Cor. 1:20). Again, "If ye be Christ's, then are ye Abraham's seed, and heirs according to the promise." (Gal. 3:29). Furthermore, Paul tells the Gentiles that while they were once "aliens" in regard to "the commonwealth of Israel and strangers from *the covenants of promise*," they are, in Christ Jesus, not such any longer. (Eph. 2:11-13). Paul says in Philippians 3, of Christians, "*We are* the circumcision, who worship God in the Spirit, rejoice in Christ Jesus, and have no confidence in the flesh..." He writes to the Corinthian Christians that "*our* fathers were under the cloud, etc.," thus indicating that Christians are, in some real sense, descendants of the Jews who left Egypt. Furthermore, every

---

[13]Though more evidence for our interpretation is not wanting. Cf. 1 John 3:17; 1 Peter 5:9; James 2:15, 16; Hebrews 13:1-3.

[14]See Appendix A on the hermeneutical principle of the Dispensationalist.

major metaphor used of Israel in the Old Testament is ascribed to the Church in the New: The Beloved of God, The Children of God, The Flock, The House of God, The Kingdom of God, The People of God, The Priests of God, The Bride of God, The Chosen People.[15] This is the manifest testimony of Scripture, and examples could be multiplied.

Dispensationalists seem not to notice the fact that the New Testament Church was originally, an assembly of Christ's people "called out" from among the Jews.[16] Thus, the first churches, constituted as they were of Jews, formed the basis of the New Testament Church,

---

[15]I have made use in the sentence above of the outline of Charles D. Provan in *The Church Is Israel Now* (Vallecito, CA: Ross House Books, 1987). Provan has demonstrated, incontrovertibly, that the New Testament sets forth the Church as a New Israel. (I must note, however, that his treatment of Romans 11 is wholly inadequate). Of course, this was also the position of the Reformers and Puritans who are favorably quoted in this foreword. I emphasize this fact since it once again proves that covenant theology and anti-Semitism are not simply strange bedfellows, they are antithetical, when accompanied by a Biblically informed view of Law and the future restoration of the Jews. There need not be a problem in regarding the Church as Israel if we bear in mind that "Israel" may be used in different senses, the sense in any given passage to be determined by the context and other sound hermeneutical principles. For example, Matthew very definitely portrays Jesus Christ Himself as the *True Israel* See Matthew 2:15. In fact, the whole of Matthew, and most especially his early chapters, so powerfully portrays Jesus Christ as Israel that (as one commentator put it), "you'd have to have a block of cement on your shoulders, instead of a head, to miss it." Descent into Egypt followed by going through the waters (of baptism—cf. 1 Corinthians 10:1,2), into the wilderness, up to the mountain from which He expounds the Law, etc. Now, Jesus' being the True Israel does not preclude the Church from being the spiritual Israel. Neither does the Church's being spiritual Israel preclude the physical descendants of Abraham, Isaac & Jacob from being referred to as Israel in a physical sense. The sense in which they are not *now* Israel is the sense in which I argue, after Paul, they *will* fully be. To argue that "Israel" throughout Romans 11 refers to the church, therefore, is not merely unnecessary, it is ludicrous. Try reading it that way: "Israel has experienced a hardening in part until the full number of the Gentiles has come in." (v.25) *The Church has experienced a hardening in part?* Or, "Salvation has come to the Gentiles to make *the Church* jealous"? (v.11). No! Obviously, Scripture uses "Israel" in different senses, as it does "children of Abraham." This is proved conclusively by an examination of our Lord's words in John 8. At verses 55 and 37 Jesus freely acknowledges that the Jews with whom He was speaking were Abraham's children. "I know that you are Abraham's descendants." He immediately shows that there is another sense in which they were *not* such, when He says, *If* you were Abraham's children, etc." His awful conclusion, based on their unbelief and conduct, is in verse 44: "You are of your father the devil." The unbelieving Jewish people today are covenant-breaking children of Abraham. They will one day be covenant-*keeping* children of Abraham, part of the New Israel, the Church. This is a certain and sure promise of God, who cannot lie.

[16]See Appendix B for a brief discussion of Church and Synagogue.

the New Israel, to which Gentiles were eventually added. That Gentiles currently make up the majority does not change the fact that they were grafted on to Jewish stock.

Has the Church Replaced Israel?

(2) Oy vey, what a confused statement! First of all, "the Church" has not forever taken Israel's place because "Israel" was the Church throughout most of the Old Testament. The major difference now is that Israel is no longer confined geographically or racially. It is more sound to speak of the church as growing out of Old Israel, or being ingrafted. Secondly, to hold to this *does not require a rejection of the hope of a future Jewish restoration.* One of the finest Christian gentlemen of this century, Geerhardus Vos, was a brilliant and committed Amillennialist. He puts the lie to Mr. Lindsey's generalization with the following statement (note how carefully phrased and qualified his thoughts are): "The elective principle, abolished as to nationality, continues in force as to individuals. And even with respect to national privilege, while temporarily abolished now that its purpose has been fulfilled, there still remains reserved for the future a certain fulfillment of the *national* elective promise. Israel in its *racial* capacity will again in the future be visited by the saving grace of God."[17] Now compare this with Mr. Lindsey's second assertion, above.

Any Moment?

(3) First, some Amil's do hold to the any-moment possibility. Second, if Israel had to be in the land (as Dispensationalists hold) before the tribulation could start, and if the rapture has to occur before the tribulation (as Lindsey holds), then the rapture could not have occurred until Israel was in the land. Since Israel was not in the land with sovereignty until 1948, the rapture could not have occurred until then. If it could not have occurred until then, it could not have been imminent for the preceding 1900 years. That means that, for 1900 years, anyone who thought that Jesus could come back at any moment was wrong. He could not, for an intervening event was required. If belief in imminency is required for godliness, then for 1900 years no Christian could attain unto that for which they were

---

[17]*Biblical Theology* (Edinburgh, Scotland: Banner of Truth, 1974) p. 79. emphases his.

saved. Third, contra Lindsey, the Kingdom of God is *already established* and is therefore not an intervening event required by either Amillennialists or Postmillennialists in order for Christ to return.

I believe that what Mr. Lindsey meant was that Postmillennialists (*only*—but remember that he was giving a purported summary of what A- and Post- have *in common*) expect a certain fullness of manifestation of the Kingdom, so that Christ's rule from heaven is universally and happily acknowledged before His return. However, the precondition of this manifestation is not held by any to be *self*-purification! It is the Messiah, our Husband, who sanctifies and cleanses His church by the washing with water through the Word (Eph 5:26). If it is asserted that the Church must believe and obey all of God's Word sincerely before they might rightly expect such a blessed manifestation, I would answer that such trust and obedience is itself a manifestation of the Kingdom (Matthew 6:10). When the Church returns, by the grace of God, to an ardent embrace of the Law of God as the Rule of Righteousness, we may rightly expect an ever-increasing display of God's righteous rule over the earth. "You ought to live holy and godly lives as you look forward to the day of God *and speed its coming*." (2 Peter 3:11,12).

What Post- and Amillennialists have in common, therefore, is *not* a particular notion of imminency, but rather the conviction that Christ's return is a singular and final event, concurrent with *the* resurrection of the righteous and the wicked,[18] marking the consummation of God's redemptive program in space, time and history. Many A-'s and virtually all Post-'s believe the restoration of the Jews will certainly occur before the Second Coming.

---

[18]The multiplicity of resurrections required by the Dispensational system was one of their teachings which became impossible for me to believe as I examined it against the Scriptures. Everywhere in Scripture we are given the impression that *one grand day of judgment* is to be held, and this will occur at Christ's return. See, for example, Acts 17:31: "He has set *a day* when He will judge the world with justice by the Man He has appointed." Also John 5:28-29:"(T)*he hour* is coming in which *all* who are in the graves will hear His voice and come forth—those who have done good, to the resurrection of life, and those who have done evil, to the resurrection of condemnation." (Cf. also Acts 24:15.) Dispensationalists, on the other hand, have a resurrection of the New Testament era saints before the tribulation, a resurrection for the tribulation era saints immediately after the tribulation, a resurrection of the wicked immediately after the millennium, and one of uncertain placement for the Old Testament saints! Furthermore, the preparation of the "millennial saints" for eternity requires yet another "resurrection," one which, even on their hermeneutical principles, they have not been able to discover in Scripture. They just figure that *it must* happen somehow. If you find this all too confusing, you've just joined a growing club. Welcome home to the Reformed faith.

Mr. Lindsey's summary of the supposedly common points of Post- and Amillennialism call for another observation which is both disturbing and encouraging: His real problem is *not* with Christian Reconstructionists—*it is with the Reformed faith.* Throughout his book, under the guise of exposing nefarious Reconstructionist beliefs, he repeatedly attacks only tenets of the received Reformed faith.[19] His problem is principally with *covenant theology*. It should be understood by the reader that anti-Semitism is a charge frequently leveled by Dispensationalists against Reformed-covenant theology.[20] Perhaps too many Reformed folk have given justification to the charge. Whether that be so or not, it is unfortunate that this prejudice against Reformed theology still haunts many, and has probably been exacerbated by Mr. Lindsey's book. What is encouraging, though, is that in leveling his sights at Reconstructionists, we find a tacit acknowledgement that Reconstructionism is having good impact

---

[19]It is true that Lindsey focuses on Postmillennial hermeneutics in particular, but, as I will attempt to show shortly, that is the historic Reformed norm. It was only after the turn of this century, especially after World War I, that this robust future orientation subsided. Dr. J. T. Duffield in a discourse delivered on October, 1866, referred to Postmillennialism as "the *common* theory." (emphasis his). And writing in 1911, Dr. Edward D. Morris wrote (seemingly without fear of contradiction) that, "It is a fact of deep significance that the Christian Church through all the ages, and never more strongly than now, has been animated by an unswerving conviction that...a grand future is yet to come to our race, and that *this result is to be secured through the Gospel.*" (emphasis mine). Morris proceeds to specifically discount social-gospelism and Premillennialism, the latter of which he says has not found "more than slight and occasional acceptance within the church." *Theology of the Westminister Symbols*, (Cincinnati, OH: Published by the Faculty of Lane Seminary), p. 729. And still today, in 1990, Postmillennialism is acceptable in virtually every Reformed denomination. It is being reembraced by more and more Reformed daily.

[20]When I became more consistently Reformed (I had always, as a Christian, been soteriologically Calvinistic) I was subjected to much abuse by my Dispie friends. Our congregation was evicted from the premises we had been renting from Dispensationalists. We became the subject of many rumors, chief among which was the charge that I had become anti-Semitic! Perhaps I should note that, typical of church gossip, no one ever *asked me* what my views on Israel or the Jews were. It was simply a case of: If you are not Dispensationally Premillennial, you are anti-Semitic. Lindsey's book is merely 283 pages of the same "reasoning." It is having its intended effect amongst those involved in Jewish outreach. Sid Roth, Charismatic broadcaster of "Messianic Vision," wrote in his February, 1990 newsletter, "History is about to repeat itself! Hal Lindsey,...a recent guest on the Messianic Vision, has observed that there are certain movements within the church today that deny God's special calling on the Jewish people. According to Lindsey, the teachings of these movements could lead both the church and Israel to disaster." And so on. It is very difficult to have constructive discussions in such an hysterical environment.

on the Church, being effective in its efforts to call the Church back to her Reformed heritage. This is good news for the well-being of both the Church *and* the Jews.

Some Common Ground

There *are* many points of concern which I share, sometimes wholeheartedly, sometimes reservedly, with Mr. Lindsey. Dispensationalists are not enemies, they are brothers.[21] Aside from our mutual expressed allegiance to a common Lord, together we hold many vital and fundamental truths, particularly, a high regard for Scripture as being the very words of God. I also share his belief that doctrine has consequences: What we believe certainly effects what we do, and this goes for churches and cultures, as well as individuals.

I am also sympathetic with his frustrations in getting some Reformed brothers to even consider whether the modern State of Israel *may*, in fact, be prophetically significant. Their reluctance is interpreted by Mr. Lindsey as stemming from anti-Semitism. Whether or not that is so, it is disturbing to see the hedging, hemming and hawing—disturbing and unnecessary. After all, the question of interest among the Reformed regarding the Jews in the mid-nineteenth century, as will be shown, was not their spiritual restoration—that was a given. Rather, it was whether the prophecies regarding their future required their restoration to the land. This question is answered by Dr. Brown in the affirmative,[22] and in a manner that requires

---

[21]Seeing that we find ourselves at what may be the beginning of a period of testing and purification for the Church, I have no desire to drive wedges between those who sincerely profess allegiance to Christ. Someone has said that the Millennium is a thousand year period of peace about which Christians fight. The conflict between the two great religions of our day, Christianity and Humanism, is a greater, and accelerating, fight. It is no accident that God would bring to the forefront of Christian thought at this time *the* critical question which divides the two religions: Who is King, Christ or Caesar? It cannot be doubted that the providences of God will thrust us all closer together should we begin to answer this question in the face of persecution. Unless we judge ourselves, God Himself will purge the inconsistencies between our professions of Jesus as Lord, and our theologies & lives. While it may be that Christians facing the lions together didn't quarrel about millennialism, we can be sure that an apprehension of Christ's Lordship is what bolstered them throughout their ordeals. Compare Stephen's source of grace and courage in Acts 7:54-56. The millennial question, particularly as it bears on the Kingship of our Messiah, requires careful and Scripture-guided thought. While we are thinking, let us remember: Rome lost—Christ still reigns. (See Psalm 2.)

[22]For the negative reply, the reader is referred to the appendix of Volume 1 of Dr. Patrick Fairbairn's *The Typology of Scripture* (T&T Clark, 1847 edition). The appendix is entitled, *ON THE BEARING WHICH THE RELATION THE*

serious consideration. Since God in His providence has answered *part* of that old controversy by bringing Jews back *to the land*, it hardly seems fair for the Reformed to ignore or dismiss the possibility, *a priori*, of that return having *any* prophetic significance.

Anti-Zionism Does Not Equal Anti-Semitism

Permit me to offer this analysis. On the return of Israel to the land in unbelief, the Dispensationalists place almost all their emphasis on the return, while the Reformed tend to see only the unbelief. We should try to evaluate and regard *both* from a Biblical perspective. Mr. Lindsey and his sympathizers certainly minimize the seriousness and implication's of the militant anti-Christian unbelief in Israel.[23]

FAMILY OF ABRAHAM HELD IN RESPECT TO THE EARTHLY INHERITANCE, HAS ON THE QUESTION OF THE RESTORATION OF THE JEWS TO PALESTINE. Also, Charles Hodge surveys both in his *Systematic Theology* (Grand Rapids, MI: Eerdman's, reprinted 1982), Volume 3, pp. 807-811.

[23]That modern Israel is not favorably disposed to the evangelical Christian religion is rarely admitted by Dispensationalists. I am sure their motive for hiding the fact is a noble one: they do not wish to inflame anti-Jewish sentiment. As I indicate at several points in this foreword, I share this concern. However, the reader should know that when we discuss the modern State of Israel, we are not discussing a country that is neutral toward Christianity. Missionary activity continues, but that is despite official efforts to curtail it. Furthermore, Jewish Christians (as of this writing) have been officially barred by the High Court of Justice from making *aliyah* (returning "up" to Zion, as it were) under the Law of Return (which gives preferential treatment to Jewish immigrants). A case is currently being conducted in Israel seeking to overturn this ruling. Involved in the case are many of the difficult questions that flow from the main one: who is a Jew? The critical nature of this question for Israel was seen in 1989 when there was a strong push to disallow any conversions but orthodox to be considered valid for "aliyah" purposes. This effort caused great consternation among American Jews, most of whom are Conservative or Reformed, since Israel would effectively be telling them that they are not authentically Jewish. It caused grief for Israeli political leaders who recognize that most of the American dollars contributed to Israel come from Conservative and Reformed Jews. The measure died. Of course, an equally interesting question is why Messianic Jews would so fervently desire to be recognized by unbelieving Jews as Jews. On unbelieving Jewish principles it is not possible. The Reformers did not beg Rome to regard them as true Christians. They appealed to the Scriptures, not unbelievers. Jewish Christians must do the same. Messianic Jewish efforts to be recognized as another branch of Judaism are obscurantist and retrogressive, just as the High Court of Justice in Israel affirmed. "Messianic Judaism" is the schizophrenic off-spring of Dispensationalism. This is a theological observation, please note. I have personal respect and affection for many within the movement. Moreover, I share not a few personal, adiophoric proclivities with my Messianic brethren. The desperate desire to be acknowledged as true Jews by unbelievers, however, is sad. I think we can see here a tension that has resulted from the Dispie Church/Israel distinction. Believing physical offspring of Abraham really are the

However, even some modern Jews reject the legitimacy of the modern State of Israel. This helps us to see the danger of equating anti-Zionism with anti-Semitism.[24] Consider the following excerpts from an advertisement that ran in the New York Times in May, 1988. It was placed by "American Neteuri Karta (Friends of Jerusalem)," Rabbi E. Schwartz, Box 1030, New York, NY 10009:

> According to Torah we Jews are obliged to state the Jewish belief regarding this issue. Before the Almighty gave us the Holy Land 3260 years ago, He made these conditions: If we will abide by the Torah, it is ours, if not, we will be expelled. Alas, we sinned and were exiled from the land...*Only through complete repentance will the Almighty alone, without any human effort or intervention, redeem us from exile.* At that time there will be universal peace. This will be after the coming of Moshiach...
>
> The following oaths were imposed on us by the Almighty: We should not rebel against the nations and we should remain loyal citizens; We should not leave exile ahead of time. Even if the land would be given to us by all the nations, we are not allowed to accept it. (Talmud Tractate Ksubos 111)
>
> Jews remained faithful to these oaths for over 1800 years until the advent of the Zionist atheist idea, concocted by an atheist. He rejected our beliefs and claimed that we were exiled because of our military and economic weakness. In the ensuing years the Zionist movement gained control of Palestine...
>
> *The true Jews remain faithful to Jewish belief and are untainted by Zionism.*
>
> Even if the Palestinians were forced to surrender claim to all Palestine, we are forbidden to accept it...
>
> Let the world know that Zionism and Judaism are diametrically opposed and their use of the name "Israel" is a falsification. The Zionists have no right to speak in the name of the Jewish nation. (emphases in the original)

This is a remarkable statement. Imagine if it was signed by a Christian Reconstructionist instead of a Jewish Rabbi. Look out! Mr. Lindsey, and most other Dispensationalists whom I have read or met, have so hitched their wagons to the modern State that the sentiment expressed here would undoubtedly be regarded not only as anti-Semitic, but as heretical. While anti-Semites do use Israel the State as

---

True Jews. That implies (doesn't it?) that unbelieving Jews are not. Our efforts, therefore, should not be directed at receiving their approval, but directed at God in prayer to bring about their conversion. *God has marvelously ordered things so that not even modern Israel can define a Jew until they recongize Messiah as the Definer.*

[24]Though I would encourage Reformed critics of Zionism to carefully communicate the fact that they do distinguish the people from the land.

a convenient whipping boy to vent their perverted hatred, one ought to be given the right to insist upon a distinction between the people and the land. Dr. Brown, who argues for a literal future restoration of the Jews to the land, would nevertheless endorse Rabbi Schwartz's statement as one which essentially agrees with his main point. Says Dr. Brown, "As their sins were the *cause*, and their dispersion the *effect*, so their conversion, removing the cause of their present dispersion, shall be accompanied by their return, under the Divine favor, to their father-land. The covenant-*favor* and the covenant-*land* go hand in hand." Rabbi Schwartz omits only the fact that this repentance will be in terms of Israel's recognition of the Messiahship of Jesus.

The question of *where* they will be converted, then, is of secondary importance to the *fact* of their future conversion.[25] Just weight must be given, to be sure, to the reality of the Jewish presence, three and a half million strong now, in the land. This could not have occurred but for the Providence of God, all must agree. Yet for all we know, it is possible that there may be another dispersion with a regathering a thousand years hence. We hope not and we doubt it, but we simply do not know. What you will find Dr. Brown arguing is that *we do know* that their *title* to their land is permanently linked to their faith in such a way that they may not *claim* the land as "theirs" apart from that faith. "I am not here arguing that the Jews will be converted in the countries of their dispersion, and then transported to Palestine. For all I know, they may all be in Palestine ere they get the 'new heart' promised to them. Not a few of them are there already [This was written in 1861—SMS]. In a few years many more may flock thither...(However), the only light in which the eventual restoration of Israel is held forth in Scripture is as the Divine sequel and public seal of Reconciliation to the (then) contrite and converted nation." And again, "The only future possession of Canaan which I believe in is...the possession of it by Israel circumcised in *heart*."[26]

Thus I join Mr. Lindsey in his concern about and condemnation of anti-Semitism, so long as it is not confused with anti-Zionism. I *have* heard and read what might be construed as anti-Jewish sentiments expressed by so-called Reconstructionists. This is indeed

---

[25]I rather suspect that it will occur both within and without the land of Israel.

[26]The evangelical zeal of David Brown is matched only by his fairmindedness. He walks a balanced path with such manifest reverence for Scripture that I am sure he will win many from both the extreme "literalist" camp (Dispensationalists) and the extreme "spiritualist" camp (Amillennialists).

disturbing. It is no less disturbing when I hear anti-Semitic remarks from Dispensationalists, a reality of which Mr. Lindsey appears unable to conceive. Nevertheless, some of the more ignorant statements I've heard made about my people in the last dozen years have fallen from the lips of bona fide Dispensationalists.

Be that as it may, I hope to make this much clear: *There is absolutely no necessary connection between the theology of Christian Reconstructionism and anti-Semitism.* In fact, most Reconstructionists regard themselves as being consistent exponents of the theology expressed in the great confessional statements of the Reformation, particularly its finest, the *Westminster Confession of Faith.*

Calvinism Is Not Lutheranism

This knowledge would have aided Mr. Lindsey in his analysis and kept him on a narrower, more responsible track. He seems unable to distinguish, for example, between Lutheranism[27] and Presbyterianism. Instead of tracing Reconstructionism to Luther and his theology as it developed in Germany, *he should have traced it to Calvin* and the development of his theology in the British Isles and the Netherlands. Though not a few Lutherans fervently believe in and pray for the spiritual restoration of Israel, it may well be that the roots of Post-Reformation ecclesiastical anti-Semitism are to be found in Luther's theology. How Lindsey has overlooked this possibility, especially in view of the fact that the holocaust began in a Lutheran nation, is difficult to understand. Perhaps it was because the similarities between Lutheran theology and Dispensationalism in their antipathy to the Law in the life of the believer are so striking. The suggestion that there is a radical hostility, rather than a Divine complementarity, in the principle of Law and the principle of Grace, is a distinguishing mark of both systems as over against the Reformed faith. From Luther's hostility to the Law of Moses it was only a short step to hostility toward the people most obviously associated with that Law, i.e., the Jews. On the other hand, it was the Calvinists'

[27]The reader is invited to send for the lectures on "The Law of God in Church History", by Dr. Peter Lilback, for an enlightening review of the different views of Lutherans and Calvinists on this subject. The lecture was part of a series sponsored by The New York Cooperative Academy for Reformed Theology, and can be obtained by writing to Messiah's Tape Rack, Messiah's Christian Reformed Church, 2662 East 24th Street, Brooklyn, NY 11235. There is no set price; contributions are accepted.

love for the Law that contributed to their appreciation of the Jewish people.

Roots of Love and Freedom

Of course, had Lindsey emphasized the important distinctions between Lutheranism and Calvinism he would have lost out on his most sensational (and irresponsible) image, viz., the linkage of Reconstructionist theology with Hitler. What he would have found, instead, was the source of the political and social emancipation of the Jews in the Western world, which is quite a different thing. In addition to finding the specialness of the Jews written into their very confessions and church orders, in addition to finding the birthplace of Jewish missions, he would have discovered countless stories of the love and sacrifice of Reformed Christians for the Jewish people over the centuries.

May I stress this? Christians who tenaciously held to the very doctrines which Mr. Lindsey regards as sure precursors to another holocaust,[28] these same Christians regarded the Jews as covenantally unique, not infrequently risking their lives for them. To use Mr. Lindsey's argument by association, it is no accident that Corrie Ten Boom's family performed their courageous acts of heroism on behalf of the Jews *in Reformed Holland.* Not long ago, I met a man, a member of the Christian Reformed Church (my own denomination) who recounted to me how his family repeatedly risked their welfare, their very lives, by hiding Jewish youngsters in their homes during World War II. When the Nazis would approach to conduct searches, the family would hurry the children out the back of the house where there was a lake. They were given straws to breathe through as their bodies remained out of sight under water, until it was safe. The dear, very Reformed brother who related this story to me, cried as he told it. His experience, with variations, is not uncommon.

In the last 2,000 years the Jews have enjoyed their most extensive freedoms in, and have made their greatest resulting contributions to, Reformed and Calvinist countries. They had been banished (for example) from Romanist England in 1290. It was the Puritan, Oliver Cromwell, Lord Protector of the Commonwealth, who insisted and eventually succeeded in re-admitting the Jews in 1656. During the

[28]That is, one Church from Adam to the end of time, covenantal continuity, validity of Old Testament Law, etc.

controversy that led up to this change in policy, Thomas Collier produced a work, dedicated to Cromwell, in which he wrote,

> "Oh, let us respect them...Our salvation has come from them! Our Jesus was of them! We are gotten into their promises and privileges! The natural branches were cut off, that we might be grafted on! Oh, let us not be high-minded, but fear. Let us not, for God's sake, be unmerciful to them! No! let it be enough if we have all their (spiritual) riches."[29]

Please note well that this man who so fervently pleads for toleration toward the Jews and for humility on the part of Christians, at the same time unmistakably holds the conviction that the Church is heir to the promises made to the Jews, a theological conviction which Mr. Lindsey singles out as the error which leads to holocaust! Yet, it was this very argument that contributed to their restoration in England.

The following excerpt is from a history of the Scottish Covenanters, forwarded to me by Gerry Wisz, an Elder in an Orthodox Presbyterian Church. It is yet another illustration of the almost uniform love and concern for the Jewish people among the historic Reformed.

> (S)trict Covenanters...organized what were known as "Praying Societies" or "Society Meetings." These were private religious meetings of small groups of Covenanters, held secretly, by which they maintained their identity and refreshed their souls when field conventicles could not be held. Walter Smith, a minister who was executed in 1681, drew up a set of rules for such meetings, entitled "Rules and Directions anent Christian Meetings, for Prayer and Conference to mutual edification, and to the right management of the same." It is interesting to note that under rule 23 the following are listed as matters for prayer:
>
> "1) That the old off-casten Israel for unbelief would never be forgotten, especially in these meetings, that the promised day of their ingrafting again by faith may be hastened..."

The concern expressed at the top of the Covenanter's prayer list was already a tradition by 1681. In the Directory for the Publick Worship of God, adopted by the General Assembly of the Kirk of Scotland on February 3rd, 1645, we read under "Publick Prayer before the Sermon," these words: "To pray for the propagation of the gospel and kingdom of Christ to all nations; for the conversion of the Jews, the fullness of the Gentiles, etc."

---

[29]Quoted by H. Graetz, *History of the Jews* , (Jewish Publication Society of America, 1956), Vol V., p. 46. The brackets in the quotation are Graetz's.

Much more could be said. It was in English and Scottish churches in the first half of the 19th century, that a good number of missions to the Jews were established. The first denominational ministry to the Jews is an honor belonging to the Scotch Presbyterians, people who *ardently* believed all the things Mr. Lindsey suggests go to make up anti-Semitism (i.e., covenant theology, the validity of the Law of God, and postmillennialism). A Committee was appointed by the General Assembly to investigate the condition of the Jews world-wide, their numbers, location, status, etc. Twelve lectures were given, including perspectives on the Biblical teaching regarding the Jews and their future. These were published in "Lectures on the Jews," by the Presbyterian Board of Publication, Philadelphia, PA, in 1840. I quote from the introduction: "Such is the Act of the Church of Scotland in reference to God's ancient people—the first Act, it is believed, in which any Christian church, as a church, has expressed her deep interest in, and her earnest resolution to promote their salvation."

Roots of Frustration and Hate

Mr. Lindsey's idea that the roots of the holocaust are found, as well as bound, in Reformed Covenant theology is not true. I suggest that they *may* be discovered in theologies which both ***a)*** deny the future restoration of the Jewish people to full and blessed covenant-keeping status, and ***b)*** are Antinomian (against the Law of God as normative). It is evident that Reconstructionists are guilty of neither of these positions. Dispensationalists, on the other hand, are often guilty of Antinomianism, *and* have corrupted the Biblical hope connected with the Jews' restoration, regarding it as something which will occur after the Church has left the earth. Should the modern State of Israel remain in unbelief for, say, another hundred years, the most fanatical anti-Semites *may* be found to issue forth from the Dispensational school. This danger has been recognized by modern Jews, many of whom are more than a little uncomfortable with the support Israel receives from Dispensationalists, being, as it is, so obviously linked to the Dispensationalist eschatological scheme. It was, after all, Luther's disappointed expectations in seeing the Jews' *soon* conversion, coupled with the antinomian elements in his theology, which led to some of his more virulent, famous anti-Semitic sentiments in his later years.

If the hope of the restoration of the Jews is to be realized, as I and other Reformed folks believe it will, *before* the Second Coming of

Christ, than it must come about, at least in part, through the provocation to jealousy spoken of by Paul in Romans 11. *What else could provoke my people to jealousy if it is not their beholding the Gentiles as heirs and enjoyers of all the covenant promises and blessings?* The precondition for the enjoyment of covenant blessedness, however, has always been and will always be a wholehearted obedience to the Law of God which stems from a true faith. *Thus, Dispensational Antinomian theology may actually be the single largest evangelical obstacle to fruitful Jewish missions today, and Reconstructionism its brightest hope.*

Getting Personal

It is at this point that I must speak from a personal interest in this issue. My heart's desire and prayer to God for Israel is that they be saved. I have been a missionary and minister to the Jews for more than ten years. I will never forget a conversation I had with two orthodox Jews while I was still a Dispensationalist. Naturally, the subject of the Law of God came up. I, a good and faithful adherent to the Dallas Theological Seminary brand of Dispensationalism, informed these pious Jews that the Law of God is not binding in this era. The conversation was interrupted by an awkward pause. They just looked at me like I was from Mars. The *thought* that the holy Law of the holy God of Israel could be *dispensed with* filled them with revolting horror and disbelief. What sort of religion, they thought, could Christianity be if it could make Psalm 119 irrelevant, if it no longer expressed the feelings of the covenanted man?

Though it would take me some years to put the pieces together, I can now look back on that conversation as a key to my present understanding of the philosophy of Jewish missions. A Dispensational church cannot reach, cannot provoke to jealousy, *orthodox* Jews. This is extremely significant. Of course, it poses no problem for the Dispensationalist because he doesn't really believe that the Jews are going to be reached anyway. Not in this Dispensation, at least. But if the Jews *are* to be converted prior to the Second Coming, and if the primary means[30] of their conversion is to be the preaching of the

---

[30]Viewed from our human perspective, of course. The sovereignty of the Holy Spirit in conversion is fully and freely acknowledged. Nevertheless, we know for a fact from Scripture that God has appointed *indispensable means* by which His will is carried out. Thus Paul says, "How can they call on the one they have not believed in? And how can they believe in the one of whom they have not heard? And how can they hear without someone preaching to them? And how can they preach

Word issuing forth from a church that provokes them to jealousy, then that Church must be one that honors, that loves, that obeys every Word of God, including His magisterial Law.

The Reformed Faith: A Foundation for Hope

Thus, far from providing a foundation for anti-Semitism, insofar as it recognizes the permanent validity of the holy Law of God, Reformed theology, even that theology which is called Reconstructionist, paves the theological road which leads to the greatest blessing which this earth will ever experience prior to the consummation: The restoration of the Jewish people to the faith of their Fathers. For historic Reformed theology is not only characterized by high regard for the Law, but also by that other indispensable conviction, mentioned above: That all Israel shall be saved, *in God's time*. That salvation will result in such great blessing for the world that Paul says it will be as "life from the dead."

Mr. Lindsey may, in some cases, accurately note the symptoms; he simply errs in identifying the underlying cause.[31] Reformed and Presbyterian churches have, historically, been the bright, shining

---

unless they are sent?" I simply add, *Why **should** they be believed if they preach against the Law of the Sender?*

31Since Reformed theology is solidly Biblically based, his charges against Reformed theology are actually, though indirectly, complaints against the teachings of Scripture. One ought to be careful when one deals with the Word of God. This is why I believe the balance offered by Dr. Brown is so very necessary for us today. Surely we all recognize that there is more than one strain of texts relating to the Jewish people in the New Testament. The temptation is to look at only the one that will fit one's system. We might call this selectavision, a good term to describe the process by which we scan, evaluate and absorb information. It works like this: At a management seminar participants were asked to look around the room for green objects. After a reasonable time, the facilitator asked the group to close their eyes and name red articles in the room. No one could name a single object, even though the room was filled with red things. (see my article, *Ministry Among Jews* in *Heirs of the Same Promise*, edited by Wesley D. Balda; National Convocation on Evangelizing Ethnic America, 1984; pp. 89ff.) The "Jewish Question" has witnessed adherents who tend to see *only* verses like, "The Jews, who both killed the Lord Jesus and their own prophets...they please not God, and are contrary to all men," and, "As concerning the gospel, they are enemies for your sakes," and, "(They) fill up their sin always; for the wrath of God is come upon them to the uttermost;" *or* they see *only* verses like, "As touching election, they are beloved for the father's sakes," and, "My heart's desire and prayer to God for Israel is, that they may be saved," and, "God's gifts and calling are irrevocable." *Both* sets of verses are Scriptural, both must be considered. One is not necessarily anti-anything simply for carefully taking account of all Scriptural data. But again, caution must be exercised that one does not become guilty of "selectavision."

exceptions, holding forth this Scriptural hope as a beacon, sometimes a banner under which they conducted their missions. Patrick Fairbairn summarized the three major opinions regarding the future of the Jews current in 1864:

> The Jews hold, and on *their* principles, indeed, consistently hold, that according to prophecies of Old Testament Scripture, they shall, as a people, be gathered from their dispersions by the Messiah, and restored to their ancient territory—that there the temple shall again be rebuilt, and its worship set up anew, after the handwriting of Moses—and that, thus established and presided over, they shall stand politically at the head of all the nations of the earth. Such, generally, is the Jewish expectation; and there are not wanting, especially in the present day, evangelical Christians who entirely concur with the Jews in their interpretation of the prophecies, and confidently anticipate, not only a restoration of the Jewish people to the land of Palestine, but also a reinstitution of the rites and services of the law, to be performed in a Christian spirit, and frequented by Christian worshipers.
>
> A much larger portion, however, concur only in so far as the national restoration to Palestine is concerned, along with a certain preeminence in honor and Christian influence beyond what shall be possessed by any other people in Christendom.
>
> And another portion of Christian interpreters—also a very large one—deeming it impossible to divide, in the work of interpretation, between the national restoration of the Jewish people, and the reestablishment of their ancient polity and worship, reject the one as well as the other, and hold, that the proper meaning of the prophecies, in so far as they bear on the future of Israel, is to be made good simply by the conversion of the people to the Christian faith, and their participation in the privileges and hopes of the church of Christ.[32]

The Jews and the Kingdom

All classes of interpreters held to the spiritual restoration of the Jews, but Mr. Lindsey has made allegiance to the interpretation of prophecy as held by *unbelieving* Jews to be the litmus test by which one must prove that he is *not* anti-Semitic! This makes Amil's and Postmil's guilty until proven innocent, and that because they demur from unbelief. The implications of this are enormous, for, since the Jewish interpretation is substantially the same as it was in the time of Jesus, it is a virtual admission that the unbelieving Jews of Christ's day were *right* in crucifying Him. Dispensationalists hold that the Jewish Kingdom expectations were *correct*. If the unbelieving Jews

---

[32]Taken from "Fairbairn on Prophecy" (Edinburgh: T&T Clark), by Albertus Piters in, "The Prophetic Prospects of the Jews" (Grand Rapids, MI: Eerdmans; 1930). pp. 90-91.

were right, Jesus must have been wrong. The standard Dispensational rhetoric holds that Jesus offered the Kingdom to the Jews but they refused it. By "the Kingdom" they understand that reign and economy which is described by Fairbairn, above. The fact is, however, that the Scriptures, far from presenting the Jewish people of Jesus' day as *rejecting* this sort of Kingship, tried to force it upon Him. *It was Jesus Christ who rejected the Jewish conception of the Kingdom.* This we read in John 6:14,15:

> After the people saw the miraculous sign that Jesus did, they began to say, "Surely this is the Prophet who is to come into the world." *Jesus, knowing that they intended to come and* ***make him king by force***, withdrew again into the hills by himself.

In the verses following, Jesus teaches them the proper, spiritual conception of the Kingdom.[33] When Jesus was crucified, the God-ordained sign above His head constituted a universal (three-language) proclamation of fact: Jesus of Nazareth *is* the King of the Jews. "In the Acts of the Apostles we can see the large place which the *present* kingship and kingdom occupied in the thinking and teaching of the Apostolic church (Acts 2:33-36; 4:10-12; 5:29-32; 10:34-42; 13:34-42; 13:22-41; 15:14-17; 17:6-7; 28:23, 31). Always, it is the idea of sovereignty, authority, judgment, power, and majesty which are prominent, but always in the interest of spiritual redemption."[34] This

---

[33]That the Kingdom is spiritual does not mean that it has no earthly implications. It certainly does! But, as Jesus said, His Kingdom is not of this world, meaning, its source, or origin, is not here. It is not established by sword and revolt, though it is certainly established. By His rule from heaven He is ever extending its reach and sway through the Gospel and its fruit. (Write: *Christian Reconstruction Today* [newsletter #2 Nov./Dec. 1988], c/o Still Waters Revival Books; for an extended exegetical view of this verse).

[34]Roderick Campbell, *Israel and the New Covenant*, (Philadelphia, PA: Presbyterian & Reformed/ Geneva Divinity School Press, 1954), p. 130, footnote 1. It is worth pointing out that this 1954 book was reprinted (n.d.) in the 80's by Reconstructionists. Throughout the book there is sensitivity and compassion displayed toward the Jews from a mature Christian perspective. For example, in his preface, Mr. Campbell hopes that his efforts "will help our neighbors of the Jewish faith to see that we, who accept Jesus as the Messiah of Israel and the Mediator of the New Covenant, have not departed, as the Orthodox Jew [and the Dispensationalist?—SMS] has supposed, from the world-embracing Salvation toward which the great prophets of Israel so clearly point the way." (p. xiii). And again, on p.3: "Christianity...recognizes in Orthodox Judaism a misguided but worthy contender—the only one which has anything like a solid basis for its claim." Are these the words of an anti-Semite? I offer just one more example of Mr. Campbell's thoroughly Christian attitude toward the Jews. He wonders if "those who turn away from the thing they know as Christianity are wholly ignorant of

is the Kingdom which will explode with power and *joy* when God brings the Jews back to Himself.

A Reminder for the Reformed

Turning our attention from Mr. Lindsey and Dispensationalists, we would now remind our Reformed brothers and sisters of their own historic faith.[35] That the Jewish people, as a people, will turn in true faith to their Messiah, before His return is a plain fact of Scripture and has been held as such by the vast majority of Reformed and Presbyterian interpreters since the Reformation. Long before the Reformation, the Apostle Paul was very concerned to impress this truth upon the hearts and minds of Gentile Christians:

> "I do not want you to be ignorant of this mystery, brothers, so that you may not be conceited. Israel has experienced a hardening **in part until** the full number of the Gentiles has come in. And so all Israel shall be saved."[36]

He says expressly, "I do not want you to be ignorant," lest the Gentiles proudly imagine that their own (false) ideas about the covenant future of the Jews were correct.[37] Paul's concern that failure to understand the place of the Jews in God's redemptive program might result in Gentile arrogance has been painfully proved valid, and that repeatedly throughout church history. Whenever the truth and hope of Romans 11 faded, dark days for the Jews would follow.

The most important phrases in this text must not be overlooked: ***In Part*** and ***Until***. God's judicial hardening of Israel was neither

---

what true Christianity really is." F.F. Bruce is then quoted for support: "There is too much substance in the Jews' complaint that Christendom has hidden the face of Christ from them." (p. 10).

[35]That this reminder is necessary can be seen from this excerpt from a letter written by a Reformed minister to a friend. (The minister gave him permission to share it with me.) "The Jews *were* God's people in the O.T., and that is what makes them special in a sense, but they are no longer God's holy people today. In no way. They are just like any other nation, except they were the original recipients of God's grace. Schlissel agrees with you here (sad to say), but that's where Schlissel and I disagree. I think he's mistaken, because he is a Jew. He has a blind spot." Many blind spots I may have, but I trust that the good Dr. Brown, H.G. (Honorable Gentile), will remove the cataract which prevents many of my Reformed brothers from seeing the Biblical significance of the Jews. They are unique covenantally, apologetically and eschatologically.

[36]Romans 11:25, 26.

[37]Cf. Charles Hodge, *Commentary on Romans* (Grand Rapids, MI: Eerdmans, reprint), p. 373.

total nor *permanent*;[38] i.e., it was partial and *temporary*. In part, until. Keeping these truths in mind, St. Paul was persuaded, would prevent an arrogant spirit from rising up in the privileged Gentiles, a spirit that would profit neither Gentile nor Jew. Unfortunately, it was that very spirit, one of supreme Gentile arrogance, that gripped the church from the fourth to the sixteenth centuries! Tragically, that ill spirit is rearing its head here and there in the church again today.

The Hope Fades

As we have said, and will say again, just a century ago *all* classes of Reformed interpreters held to the certainty of the future conversion of Israel *as a nation*. How they have come, to a frightening extent, to depart from their historic positions regarding the certainty of Israel's future conversion is not our subject here.[39] I suspect that a dynamic similar to that which led us away from consistent social action was at work. What I mean is this: *Early* in this century the doctrines of social mercy were being corrupted by the liberal churches into a social "gospel." The modernist liberals envisioned a universal brotherhood of man, not through the work of the Holy Spirit powerfully converting people through the preaching of the Word of Christ, but rather, and simply, through good works (and the force of evolution). This dangerous heresy produced a pendulum reaction in churches concerned with preserving their orthodoxy. They were so afraid of being associated with this heresy that they actually distanced themselves from good works, to an extent. They lost a bit of that good old holistic Reformed world-and-life view in the bargain.

Similarly, the hope of the future conversion of the Jews became closely linked, at the turn of the century and beyond, with Premillennial Dispensationalism, an eschatological heresy.[40] This,

---

[38]Nearly all Reformed interpreters recognize the former; it is the latter that they lately stumble over. Yet, it is equally a true teaching of Scripture.

[39]Any seminarian wishing to study this topic should contact Messiah's Christian Reformed Church and inquire about our scholarship fund for such an enterprise.

[40]The Rev. Harry Bultema, a minister in the Christian Reformed Church, early in this century "taught that there was an *essential* difference between the New Testament Church, as the body of Christ, during the so-called 'Church-Age', and the Jews, while he held also that our Lord Christ was not, in the accepted sense of the term, the *King* of the Church, but only its head. The Synod of 1918 declared officially that the Church of all ages was essentially *one*, and that Christ is the King of the Church in the juridical sense of the term. Unfortunately, the Rev. Bultema and his following in his own congregation (First CRC, Muskegon) and in about half a dozen other places, refused to accept the decision of Synod and formed a new

necessarily, one might say, soon became bound up and confused with Zionism. Christians waxed loud about the return of the Jews to Israel being a portent that the Second Coming is nigh. It thus seemed impossible, for many, to distinguish between the spiritual hope of Israel and their political "hope." Many Reformed, therefore, abandoned both.[41] Christian Reconstructionism, insofar as it is a revival of the historic Reformed concern for the Jews, should be *welcomed* by all who profess to love the Ancient People.

The Reformed and the Land

While we have been careful to distinguish these two questions, would it surprise you to learn that the Jews' geographical restoration was once widely held by Reformed folk to be the Scriptures'

---

group on September 15, 1920, organizing as 'Berean Reformed.' As Dr. C. Bouma expressed it in the *Calvin Forum*, October, 1944, 'The charge is sometimes made that the 1918 Synod condemned any one believing in the premillennial coming of our Lord. The fact is that the position repudiated was the denial of the present Kingship of Christ over His Church, and the denial of the continuity of the Old and New Testament dispensations of the Church.'" (Dr. Henry Beets, *The Christian Reformed Church*; [Grand Rapids, MI: Baker, 1946], p. 107). The Synod of 1918 could have gone even further by insisting on the Biblical teaching of Christ's present Kingship over *all* the earth, not just the Church. This is Scripture's testimony, and a necessary one to bear. Ephesians says, "He is head over *all* things *for* the Church." Again, in Matthew, "*All* authority...on earth has been given to (Him)." He *is* "the King of kings and Lord of lords." By Him kings reign. This is very important. (See Acts 4:25,26; John 17:2; 1Peter 3:22; Eph.1:18-23; 2 Thess. 1:8; Phil. 2:9-11; Heb. 1:3,8; etc.) If Jesus is *not* presently the Universal King, aside from Scripture's testimony being undermined on this point, the disobedience of earthly kings would not have the character of *rebellion* which Scripture insists it has. In Psalm 2 God commands all the earthly kings to submit to His Son (when He is once installed), or perish. The New Testament repeatedly refers to Psalm 2 as having been fulfilled in Christ. He is *now* enthroned. Thus, refusal to submit does not leave a ruler as a neutral party, but a guilty seditious one, in danger of the wrath of the Son. The message of the church is that, since *God* has installed Messiah Jesus as *the* Mediatorial Sovereign ruling heaven and earth, *all* must seek refuge in Him (and those who do will not be turned away) or be destroyed. John Brown, in his commentary on Hebrews (Banner of Truth, 1983 reprint) puts it this way: "The declaration...that the Messiah sits on the throne of God, at the right hand of His divine Father, is just equivalent to a declaration that He is the Ruler of the universe." (p. 67. In addition to 1 Cor. 15:25, he adds these pertinent references—Jn. 5:22, 23; Mt. 18:18; and Col. 1:15-17). Therefore, the Synod of 1918 did well in recognizing the issue of Christ's *present* Kingship as unacceptably degraded in the Dispensational scheme, but they could have done better. Jesus is Lord! Cf. also with William Symington, *Messiah the Prince* (Edmonton, AB: Still Waters Revival Books, [1884], 1990).

[41]Though the largely Amillennial Christian Reformed Church has a long history of missions to the Jews.

teaching? No less an exegete than John Owen maintained, "The Jews shall be gathered from all parts of the earth where they are now scattered, and brought home into their homeland."[42] More recently, and some would say, modestly, Dr. Hepp of Amsterdam, when asked if, in his judgment, the prophecies of the Bible required the national restoration of the Jews in Israel, replied, "Ik weet het niet, ik weet het niet." (I do not know, indeed, I do not know.)[43] In 1853, Dr. J.J. Janeway was not so tentative. He wrote a book, *Hope for the Jews, or, The Jews Will Be Converted to the Christian Faith; and Settled and Reorganized As a Nation, In the Land of Palestine.*

It is possible, as I have said, that the State of Israel, as it exists today, is, in fact, not the fulfillment of prophesy. It must be understood, however, that Reformed theologians were not always antipathetic to the idea of a national restoration of the Jews to the land. Valpy (in Scott & Henry at Rom. 11:23) comments, "This grafting in again seems to import that the Jews shall be a flourishing nation again, professing Christianity *in the land of promise...*" Scott adds (at vv. 33-36), "It is now ***generally agreed*** among the learned, that we are warranted by the Scriptures to expect a national conversion of the Jews, ***and*** their return to their own land." Why would the apparent fulfillment of the latter make Reformed scholars *less sure* of the future fulfillment of the former? Apart from my hypothesis offered above, this question baffles me. I pray that you, dear reader, will minimally grant that Elnathan Parr was correct when he wrote that "Surely the preservation of the Jews, in the providence of God, notwithstanding all their affliction, to be a people distinguished, not only in name and apparel, but in customs, ceremonies, religion, from all other nations, *argues that God has some good purpose towards them...*" Amen.[44] Those who (sometimes militantly) reject a blessed future for Israel, today see a political reality which should give their pens a pause and put their minds to work.

The Reformed and the People

While the return of Israel (the people) to Israel (the land), *may* be the beginning or the groundwork of a fulfillment of prophesy which

---

[42]*A Puritan Golden Treasury*, Compiled by I.D.E. Thomas. (Edinburgh, Scotland: Banner of Truth, 1977), p. 155.

[43]Recounted by Dr. Albertus Pieters in his introduction to *The Prophetic Prospects of the Jews, or Faibairn vs. Fairbairn* (Eerdmans, 1930), p. 8.

[44]Cited in the notes of Thomas Scott, bound with the commentary on Scripture by Matthew Henry, (Royal Publishers, Nashville, 1979).

has been eagerly awaited by Reformed believers for centuries, I will leave that whole subject to Dr. Brown. The question of the future *conversion* of the Jews to the faith of Messiah will be our concern now.

Whatever views were maintained as to Israel's political restoration, their spiritual future was simply a given in Reformed circles. Ironically, this sure and certain hope is not a truth kept burning brightly many Christian Reformed Churches today, despite the fact that the historic Dutch sympathies and sacrifices for the Jewish people can only be understood in terms of their Calvinism.[45] In fact, their future conversion aside, the Jews' very existence is rarely referred to today, and even then it is not with much grace or balance.[46]

John Calvin on the Jews

Grace and balance, however, were certainly present in the pen of John Calvin in his *Institutes of the Christian Religion*. Calvin regarded the Jews as occupying a special place in the plan and program of God. Though he does not address any convictions regarding their future conversion in the passage from the *Institutes* cited below, he recognizes very clearly their unique position in relation to God. If Calvin's mind had been the mind of the church since the fourth century—*well, much Jewish blood would have been spared*, and many Jewish souls may have been won. In this passage he plainly breaks with Roman church tradition by urging Christians to hold even unbelieving Jews in high regard.

> (T)he covenant which God had made once for all with the descendants of Abraham could in no way be made void. Consequently, in the eleventh chapter [of Romans] he argues that Abraham's *physical* progeny must not

---

[45]I have been blessed to meet more than one or two with living recollections of their own or their parents' efforts to save Jews during the war. If you can broaden my exposure on this front, *please* write to me.

[46]I met one Christian Reformed man in Canada who seemed to entertain the false-holocaust theory! (Now this is an error which Mr. Lindsey would serve the church by exposing.) Happily, this man is not typical of the Christian Reformed attitude toward the Jews. The official weekly CRC magazine, *The Banner*, has been a pleasant exception in Reformed periodicals by regularly holding the Jewish people before the hearts and minds of its readers, reminding them of the need to pray for their salvation. Furthermore, Dr. Richard DeRidder, formerly of Calvin Seminary, has for years been one of the most outspoken advocates of Jewish evangelism in the nation. While we demur from his seemingly uncritical embrace of "Jews for Jesus" we applaud his *vocalized* concern for the Ancient People.

> be deprived of their dignity. By the virtue of this, he teaches, the Jews are the first and natural heirs of the gospel, except to the extent that by their ungratefulness they were forsaken as unworthy—*yet forsaken in such a way that the heavenly blessing had not utterly departed from their nation.* For this reason, despite their stubbornness and covenant-breaking, Paul still calls them holy [Romans 11:6][47]...(T)hey are, so to speak, like the first-born in God's household...(D)espite the great obstinacy with which they continue to wage war against the gospel, *we must not despise them, while we consider that, for the sake of the promise, God's blessing still rests among them.*[48]

What Calvin so confidently asserts has been lost as a living attitude in many orthodox Reformed and Presbyterian churches today. Therefore, it is good for us to pose these questions: *Has* God forsaken His people? If He has, why do they continue to exist?

Nothing New

These are not new questions. The first was asked by Paul and twice answered in the emphatic negative.[49] "I say then, Hath God cast away His people? God forbid." (Romans 11:1). And again, "I say then, Have they stumbled that they should fall beyond recovery? God

---

[47]Calvin affirms that Scripture here teaches that *unbelieving Jews* are the ones called "holy", i.e., set apart. This is vital, for once it is admitted that a people may be called holy, even in their Christ-rejecting estate, they obviously have some peculiar relation to God. This is *never* said of any Gentile nation. I trust you see that, this being granted, we **must** admit that in the case of the Jews, we have an exceptional people, even if the venerable Back to God Hour issued a booklet proclaiming that no such exceptions exist. I would like to suggest that the Scriptures in this place (and others) teach a heretofore undefined category of grace which I believe applies to the Jews uniquely: ***Preservational grace***. This is the gracious promise of God to sustain the Jews as a people with a distinct identity, preserve them even in unbelief, until the day and generation in which He would remove the veil of blindness and bring to fruition His covenant blessedness as promised to Abraham, confirmed in Christ, and taught here by Paul. I can find no theological objection to this category in view of this passage, and certainly not when Calvin's concession is considered. Therefore, it is not correct to say that there is no difference between Jews and Gentiles *outside of Christ*, for only the Jews have been given the promise (though we as Christians alone believe it) that *they will one day savingly confess Jesus is Lord!* Please note, also, that while it is perfectly true that in the church there is neither Jew nor Gentile, the Bible does not say that outside the church there is *only* Gentile. No. Paul says, "Do not cause anyone to stumble, whether [unbelieving] Jews, [unbelieving] Greeks (Gentiles), or the church of God." (1 Corinthians 10:32).

[48]*Institutes*, IV, XVI, 16. emphases added.

[49]In order to profit from this discussion it really is necessary for the reader to read through Romans 11 before proceeding.

forbid."[50] The words of the Holy Spirit, however, were lost in their signification to the church, with devastating consequences, precisely when she needed most to understand. For the Apostle himself explains that what he has written, what he has revealed about the Jews will serve as a corrective against arrogance and overweening pride in the Gentiles. Yet, when the church began to feel her oats, instead of the face of humility and love, she turned a face of hatred and persecution toward that nation she was duty bound to love above all others.

Before the Reformation, speculations like the following, from the pen of Jonathan Edwards, were rare. "Their preservation as a distinct nation has, in many respects, been...remarkable. What are left of this people [since the reign of Trajan and Adrian] have ever since remained in a total dispersion over all the world, mixed everywhere with other people, without anything like a government or civil community of their own, and often extremely harassed by other nations;[51] though still they remain a clear and perfectly distinct nation

---

[50]I am sorry that space limitations prevent me from setting this passage in its context. You'll have to invite me to preach on this text for a fuller overview (or write Messiah's Tape Rack [address at the back of this book] for cassette copies of Steve's preaching on this subject—SWRB). Suffice to say, Paul actually began dealing in Romans 9 with the question he is first articulating in Romans 11. His entire epistle will stand or fall with this question—hence, he devotes three chapters to the answer. If God *has* rejected His people with whom He covenanted, then His Word is *not* reliable. Paul in Romans 11, is showing *how* that Word is fulfilled in regard to the standing of the Jews. First, in 11:1-10, he shows that God's Word is fulfilled via the saving of a Jewish remnant, among whom Paul reckons himself. Secondly, Paul begins at verse 11 to address the *permanent* status of the *mass* of the Jews. Have they, as a nation (the question of individual Jews was already dealt with) fallen beyond recovery? His answer could not be plainer if words are to mean anything at all. He starts out by saying, "Absolutely not!" He then proceeds to show the interest that the Gentiles, as a group, have in this question. They should be anxious to see the day of ingrafting because it will mean untold riches for the world. They should await that day in humility knowing that the very pitiful condition of the Jews is a reminder that we are saved always by grace. Covenant presumptuousness is *the* sin toward which covenant people are always inclined. Therefore, rather than boasting against the broken branches, the church of the Gentiles should fear. Furthermore, Paul says, they won't remain in unbelief forever. God is able to, and God will graft them in again, because, IN FACT, His gifts and His calling *are* irrevocable. He is fulfilling and will fulfill them in marvelous ways according to His infinite wisdom and grace. (I feel so hampered by space limitations in this summary, I can only ask you to meditate on the passage itself. It is sufficiently clear, and has been to the greater number of Reformed expositors until the Twentieth century.)

[51]Nearly all, "*Christian*" nations.

from all other people...(They are) a remarkable standing evidence of the truth of revealed religion."[52]

The Wrong Answers

Far from regarding them as a standing evidence of the truth of the Bible, the church from the fourth to the sixteenth century regarded the Jews with bewilderment or contempt, usually the latter. It was only to the church that the simple existence of this people became "the Jewish problem." It was uncomfortably necessary to reconcile the Jews' definite and distinct continuance with the Church's teaching that they had altogether fulfilled their redemptive-historical purposes. Of course, the devilish reason went, if their purpose had expired, the people might as well expire, too. Yet, they had to be accounted for, for there they were! So, attempts were made by many in the early church to do so. Sometimes irenic, mostly hostile, a great number of apologetical treatises designed to refute Judaism were issued. Justin, Tertullian, Cyprian, Hippolytus and Origen all tried their hand. The determination of the Jews to remain distinct and opposed to Christianity tried their patience. Augustine thought the Jews' purpose in this dispensation was to serve as an object lesson of the wrath of God. Chrysostom was especially virulent in his public attacks on the Jews, as was Ambrose. The former "thundered against the Jews with his bombastic and cynical eloquence; even [making] them the subject of six successive sermons."[53] Here's an example of his preaching:

> "[The Jews] are inveterate murderers, destroyers, men possessed by the devil...debauchery and drunkenness have given them the manners of pigs and lusty goats. They know only one thing, to satisfy their gullets, get drunk, to kill and maim one another...they murder their offspring and immolate them to the devil...The Jewish disease must be guarded against...The Christian's duty is to hate the Jews."

Jerome, accused of heresy because of his Jewish studies, sought to convince his opponents of his orthodoxy by assuring them, "If it is requisite to despise the individuals and the nation, so do I abhor the Jews with an inexpressible hate."[54]

---

[52]*Works*, (Edinburgh, Scotland: Banner of Truth) Vol. II, p. 495, 3.

[53]*History of the Jews,* by Heinrich Graetz, Vol II, p. 613.

[54]*Ibid.*, p. 625

"The turn in Jewish-Christian relations which followed the ascendancy of the Church in the fourth century is not a subject in which Christian readers can take any pride: there is too much substance in the Jews' complaint that Christendom has hidden the face of Christ from them."[55] "There can be little doubt that in these early centuries a theological construct of the Jew was created, which by the fourth century had lost many of its human features...The refutation and debasement of Judaism progressively became integral elements of [the church's] apologetics; among its apologists, there were signs of a rising irritation, the beginnings of a certain Judaeophobia."[56] And the more vitality Judaism enjoyed, the greater the hostility expressed toward her, because they just couldn't figure Israel out. In their theological framework there existed no place for the Jews.

Thoughts to Words to Deeds

Reality soon followed theology and the Jews were systematically and progressively excluded from life in "Christian" Europe. The stories and horrors are endless.[57] The origin of the ghetto, forced "conversions," banishments, the infamous blood libel, crusades in which crusaders were promised a ticket to bypass purgatory if they killed a Jew on the way to the "Holy Land," the burning down of synagogues with men, women and children inside, while "Christians" circled the burning building singing hymns—it's all just too much to recount. Suffice to say that Martin Luther's gibe well summarized more than a thousand years of church-synagogue relations: "If it is a mark of a good Christian to hate the Jews, what excellent Christians all of us are."[58]

---

[55]F.F. Bruce, cited by Roderick Campbell in *Israel and the New Covenant*, p. 10.

[56]Edward Flannery, *The Anguish of the Jews*, (Macmillan, 1965), p. 33, 35.

[57]Nineteenth-century evangelical scholar Franz Delitzsch observed, "The attitude of the Church to the Jews was almost willfully aimed to strengthen them in their antipathy to Christianity. The Church still owes the Jews the actual proof of Christianity's truth. Is it surprising that the Jewish people are such an insensitive and barren field for the Gospel? The Church itself has drenched it in blood and then heaped stones upon it."

[58]Quoted by N. Ausubel in *Pictorial History of the Jewish People* (Crown Publishers, 1959), p. 94. This is far different from the sentiments expressed by Marty in the early years of his enlightenment. "If I had been a Jew, and seen such stupidity and such blockheads reign in the Christian Church, I would rather have been a pig than a Christian. They have treated the Jews as if they were dogs, not men; they have done nothing but revile them. They are blood-relations of our Lord; therefore, if it were proper to boast of flesh and blood, the Jews belong to Christ

Here is a sampling of some of the acts which constituted "Christian" countenance toward the Jews during the five hundred year period prior to the Reformation (though their suffering did not then end):

Year	Event
1096-99	First Crusade. Crusaders massacred the Jews of the Rhineland. Many Jews commit suicide rather than submit to baptism.
1190	Anti-Jewish riots in England. Massacre at York and other cities.
1215	Fourth Lateran Council promulgates a canon requiring Jews to wear a distinguishing mark.
1290	Jews banished from England.
1348-50	"Holy" massacres throughout southwestern Europe when the Black Plague was blamed on Jews.
1421	270 Jews burned at stake in Vienna.
1492	Expulsion from Spain.
1496-7	Expulsion from Portugal; mass forced "conversions."
1516	First Ghetto in Christian Europe initiated in Venice.
1535	Tunisian Jews massacred.[59]

Remember, please, this is only a sampling. Viewing the plight of the Jews in Christian lands from the fourth century to the recent holocaust, one Jew observed, "First we were told 'You're not good enough to live among us as Jews.' Then we were told, 'You're not good enough to live among us.' Finally we were told, 'You're not good enough to live.'"[60]

This devastatingly accurate historical analysis was the fruit of an error, a building of prejudice and hate erected upon a false theological foundation. The blindness of the church regarding the place of

---

more than we...Therefore, it is my advice that we treat them kindly." (Graetz, Vol. IV, p. 470). Whether Luther was just using the Jews as another battering ram against Romanism, or whether he had a change of heart after years of failed attempts to convert them (interestingly, there is a record of three learned Jews having visited Luther with a view of converting *him*), "at the end of his life the German Reformer vilified the Jews in violent pamphlets." (Encyclopaedia Judaica).

59*Anti-Semitism,* p. 23. This was the result of the theological errors under the consolidation of power in Rome (Romanism).

60A paraphrase of Raul Hilberg's statement from *Destruction of the European Jews*, (New York: Harper Colophon, 1961), quoted also (more fully) in Lindsey, *The Road to Holocaust*, p. 6-7.

the Jew in redemptive history is, I believe, directly responsible for the wicked sins and attitudes described above. What the church believes about the Jews has *always* made a difference. But the church has not *always* believed a lie. In every way, not least in the matter of the proper posture toward the Jews, the bright and shining exemplar of true Christianity has been the Reformed faith.

The Exceptions and Their Rules

This has not gone unnoticed by modern Jewish scholars. One has noted that "French Calvinists were traditionally pro-Jewish, an outlook retained to a considerable extent to the present day...The role played by the Old Testament in Calvinism led the Puritan sects to identify themselves with the Jews of the Bible and reflected favorably on their attitude toward contemporary Jewry."[61]

What these scholars do not note is the role played by a more accurate understanding of the *future* of the Jews as indicated by St. Paul in Romans 11.[62] By the end of the sixteenth century, Jewish missions work was born in Reformed soil. "From the first quarter of the seventeenth century, belief in a future conversion of the Jews became commonplace among the English Puritans."[63] Cromwell, under whose rule the Jews were admitted back into England after four centuries of banishment, said, "Great is my sympathy with this poor people, whom God chose, and to whom He gave His Law."[64]

With the Reformation, a new day began for Jews living in Christian nations. Modern secular interpretations of history tend to overemphasize the Enlightenment as the cause of improvement of the Jews' position in the West, while understating the significance of Calvinism. The Reformed faith, in rewriting the rules of civilization in terms of the Bible, did not overlook the Jews and the Church's relation to them. The cherished hope of their future conversion before the return of Christ was such a confirmed belief that by the

---

[61]*Anti-Semitism*, p. 23. The book is a compilation of various articles gleaned from Encyclopaedia Judaica, published in 1974 by The Two Continents Publishing Group, 30 E. 42nd Street, New York, NY 10017. It is a most informative, objective, balanced, well-written, and disturbing compendium.

[62]For a survey of this passage and its impact on Puritan thought see Iain Murray, *The Puritan Hope* (Banner of Truth, Edinburgh: Scotland, 1975), chapter IV.

[63]*Ibid*, p. 43.

[64]Graetz, *op. cit.*, Vol. V, p. 27.

1640's it had become a confessional matter,[65] being written in one of the most important Reformed symbols, the *Westminster Larger Catechism:*

> Q. "What do we pray for in the second petition?"
> A. In the second petition, (which is, *Thy kingdom come,*)...we pray, that the kingdom of sin and Satan may be destroyed, the gospel propagated throughout the world, the Jews called, ***the fullness of the Gentiles brought in***, etc...[66]

Martin Bucer believed the future conversion of the Jews was guaranteed by Paul's teaching in Romans 11. This confidence was shared by Peter Martyr, Theodore Beza, and David Paraeus, the Heidelberg expositor, John Owen, Thomas Manton, John Flavel, Jeremiah Burroughs, David Dickson: "a list which could be greatly extended."[67]

The view that the conversion of the Jews prior to the consummation is certain was the commonly received one among the Dutch Reformed. Herman Witsius, the father of covenant theology, wrote on Romans 11:25, 26:

> "When the fullness of the Gentiles is brought in, all Israel will be saved: That is, ***as our Dutch commentators well observe***,[68] not a few, but a very great number, and in a manner the whole Jewish nation, in a full body...They depart from the apostle's meaning, who, by 'all Israel,' understand the 'mystical Israel,' or the people of God, consisting both of Jews and Gentiles, without admitting the conversion of the whole Jewish nation, in the sense we have mentioned."[69]

This extract establishes that the "spiritualized" notion of "Israel" in Rom 11:25, 26, was known to and *rejected by* the body of Dutch expositors. "During the sixteenth and seventeenth centuries several Reformed theologians in the Netherlands taught (what) would now be called Postmillennialism. Among them were such well known men

---

[65]How sad, then, that a minister was recently disinvited from a reputedly orthodox *Presbyterian* pulpit for preaching this very hope! But this decline is evident among the continental Reformed also, whose ancestors held to the very same interpretation of Romans 11 as the Puritans.

[66]Q&A 191. Scriptures quoted for support include Romans 10:1 and 11:25, 26.

[67]Murray, *The Puritan Hope*, p. 44.

[68]This makes it obvious that what Witsius is about to cite was the commonly understood interpretation.

[69]From *The Restoration of the Jews*, an extract from H. Witsius, published by George White in 1806.

as Coccejus, Alting, the two Vitringas, d'Outrein, Witsius, Hoornbeek, Koelman and Brakel...*The prevailing view* was that the gospel, which will gradually spread through the whole world, will in the end become immeasurably more effective than it is at present, and will usher in a period of rich spiritual blessing for the Church of Jesus Christ, a golden age, *in which the Jews will also share in the blessings of the gospel in an unprecedented manner*."[70]

The Dutch Demur

Since the turn of the century, most modern Dutch Reformed, following Kuyper and Bavinck, reject this historic position. Dr. Louis Berkhof, for example, acknowledges that "both the Old and New Testament speak of a future conversion of Israel, Zech 12:10; 13:1; 2 Cor 3:15, 16 and Rom. 11:25-29 seem to connect this with the end of time." He even admits that "it may be thought that Romans 11:11-32 certainly teaches the future conversion of the nation of Israel. Many commentators adopt this view." But then, strangely, Dear Dr. Louie turns around and says the correctness of this interpretation "is subject to considerable doubt."[71] (I urge you to keep this "doubt" in mind as you read the survey below of some other great minds on this passage.)

Anthony Hoekema gives what I regard as insubstantial treatment to Paul's argument in his book, *The Bible and the Future*. I was able to broach the subject briefly with Dr. H. before his passing. He was willing to discuss other possibilities.[72]

Herman Hoeksema offers a somewhat more satisfying treatment of Romans 11.[73] All who would like to find *some* justification for the wrong view of the future of the Jews, adopted by most Amillennialists, would do well to consult his comments on Romans 9-11. Nevertheless, Herman has major problems and unsupportable conclusions. He is correct when he rejects the idea of a special way of salvation for the Jews, but HH goes too far when he says we must not

---

[70]L. Berkhof, *Systematic Theology*, p. 716; cited by Greg L. Bahnsen from his article *The Prima Facie Acceptability of Postmillennialism* in the *Journal of Christian Reconstruction: Symposium on the Millennium* (Vallecito, CA: Chalcedon, Winter, 1976-77, Vol. III, No. 2.), emphasis added.

[71]*Systematic Theology*, p. 698-9.

[72]It should be noted that some Dutch Reformed hold to a brand of Amil that is very near the historic position. The element which I believe must be held by all is the certain expectation of the Jews' conversion before the parousia.

[73]In *God's Eternal Good Pleasure*, Reformed Free Publishing.

"expect a time when there shall be a widespread and very general conversion of the Jews." Paul, according to HH, "has not in mind any mass conversion of the Jews at some future time," the very notion being "certainly contrary to the immediate context." HH concludes that "'All Israel'...denotes the fullness of the elect Jews in the new dispensation."

No Way Around Romans 11

Let's consider some problems with Rev. Hoeksema's interpretation. Firstly, neither the immediate nor the broader *context* support his conclusions. One may not dismiss the second question of chapter 11, stated at verse 10, which provides the context to Paul's statements in the remainder of the chapter. Specifically, the question is, Have the Jews fallen beyond *recovery as a nation*. It may thus be seen that to regard "All Israel" as the fullness of elect Jews is just a grand begging of the question. That same definition could easily describe the Puritan's hope. They simply asserted that "the full number" includes (at least) an entire generation before the end.

Secondly, How would the fact that individual elect Jews would be saved discourage arrogance in the Gentiles, addressed as a group? A possible answer might be, "The Gentiles should realize that there will always be Jews in the Church." But Paul is not speaking about Jews *in* the church; he is now speaking about those who have been cut off-the Gentiles must not boast against *them* (v. 17-21).

In view of this, we add, thirdly, HH's interpretation utterly fails to account for verses 28 and 29, where, again, it is as clear as could be that Paul is talking about *presently unbelieving* Israel. *They (the Israel in question) are enemies* (v. 28). Surely no one would maintain that Paul has elect individuals in view here! Yet Paul says that these very enemies are *beloved* as far as election is concerned. This could mean nothing other than national election, the final fruits of which will be seen at their ingrafting, something for which the Gentiles should eagerly pray (10:1; 11:12,15).

Nor, fourthly, does Rev. Hoeksema's interpretation adequately explain the context which begins at verse 11 and includes these statements: "If their transgression means riches for the world...how much greater riches will their fullness bring" (v.12), and, "If their rejection is the reconciliation of the world, what will their acceptance be but life from the dead." HH thus ignores the very clear *two-fold* nature of Paul's argument, in which he argues for God's faithfulness in the preservation of a *Jewish remnant* (verses 1-10), and in the certainty of a *mass Jewish conversion* in the future (verses 11-36). Robert Haldane notes at verse 11, "Having proved that God had not cast away His people, by referring to the fact that even a remnant, according to the election of grace, was preserved, Paul supports his denial of their rejection by the consideration that in the process of time the whole nation shall be restored. This restoration...forms the subject of nearly the whole remainder [verses 11-36] of the chapter."[74] As I said, HH ignores this division.

In fact, fifthly, *once it is admitted that God is continually fulfilling ancient promises by saving Jews* ***as Jews*** *into the church throughout history, what principled objection is left to His fulfilling it dramatically and fully before the consummation?* It seems that the continued existence of the Jews as a distinct people with distinct promises is the very thing that irks these expositors. Yet, they themselves are forced to admit that distinct promises *are* being fulfilled *in some way*, by their own interpretation (at least of verses 1-10). Having granted, then, that the Jews enjoy a covenant promise which the Dutch and Mexicans (for example), as Dutch and Mexicans, do not, Amillennialists appear to be fighting for nothing but sheer prejudice's sake against the plain and natural interpretation of Romans 11:11-36.

Finally, if HH is right, what is the mystery about which Paul, at 11:25, 26, does not want the Romans (or us) to be ignorant? That Jews will be saved? He's already proved that long ago in verses 1-10! Is the mystery that the elect will be saved? Talk about tautologies! No. The revelation of which Gentiles should not be ignorant, that will keep them from being arrogant, is that God is not yet through with the Jews. Amen.[75]

---

[74]*Commentary on Romans* (Grand Rapids, MI: Kregel, [1853] 1988), p. 539.

[75]Charles Hodge stated the case succinctly and accurately in his commentary on Romans: "(There) shall be a full accomplishment of those prophecies which predicted the salvation of the Jews. The reason given in verses 28, 29 for the event to which Paul refers, is the unchangeableness of God's covenant and purpose. Having once taken the Jews into special connection with Himself, he never intended to cast them off forever. The apostle sums up his discourse by saying, 'As the Gentiles were formerly unbelieving, and yet obtained mercy, so the Jews who now disbelieve, shall hereafter be brought in; and thus God will have mercy on all, both Jews and Gentiles.' From all these considerations, it seems *obvious* that Paul intended here to predict that the time would come when the *Jews as a body,* should be converted unto the Lord; compare 2 Cor. 3:16. The prediction contained in this verse is to be explained by the context. The rejection of the Jews at the time of Christ, did not involve the perdition of every individual of that nation. Thousands, and even myriads, believed and were saved. So the restoration here foretold is not

A Great Cloud of Witnesses

This is not mere chauvinism.[76] This is the ***clear*** meaning of the Scripture. Says who? Says some of the greatest expositors in the history of the Christian church, across every major denominational line. What I wish to call attention to in the following excerpts is not simply the interpretation of this passage (and the sense of related passages) as given by these great men, but their uniform testimony to its ***clarity*** (*all emphases are mine)*. It is not simply the ***true*** interpretation, they maintain, it is the exceedingly and abundantly plain and certain interpretation. It is the ***necessary*** interpretation.

Jonathan Edwards: *Nothing is more certainly* foretold than this national conversion of the Jews in Romans 11.[77]

---

to be understood as including every individual of the Jewish people, but simply that there is to be a national restoration."

[76]In fact, it is strictly a Biblical argument, with historical support. It should not be assumed, however, that I am unaware of the startling disproportion of the Jewish contribution to civilization compared to their numbers. Countless examples could be cited. I was recently discussing great musicians of the Twentieth century with a musician friend. How is it that *the greatest* pianist of this century is a Jew, Vladimir Horowitz? James Hilton wrote these words of praise: "If by some dispensation a man born deaf were to be given hearing for a single hour, he might well spend the whole time with Horowitz...(It is) as if the instrument itself had never known what it could do until Horowitz came along." Similarly, the greatest violinist was Jascha Heifetz, a Jew. One reviewer referred to his "incredible tone and virtuosity, purity of intonation, and those superhuman doublestops." After Heifetz' passing, many have come to regard Isaac Stern, another Jew, as his replacement. Why is it that Jews so consistently go *to the top* of their chosen fields? For I use this one segment of one field—classical music—as typical. Even there, I didn't mention Arthur Rubinstein, Yehudi Menuhin, Yitzchak Perlman, etc., etc. Beyond classical, we'd have to consider Irving Berlin, George Gershwin, Oscar Hammerstein and Benny Goodman—for starters. The same prominence has been achieved in science and medicine. About still another field of endeavor, one writer quipped, "Quick. Name three leading economists who aren't Jewish." Whatever enterprise has been opened to them, in that the Jews have excelled. Except sports! When one keeps in mind that we are talking about a people who comprise about .4% of the world's population, roughly comparable to the number of Sikhs, and slightly more than Shamanists, we realize we are talking about a special people *by any standard.* How could Christians deny both their Bible and their own eyes by asserting that the Jews are, "No Special People"?! But I seem to be starting another article.

[77]*Works* (Edinburgh, Scotland: Bannar of Truth, 1979), p. 607. Edwards was no slouch and was not given to injudicious language. When he says "nothing is more certainly foretold" than this, well, I think it would be hasty to dismiss his emphasis without a thought.

John Murray: If we keep in mind the theme of this chapter and the sustained emphases on the restoration of Israel, *there is no other alternative* than to conclude that the proposition, "All Israel shall be saved," is to be interpreted in terms of the fullness, the receiving, the ingrafting of Israel *as a people*, the restoration of Israel to Gospel favor and blessing, and the correlative turning of Israel from unbelief to faith and repentance.[78]

John Brown: The apostle...represents the restoration of the Jews as *not only possible and probable, but as certain.*[79]

Lefevre d'Etaples (Faber): The final conversion of (the Jews) in the last ages is here *fully and explicitly* set forth.[80]

Robert L. Dabney: The promise of Israel's ingathering is *clearly* stated.[81]

David Brown: (on 11:26) *Clearly* the meaning here is the Israelitish nation at large. To understand this great statement, as some still do, merely of such a gradual inbringing of individual Jews, that there shall at length none remain in unbelief,[82] is to do manifest violence both to it and to the whole context. *It can only mean* the ultimate ingathering of Israel as a nation, in contrast with the present remnant.[83]

Robert Haldane: (on v. 25) Here is the *clearest attestation* that the blindness of the Jews will yet cease, not only as to individuals, but as to the body.[84]

---

[78]*The New International Commentary on the New Testament: Romans, in loc. cit.* This passage in Romans 11 won Murray away from Hoeksema's position and back to the historic Reformed/Presbyterian position.

[79]*Analytical Exposition of the Epistle to Paul to the Romans* (Grand Rapids, MI: Baker Books [1857] 1981), p. 407.

[80]Cited in note at Romans 11:33 in *Matthew Henry Commentary on the Holy Bible and Notes by Thomas Scott*, (Nashville,TN: Royal Publishers [Thomas Nelson], 1979).

[81]*Discussions* (Edinburgh, Scotland: Banner of Truth [same in Sprinkle reprint], 1982), Vol. 1, p. 211. Dabney the Magnificent was, in this context, *refuting* the theology of the Plymouth Brethren, notorious Dispensationalists.

[82]Hoeksema, representatively, does not grant even this.

[83]*Romans* (T&T Clark, no date), p. 117.

[84]*An Exposition of the Epistle to the Romans* (McLean, Va.: MacDonald Publishing Co. [1839] 1958), p. 541. Reprinted by Kregel in 1988.

Increase Mather: I know not any Scripture containing a more pregnant and illustrious testimony and demonstration of the Israelites' future vocation (calling), *this being the chief object of Paul*, to make this known to the Gentiles in Romans 11.[85]

Christoph Luthardt: It appears to me to be *beyond all doubt* that the conversion of Israel is to precede the Second Advent of Christ.[86]

Charles Simeon: (under the heading, "The certainty of it [their future conversion]," at Romans 11:25-27) It is *assured* to them by a special promise; and that promise is ratified by an unchangeable covenant...He will, by the power of His Word and the effectual operation of His Spirit, "turn away all ungodliness from Jacob;" and make them "a holy nation, a peculiar people, zealous of good works."[87]

Matthew Poole: (Speaking as St. Paul) "God has revealed to me that He will one day call the Jews again, and restore them to His favor."[88]

Robert Ballie: We grant willingly that the nation of the Jews shall be converted to the faith of Christ.[89]

H.C.G. Moule: "All Israel," Israel as a mass, no longer as by scattered units, shall be saved, coming to the feet of Him in whom alone is man's salvation...The great event of Israel's return to God in Christ, and His to Israel, will be the signal and the means of a vast rise of spiritual life in the universal church, and of an unexampled ingathering of regenerate souls from the world.[90]

---

[85]Cited by Iain Murray, *The Puritan Hope* (Edinburgh, Scotland: Banner of Truth, 1975), p. 61. Highly recommended.

[86]Cited by Charles Hodge, *Systematic Theology* (Grand Rapids, MI: Eerdman's, 1982), Vol. III, p. 807.

[87]*Expository Outlines on the Whole Bible* (Grand Rapids, MI: Baker, 1988), Vol. 15, p. 444.

[88]*Matthew Poole's Commentary on the Holy Bible*, (McLean, VA: MacDonald Publishing), *in loc. cit.*

[89]Quoted in Murray and cited by Greg Bahnsen in an article, *The Prima Facie Acceptability of Postmillennialism*, which appeared in a *Journal of Christian Reconstruction: Symposiun on the Millennium*, p. 79. Ballie was a Scottish commissioner to the Westminister Assembly.

[90]*The Expositor's Bible*, (Grand Rapids, MI: Baker), Vol. V, p. 590.

Thomas Boston: There is a day coming in which there shall be a national conversion of the Jews.[91]

Philip Doddridge: O that the blessed time were come when all Israel shall be saved...Our faith waits the glorious event, but *it shall be seen*, for the gifts and calling of God are without repentance.[92]

Leslie Allen: ***All Israel*** will be saved, brought into the Christian blessings into which now only a remnant of the Jews have entered. All Israel means the Jews as a collective whole...The phrase is obviously contrasted with ***part of Israel,*** and *Israel* consistently refers to the Jews in chs. 9-11.[93]

Matthew Henry: The blindness *will be* removed from Israel, and the nation saved from its rejected and dispersed state, and must at last become true believers.[94]

Geoffrey Wilson: There is to be a spiritual restoration of Israel as a nation...the central thrust of the Apostle is *unmistakable.*[95]

James Durham: Whatever may be doubted of their restoring to their land, yet they shall be brought to visible church state.[96]

John Trapp: The blindness (of Israel) is neither total nor perpetual.[97]

Charles Hodge: There is...to be a national conversion of the Jews...to take place before the second advent of Christ. (On v. 26) Israel, here, from the context, *must* mean the Jewish people, and all Israel, the whole nation. The Jews, as a people, are now rejected; as a people, they are to be restored.[98]

---

[91]Murray, *op. cit.* p.113.

[92]Quoted in Henry & Scott, *op. cit.*

[93]Howley, Bruce & Ellison, Editors; *The New Layman's Bible Commentary, in loc. cit.*, (Grand Rapids, MI: Zondervan, 1979).

[94]*in loc. cit.*

[95]*Romans* (Edinburgh, Scotland: Banner of Truth, 1969), p. 194.

[96]Murray, *op. cit.* p. 61.

[97]*Trapp's Commentary on the New Testament, in loc. cit.* (Grand Rapids, MI: Baker, reprint 1981).

[98]The first sentence of this quote is from his Systematics (Vol. III, p. 807). Hodge adds this interesting note to the subject in his commentary on Romans (from

A.A. Hodge: Paul, in Romans 11:15-29, both asserts and *proves*...the future general conversion of the Jews.[99]

F.F. Bruce: Israel's blindness is only partial, and only temporary...The new covenant will not be complete until it embraces the people of the old covenant.[100]

John Bengel: (Since) the conversion of Israel is a mystery...they should be treated with patience who do not recognize it so quickly, and we should hope for the time when all will recognize it.[101] The conversion...will not be partial, but will include all Israel.[102]

Richard Sibbes: (At) the conversion of the Jews there will be much joy.[103]

Robert Leighton: *Undoubtedly*, that people of the Jews shall once more be commanded to arise and shine, and their return shall be the riches of the Gentiles.[104]

William Perkins: The nation of the Jews shall be called, and converted to participation of this blessing; when and how, God knows; but that *it shall be done before the end of the world* we know.[105]

Thus we have a sampling of how some of the most pious and learned men in the history of the Church of Christ regard the question of the future of the Jews. For them, Scripture, as the inspired

---

which the balance of the quote is gleaned), p. 380: "It is *through the mercy shown to the Gentiles*, according to Paul, that the Jews are to be brought in, which implies that the former are to be instrumental in the restoration of the latter." This places a positive obligation on the Gentiles to seek through prayer, mercy and Word, the ingrafting of the Ancient People. In fact, on p. 381, he says that the mutual relation between the Christian church and the Jews should produce in the minds of *all the followers of Christ*, 1) a sense of obligation, 2) sincere compassion, 3) the banishment of all ill feelings of contempt toward them, and 4) an earnest desire for their restoration. AMEN!

[99]*Outlines of Theology* (Academie Books :Zondervan, 1972), p. 571-2.

[100]*Tyndale Commentaries—Romans, in loc. cit.*

[101]This foreword is dedicated to that hope.

[102]*Bengel's New Testament Commentary*, (Grand Rapids, MI: Kregel), *in loc. cit.*

[103]*A Puritan Golden Treasury*, compiled by I.D.E. Thomas, (Edinburgh, Scotland: Banner of Truth, 1977), p. 156.

[104]*Ibid.*, p. 157.

[105]*Ibid.*, p. 156.

Word and words of God, ***left no room for doubt as to the absolute certainty of the national conversion of Israel prior to the consummation.*** In no case can these sentiments be attributed to a "party spirit." We have quoted Presbyterian, Independent, Anglican, Reformed, Baptist—even Lutheran. None of these men, to my knowledge, can be called a Dispensationalist. Most held to the Reformed confessions. **Some helped write them!** The views expressed are those of the historic Christian church, recaptured at the Reformation and being brought to the fore once again by the work of Christian Reconstructionists. These views above are not the rantings of fanatical (or even sane and sober) Premillennialists. As a matter of fact, the author of a mid-nineteenth century article appearing in *The British and Foreign Evangelical Review* believed it appropriate "to state emphatically that he has no sympathy whatever with any Millennarian theory [i.e., Premillennialism—SMS], and that he considers all such ideas, and especially such as involve the personal reign of our Savior, as merely carnal and Judaizing."! Yet, he was able to assert, just as clearly:

> We believe that it is not denied by any considerable number of Christians, or by any respectable class of interpreters, that the Jews, as a nation, will be converted to Christianity, and that this event is immediately connected with stupendous events in the future...*This is so clearly taught in the eleventh chapter of the Epistle to the Romans that one could scarcely deny it and retain his Christian character.*

How the Mighty Have Drifted

Scripture didn't change since that was written, but the prevailing Reformed sentiment certainly has! The regret expressed 150 years ago by Charles Simeon, is even more applicable today:

> It is lamentable to observe how "wise" the generality of Christians are "in their own conceits," in reference to this matter: how contemptuously they speak of the Jews, as if they were by nature worse than ourselves; and as if they were never again to be restored to the favor of their God. But, if we bear in mind what they once were, and what they are yet destined to become, we shall regard them with veneration, for their fathers' sakes, and seek their welfare with earnestness for their own sakes.[106]

---

[106]*Expository Outlines of the Whole Bible* (Grand Rapids, MI: Baker),Vol. 15, p. 445. Simeon's burden for the Jews was very great. In his index to these outlines, he provides more than two dozen references to outlines explaining prophecies relating to the Jews, their future conversion, the duty of the Christian to promote it, etc. He also lists, under **JEWS, How to Win Them**, "86 expositions on Jewish history and how to bring Jews to Christ." Though an Anglican, he was more than "in step" with the spirit of *The Directory for Publick Worship* of the Scotch

This is the heart of the faith of the Reformation as it comes to bear on "the Jewish question."[107] As you can see, the change in the fortune of the Jews in Western civilization can be traced, *not* to humanism, but to the Reformed faith. The rediscovery of Scripture brought a rekindling of the Biblical conviction that God had not, in fact, fully nor finally rejected His people. The blindness that has come upon them is *partial* (Romans 11:1-10), and *temporary* (Romans 11:11-36).

I've called in many witnesses to support what I believe to be an obvious Scripture truth. Some of these witnesses are familiar to you, some of them are obscure, but their uniform testimony is plain: God has not forsaken His people. They (the "lump", the "branches") *are* special in view of their unique relation to Abraham, Isaac and Jacob (the "firstfruit", the "root").

I Beseech Thee...

You have surveyed the evidence. Now listen to a plea:

> Be persuaded, dear brethren, be stirred up, to pray for the outpouring of the Spirit on the house of Israel. Let but the veil which is between the face of Moses, and the heart of Israel, and which has been removed from Moses' face in Christ, be removed also from their heart, and the synagogue immediately becomes the church: for if they believe Moses, they will believe Christ. But remove this veil no creature can: it is the work of God's Spirit solely and entirely. It is ours to speak to them the truth in love, if peradventure God may give them repentance to the acknowledging of the truth: to commend Christianity by our lives, adorning the doctrine of God our Saviour in all things; and above all, to pour out to God continually our heart's desire and prayer, that, by pouring out His Spirit upon them, He would lift up from their hearts the veil, which hides the Law and Gospel equally from their view.[108]

GOD HAS NOT FORSAKEN HIS PEOPLE! Join me in keeping high the vision of their future. "O to see the sight, next to Christ's coming in the clouds, the most joyful! Our elder brethren the Jews and Christ fall upon one another's necks and kiss each other."[109]

Presbyterian church, which urged that continual prayer be offered for the restoration of the Jews in the public worship of God.

[107]Do not forget that the first church council had as its first big problem, "The *Gentile* Question." See Acts 15.

[108]*Rich Gleanings from "Rabbi" Duncan*, being Evangelical Sermons, Lectures & Addresses by the Late Rev. John Duncan, LL.D. (Reprinted by Free Presbyterian Publications, Glasgow, 1984), p. 355.

[109]Samuel Rutherford, quoted in *Treasury*, *op. cit.* p. 157.

A Caution

With this vision before us, all parties involved in the current debate over Christian Reconstruction would do well to emulate the irenic spirit of the Rev. Dr. David Brown. He writes in his preface to *The Restoration of the Jews*, words which we would do well to make our own: "To controversy with the servants of Christ, and beloved friends in the Gospel, I am growing more and more averse the longer I live."

Few there will be who, even supposing that they strongly disagree with Dr. Brown's conclusions, will put this book down without the conviction that here, indeed, they have met with both a scholar *and* a gentleman. I urge this emulation even more so upon my Postmillennial brothers, in consideration of the fact that history will, we trust, prove the Postmillennial system to be the true one. Since explicit historical fulfillment is the best interpreter of prophecy,[110] not only wisdom, but prudence as well, call upon us to be patient with our Dispensational brethren, knowing for a certainty that in time, and perhaps sooner than we think, the greater number of them will behold the errors of that way and embrace Reformed truth to the glory of Christ our King. Not a few, myself included, already have.

The same holds true for our Amillennial friends in the Reformed family. While both groups have not wholly resisted the temptation to interpret the Bible in light of their newspapers, we assert that the day will come when their newspapers and the Bible will, in fact, agree. No less a personage than "Dr. Joel Nederhood, world known radio preacher for The Back to God Hour, concluded (a) keynote address (by) saying: 'I am A-Millennial. But seeing what is happening in Europe in these last few days has made me wonder if I shouldn't reconsider Postmillennialism.'"[111]

Yes, Dr. Nederhood, of course you should. But as you do, remember Dr. Brown's good advice: "The wise will not be over-hasty in interpreting specific predictions by passing events." If an interpretation is not true *to Scripture*, it will not be true in history, and will be shown to be false in the future. It is from the Scripture that we

---

[110]Dr. Brown puts it this way: "The interpretation of prophecy—besides involving difficulties peculiar to itself, with which the (church) Fathers were ill aided to grapple—is aided by nothing so much as *time*, that great unfolder of the divine purposes, and commentator on the inspired oracles."

[111]*The Counsel of Chalcedon*, Volume XI, Nos. 11&12 (January/February, 1990), p. 41. This monthly is published by Chalcedon Presbyterian Church and is available for $25 per year. P.O. Box 28357, Atlanta, GA 30358.

must gather our infallible data, and it is to the Scripture that we must look for the keys to interpretation, *not* the newspapers. Whatever may happen in the short run, we have perfect confidence that our Messiah will vindicate his rule and reign, manifestly, in the long run. In this plan, Israel is to play no small part.

The Road to Restoration

I pray that I have proven to my Dispensational brothers that Reformed Covenant theology contains no intrinsic threat for Israel, if only the covenanters bear in mind, as they historically have, that Israel *is* unique. Christian Reconstruction, in calling the Church back to its erstwhile convictions regarding the Law and the future, far from paving the road to holocaust, actually ***paves the Road to Restoration.***

I have also labored to prove to my Reformed family that Israel's uniqueness is no threat to covenant theology, if only it is borne in mind that their future ingrafting will occur as the completion (in Messiah) of the promises God made to the patriarchs. *In fact, it is only because we believe in covenant that we can fully comprehend this picture.* God has demonstrated continually throughout the Old Testament that He may fulfill promises made to one generation several generations later. A generation of Israelites received a promise of deliverance from bondage and entrance to the promised land of milk and honey (Ex 3:8). They were, indeed, redeemed from bondage, but failed to enter the promised land themselves due to unbelief. *Their children*, however, entered. Promise fulfilled-*covenantally*. So also, when Jesus says, "You shall not see me again until you say, 'Blessed is He who comes in the name of the Lord," well, the generation to whom that prophetic utterance was made is long gone. BUT THEIR COVENANT DESCENDANTS, PRAISE GOD, ARE NOT! And since God's Word, God's gifts and God's calling, are all irrevocable, what we have seen for the last two thousand years is only their suspension. There is no doubt that God will remove the veil from Israel *before* Christ returns, and all Israel shall be saved. May all God's people pray and obey toward that end. Amen.

THE RESTORATION

OF

THE JEWS

THE HISTORY, PRINCIPLES, AND BEARINGS OF THE QUESTION

by David Brown, D.D.

O to see the sight, next to Christ's Coming in the clouds, the most joyful! Our elder brethren the Jews and Christ fall upon one another; they will be kind to one another when they meet. O day! O longed for and lovely day-dawn! O sweet Jesus, let me see that sight which will be as life from the dead, thee and thy ancient people in mutual embraces.

Samuel Rutherford (1635)*

*Quoted from *The Letters of Samuel Rutherford* in *The Puritan Hope: Revival and the Interpretation of Prophecy* (Edinburgh, Scotland: Banner of Truth, 1984), p. 98.

PREFACE

PERHAPS I ought to inform the reader how this treatise originated. Many years ago I published a work on the premillennial theory of the Second advent, of which several editions have since appeared.[1] In that work the ultimate Restoration of the Jews to their own land, though not discussed, was regarded as a scriptural expectation. This gave rise to a charge of inconsistency alike on the millenarian side, for holding the Restoration of the Jews, and not also the premillennial theory; and on the anti-millenarian side, for rejecting the premillennial theory, and not also the Restoration of the Jews. Both these parties—widely as they differ from each other, alike in their principles of interpretation and in the results of them—being thus of one mind as to the inseparable connexion between the above-mentioned doctrines, I felt myself called on, alike out of deference to respected friends on both sides and from regard to my own consistency, to give to the public the grounds on which I believed that there was no foundation for the alleged connexion, and that it proceeded, in the case of both parties alike, on untenable principles of Scripture interpretation. This accordingly I did in three articles of a Magazine now discontinued, which a good while afterwards were reprinted, in an enlarged form, as one article, in the *British and Foreign Evangelical Review* for March 1855. Since then I have been repeatedly solicited to issue the whole in a separate form, not only by those who deemed it convincing, but by some who, though still inclining to the opposite view, thought that historical facts so little known, and a line of reasoning which they considered fresh, ought not to be allowed to go out of sight, as all periodical literature is apt to do. But nothing could overcome my reluctance to this step, not to speak of other studies which have since engrossed my attention; and, although able treatises have meantime been given to the public, advocating principles and conclusions the reverse of mine, I could see no sufficient reason for being again drawn into this line of investigation. To controversy with the servants of Christ, and beloved friends in the Gospel, I am growing more and more averse the longer I live.

---

[1]David Brown, ***Christ's Second Coming: Will it be Premillennial?*** (Edmonton, Alberta: Still Waters Revival Books, [1882, 7th edition] reprinted 1990).—RB.

While retaining all that I believe to be Divine truth, the air which I love to breathe, and the fellowship I delight to cherish, are those of a catholic Christianity. But having had occasion lately, in the preparation of a Commentary on the Epistle of the Romans, to reconsider the elaborate statements of the eleventh chapter, on the present standing and future prospects of the Jewish nation, I was struck with the force of the reasoning which, many years before, I had founded on that chapter, in my article on the Jews; and I candidly confess that, on reading that whole article anew, I could not but feel some regret that so much historical and exegetical matter—not elsewhere to be found, and never formally assailed—should now be all but inaccessible. And the desire for its separate publication having at that time been anew presented to me, and somewhat emphatically, by competent judges, whose attention had been specially directed to the subject, I was induced at length to comply with it—not with the intention of re-opening old controversies, which I fondly trust it may not, but simply as my contribution towards the settlement of a question involving some difficulty.

It is not impossible that the calamitous events which are directing all eyes at present to Syria, and the consequences of them, may by and by impart to this subject a new interest. But the wise will not be over-hasty in interpreting specific predictions by passing events, but, while standing on their watchtower, will entrench themselves in great general principles. "We have also a more sure word of prophecy, whereunto we do well that we take heed, as unto a light shining in a dark place, until the day dawn, and the day-star arise in our hearts."

If in this work I have omitted all notice of some passages which many would expect to be discussed in a work professing to treat of the Restoration of the Jews, it is either because I believe that they have nothing at all to do with the Jews, (such as Rev. xvi. 12,) or because they required more criticism than my limits would admit, (as Isa. xviii.; Ezek. xl.-xlviii.,) or simply because their testimony either way appeared to me indecisive.[2]

ABERDEEN, *February* 1861.

---

[2]As certain of David Brown's historical references may seem a little obscure to those unfamiliar with Church history, it has been brought to my attention that some readers may find it more profitable, after reading the "Introduction;" to proceed to the "Part Second—The Principles of the Question;" continuing to the end of the book; then, returning to read the "Part First—The History of the Question" last.—RB.

INTRODUCTION

The present standing and future prospects of the Jewish nation can be determined only by an appeal to the living oracles. It is purely an exegetical question. As such, it is a question both of difficulty and importance, involving, as it does, all the great principles of biblical interpretation. As it respects the Jews themselves, it raises the interesting inquiry, whether that people, so long "scattered and peeled, meted out, and trodden down, and wonderful from their beginning hitherto," have already accomplished their national destiny, or what further may be in reserve for them? And as one of the great questions touching the prospects of the Church, and the state of the world in the latter day, it possesses far more than a speculative interest.

The descendants of Abraham present a spectacle altogether unique in the history of nations, whether politically, socially, or religiously considered. Forty centuries have run their course since the father of the faithful was summoned out of Ur of the Chaldees to become "a great nation." That great nation still lives. Its identity is unquestioned. They are the same people who, when stretched forth in the plains of Moab and beheld "from the top of the rocks, as the valleys spread forth, as gardens by the river's side, as the trees of lign-aloes which the Lord hath planted, and as cedar trees beside the waters," kindled the inspiration of Balaam, and wrung from the hireling that remarkable prediction, "*Lo, the people shall dwell alone, and shall not be reckoned among the nations.*" From that hour to this have that wonderful people dwelt alone. The mightiest nations that ever the world saw—the ancient Egyptians, the Assyrians and Chaldeans, the Carthaginians, and even the Romans—are no more. The names of some of them still exist; the territories they occupies are still possessed; their blood flows more or less in the veins of some modern peoples; but the races have changed, and no nation now existing can trace its descent through any thing approaching to the period during which the Israelitish race have continued an unmingled and universally recognized people.

"Were there"—says the late lamented Dr. Isaac Da Costa of Amsterdam, himself a distinguished Israelite—"Were there now in existence an individual who could with certainty trace his pedigree from one of the ancient Greek or Roman families, with what care and interest would such a circumstance be investigated as a living remnant of antiquity! And yet Israel, the very Israel whose annals extend to the most remote periods of sacred and profane history, still remains, not as a remnant only, consisting of a very few solitary individuals or families, but the whole body of the people still exists, scattered over every part of our globe."[1]

But the circumstances in which they have been preserved enhance prodigiously the singularity of their preservation, baffling every attempt to explain it on ordinary principles. Not less contrary to the laws of nature was the widow's barrel of meal not wasting and her cruse of oil not failing, in spite of the daily use that was made of both, than is the continuance of the Hebrew race in direct contradiction to all the laws by which nations are affected. When a people are driven from their fatherland in such numbers that comparatively few are left behind; when, instead of being kept together in their banished state, they are dispersed amongst the nations; when they are denied the privilege of possessing land, or any fixed property whatever; when their unwearied efforts to acquire even moveable property are thwarted from time to time, their goods ruthlessly seized, and themselves subjected to insult and persecution, in not a few cases even unto blood—there is no instance of any nation long surviving treatment like this. Under such usage, when persevered in for any length of time, tribes and peoples melt away by degrees, either becoming extinct altogether, or mingling with and merging into the nations in whose territories they reside. But though this is the treatment which the Jews have met with, this is not the end to which the Jews have come. Under this grinding, wasting process, they have not been extirpated, they have not been absorbed, even their numbers have not been diminished. "The common occupancy of their native soil," says the eloquent and sagacious *Milman*, "seems in general the only tie that permanently unites the various families and tribes which constitute a nation. As long as that bond endures, a people may be sunk to the lowest state of degradation; they may be reduced to a slave-caste under the oppression of foreign invaders: yet favourable circumstances may again develop the latent germ of a free and united nation; they may rise again to power and greatness, as well as to independence. But when that bond is severed, nationality usually becomes extinct. A people transported from their native country, if scattered in small numbers, gradually melt away, and are lost in the surrounding tribes; if settled in larger masses, remote from each

---

[1]Israel and the Gentiles: Contributions to the History of the Jews from the earliest times to the present day. By Dr. Isaac Da Costa of Amsterdam. Translated from the Dutch. London, 1850: pp. 4, 5.

other, they grow up into distinct commonwealths; but, in a generation or two, the principle of separation, which is perpetually at work, effectually obliterates all community of interest or feeling. If a traditionary remembrance of their common origin survives, it is accompanied by none of the attachment of kindred; there is no family pride or affection; there is no *blood* between the scattered descendants of common ancestors, for time gradually loosens all other ties; habits of life change; laws are modified by the circumstances of the state and people; religion, at least in all polytheistic nations, is not exempt from the influence of the great innovator.The separate communities have outgrown the common objects of national pride; the memorable events of their history during the time that they dwelt together, their common traditions, the fame of their heroes, the songs of their poets, are superseded by more recent names and occurrences; each has his new stock of reminiscences in which their former kindred cannot participate. Even their languages have diverged from each other. They are not of one speech; they have either entirely or partially ceased to be mutually intelligible. If, in short, they meet again, there is a remote family likeness, but they are strangers in all that connects man with man or tribe with tribe. *One nation alone seems entirely exempt from this universal law.*"[2] "It is calculated," says this historian in another place, "that there exist between four and five millions"—more recent and accurate calculations give about seven millions—"of this people, descended in a direct line from, and maintaining the same laws with their forefathers, who, above three thousand years ago, retreated from Egypt under the guidance of their inspired lawgiver.
. . . .They are still found in every quarter of the world, under every climate, in every region, under every form of government, wearing the indelible national stamp on their features, united by the close moral affinity of habits and feelings, and, at least the mass of the community, treasuring in their hearts the same reliance on their national privileges, the same trust in the promises of their God, the same conscientious attachment to the institutions of their fathers."[3]

But if this be marvellous in our eyes, the condition in which they exist must be much more so. We might imagine them existing as a race of hewers of wood and drawers of water, abject dependents on the power and bounty of other nations. But instead of this, such is their wealth, that without them the sovereigns of Europe would be

---

[2]History of the Jews, book viii., vol. i., pp. 326-328: second edition, 1830. Some of the peculiarities above noted have, to a certain extent, been realised in other nations; but the statement as a whole carries resistless conviction.

[3]Book xxviii., pp. 417-424.

paralyzed in the execution of their gigantic undertakings. To them they must look when vast sums of money are required on a sudden. The sinews of war are supplied by them. "Their wide-extended and rapid correspondence throughout the world," which notoriously outstripped Napoleon's couriers, "and the secret ramifications of their trade, which not only commanded the supply of the precious metals but much of the internal traffic of Europe, and probably made great inroads on his continental system"—in a word, their being invariable auxiliaries of a commissariat in every quarter of Europe—all this has been advanced to account for the great conqueror's desire to gain the confidence of this singular race. But more than this: "Among the Jews," says Da Costa, "fresh vigour displays itself in every department of the arts and sciences; in Germany, the sons of Israel are distinguished professors of philosophy, letters, astronomy, and jurisprudence. Like their forefathers, before the catastrophe which put an end to their political existence, the descendants of Abraham for the last half century have again borne arms with honour. The poetic harp of Israel sounds for the first time to European accents, and Israelitish names are found the greatest masters of music in our day. In almost every part of Europe, Israelites afford to the country of their sojourn the benefit not of riches only, but of talent, genius, and learning."[4] Is there any parallel to this in the history of nations? If there be such a thing as a moral miracle, traversing all the fixed laws of the social and political worlds, this surely is one; and if it be a miracle at all, it is a *standing miracle.*

But the crowning circumstance remains to be noticed. These singularities in the Israelitish history are the literal fulfilment of Divine predictions, while the *judicial* character of their dispersion and sufferings invests the subject with an interest truly awful. In them *Miracle, Prophecy,* and *Retribution* have all their living monuments. In them the truth of revelation, and the commanding presence of its Author in the world, have their abiding witness. Shall I add, that from them has issued the LIGHT and LIFE of the world? Jesus of Nazareth—"over all God blessed for ever"—was a Jew, a lineal descendant, according to the flesh, of Abraham and of David; and that peculiar appearance, that characteristic expression, which no one can accurately observe in the Jewish countenance without knowing it all the world over, is fitted to bring before us, in the most lively and affecting manner, the external features of that adorable one "who dwelt among us," and stamps the nation with unutterable and undying interest.

---

[4]Israel and the Gentiles, pp. 12, 13.

PART FIRST

THE HISTORY OF THE QUESTION

An outline of the literature of the question, distributed into periods, may suitably introduce the exegetical discussion of it.

CHAPTER I

THE PATRISTIC PERIOD

Although the primitive Church is known to have been divided from the very first on the question of the Premillennial Advent and Personal Reign of Christ on the earth, it is a curious fact, and one that will probably startle my readers, that the national and territorial restoration of the Jews not only never entered into the controversy at all, but seems not to have been believed in by either of the parties. That the opponents of the Personal Reign should have denied to the Jews the repossession of Canaan will to many seem natural enough, and to none very surprising. But that the expectants of the Personal Reign should in this particular have agreed with their opponents will to most appear scarcely credible. None of our Church historians notice the point. Mosheim, Lardner, Burton, Kaye, Neander, Gieseler, and all careful investigators of the original sources, have dwelt more or less on the Millennial controversy, as it was agitated in the primitive Church; but as this *Jewish* element formed no part of the dispute, the attention of the historians has not been directed to it, and I have been forced to investigate the subject for myself.

It was their general principles of prophetic interpretation that brought both parties to the same conclusion regarding the Jews. Both took the same view of their standing under the Gospel which is now held by those who *deny* the territorial restoration. Considering the distinction between Jew and Gentile to have been utterly and to all effects done away in Christ, they understood those predictions which relate to the restored condition of "Israel," "Judah," "Jacob," "Zion"—in short, the covenant-people—simply of the *Christian Church*, or believers in Christ. Here both parties were entirely at one. The point at which they diverged related to the *sense* in which this predicted glory of the Church upon earth was to be realized; the one party, the opposers of the Millennium, understanding it of the moral effects of Christianity in moulding character, renovating society, and bringing the world into subjection to God; while the other party, the expectants of the Personal Reign, applied it to the millennial state of the earth under Christ and the risen saints. With the former party, *Israel* resettled felicitously in the land of their fathers meant *the Church* in a prosperous condition and near to God: with the latter party, it meant the Church of Christ too, but either that portion of it that is to rise and reign with Christ, or such as, being found alive at His coming, shall continue alive during the thousand years under government of the risen saints, What predictions were to be understood of the one class, and what of the other, seems to have been determined very arbitrarily; and at times the two classes seem to run into each other, the resurrection state being brought down to a condition very little above the present, while the prophetic pictures of things temporal are sublimated into something adapted to a superior state.

A few extracts from the millenarian fathers will sufficiently confirm these remarks.

If the "Epistle of Barnabas" was written by Paul's companion of that name,[1] and if his sentiments are correctly reported by Whitby and Gieseler, we ought to begin with him. Geisler[2] speaks of "the millenarianism of the epistle," referring to chapter xv. But its millenarianism is limited to the expectation of a personal Antichrist, and of a sabbatical millenary thereafter: in every other respect, its exegesis—if we may dignify its principles of Scripture interpretation by

[1]But for internal grounds of suspicion, the unhesitating testimony of *Clement* of Alexandria, of *Origen*, of *Eusebius*, of *Jerome*—with nothing to oppose to it—would settle the question in the affirmative. Accordingly, from Isaac Vossius, who in 1646 published a corrected text of it, to Hefele, whose first edition of the "Apostolic Fathers" was published in 1839, this epistle has found powerful defenders, including our own Pearson, Cave, Wake, and Lardner. Gieseler also declares for it. But the array of names against it includes some of the greatest, and our own Jeremiah Jones and Dr. Burton are in the number. Their objections, however, are purely internal, and amount just to this, that no companion of the Apostle Paul, and still less one so eminent among the apostles as Barnabas, could have spiritualized the Old Testament in the way this writer does, and generally, that such a man could not have written such an epistle. Those who have traced the vast disparity between the most valued remains of apostolic but uninspired antiquity and the canonical writings, will hesitate to pronounce this line of argument quite conclusive. But in the present case its force is very great.

[2]Ecclesiastical History. First Period, (XX) 35, note 1. (Clark's Translation.)

such a name—is the reverse of millenarian. "St. Barnaby," says Whitby, "is very positive that the very temple which was destroyed by their enemies shall be rebuilt gloriously."[3] But "Barnaby" says nothing of the sort, or rather, if he is "positive" at all, it is in saying just the reverse—that the temple is henceforth to be erected in the heart.[4] And yet Whitby is referred to as an authority on the opinions of the fathers in such matters, by Vitringa and other learned men, who were quite as competent to judge as Whitby himself, but who, as their studies lay in other directions, were ready to take on trust what appeared to be the fruit of accurate research in this well-known author. I shall have occasion presently to notice another of his mistakes. Passing from Barnabas then, I may say a word or two about

1. CERINTHUS, a contemporary of the apostle John, whose millennial scheme appears to have been of the most sensuous description, but about whom, on this subject, opinion is very much divided. Eusebius, on the testimony of those who, being themselves engaged in the millennial controversy, were likely to understand it, represents him as teaching "that after the resurrection the kingdom of Christ would be terrestrial, and consist in feasts, *sacrifices, and slaying of offerings,* and that the flesh would again live in Jerusalem, subject to desires and pleasures."—(*Καὶ πάλιν ἐπιθυμίας καὶ ἡδοναῖς ἐν Ἱερουσαλὴμ τήν πολιτευόμενην δουλεύειν*)[5] On the other hand, some of the most learned historians[6] are inclined to suspect that Cerinthus has in this case been misrepresented, there being no evidence that his millennium was essentially different from that of other millenarians. Perhaps there is some truth in both statements, as Ebionite and Gnostic elements are mixed together in his system—if so it may be called. But observe how clearly,

2. IRENÆUS, Bishop of Lyons in the latter half of the second century, distinguishes between the two states, the mortal and the incorruptible, and the two classes of saints, in the following passage.

---

[3]"Treatise of the True Millennium," in Paraph. and Comment. on N.T., ii. 692. Ed. 1760.

[4]In Hefele's edition, the following is the heading of chap. xvi.: "*That not the temple of the Jews but the spiritual temple of Christians is pleasing to God.*" After describing that temple of God which was to be built in the last days, and which, he says, is now in process of erection, as consisting in the purified and obedient hearts of men under the Gospel, he closes this chapter with the words, "This is the spiritual temple built for the Lord."—(*Τουτέστι πνευματικὸς ναὸς οἰκοδομούμενος τῷ Κυρίῳ.*)

[5]Hist. Eccl., 1. iii. c. xxviii.

[6]Mosheim, De Reb. Christ. ante Const., cent. i.; Lardner, Credibility, vol. iv. 689, 690; Neander, Hist., ii. 82-88—(Clark.)

Having spoken of the resurrection of the just to reign on the earth after Antichrist's destruction, he goes on to say:—

"And those whom the Lord shall find in the flesh, expecting Him from heaven, having endured tribulation, and escaped the hands of the wicked, these [not the raised saints, but those 'found in the flesh'] are they of whom the prophet says, 'And they that are left shall be multiplied on the earth.' And as many of the faithful as God hath prepared for this to be 'the left that shall be multiplied on the earth,' and to come under the government of the [raised] saints, and *to minister at this Jerusalem*," &c. (. . . ."et sub regno sanctorum fieri, et ministrare huic Hierusalem.")[7]

But the line of demarcation, here so distinctly drawn, hopelessly escapes us in other passages of the same father; the consequence of which is a complete jumble. The two following specimens will give the reader an idea, the one of his principles of interpretation, the other of his notion of Jewish restoration:—

"In saying to his disciples, 'I will not drink henceforth of this fruit of the vine until that day when I drink it new with you in my Father's kingdom,' . . . . He promised to drink of a species of wine with His disciples—thus announcing both the inheritance of the earth, on which this new kind of wine would be drunk, and the fleshly resurrection of His disciples. . . . . But He cannot be understood as drinking of any kind of wine above, as set down in the supercelestial place with His disciples; nor are they disembodied spirits who drink it, for it is the property of flesh, and not of spirit, to drink wine. Hence the Lord said, 'When thou makest a dinner or a supper, call the deaf, the blind, the beggars, and thou shalt be recompensed at the resurrection of the just.' And again He saith, 'Whosoever shall leave fields,' &c., 'for my sake, shall receive an hundredfold in this world, and in the world to come life eternal.' For what are those hundredfolds in this life, and the dinners spread out for the poor, and the suppers which are rendered back? They refer to the times of the kingdom—that is, the seventh day, which is sanctified, in which God hath rested from all His works which He hath made, which is the true Sabbath of the just, in which they shall do no terrene work; but they shall have a prepared table spread out by God, who shall feed them with all dainties. To the like effect is the blessing wherewith Isaac blessed his younger son Jacob, saying, 'Lo, the smell of my son is as the smell of a field which the Lord hath blessed. But the field is the world; and therefore he added, 'God give thee of the dew of heaven, and of the fatness of the earth, and plenty of corn and wine,' &c.

---

[7]Adv. Hær., 1. v. c. xxxv.

. . . .The predicted blessing indubitably belongs to the times of the kingdom, when also the creature [or creation,] renovated and freed, shall bear plenty of every kind of food, ('quando regnabunt justi surgentes a mortuis, quando et creatura renovata et liberata multitudinem fructificabit universa esca,' i.e., for 'the just rising from the dead,' as the whole scope of the passage shews,) through the dew of heaven, and the fruitfulness of the earth: even as the presbyters, who saw John, the Lord's disciple, relate that they heard from him, as the Lord taught concerning those times, saying, 'The days shall come in which there shall grow vines, each having ten thousand boughs, and on one bough ten thousand branches, and on one branch ten thousand shoots, and on one shoot ten thousand clusters, and on every cluster ten thousand grapes, and every grape when pressed shall yield five and twenty metretæ of wine [little short of 300 gallons]. And when one shall have laid hold of one of these sacred clusters, another shall cry out, I am a better cluster, take me, and by me bless the Lord. In like manner; also, that a grain of wheat shall yield ten thousand ears, and every ear have ten thousand grains, and every grain ten pounds of fine clean flour; and so of all other fruits, and seeds, and herbs, according to their natures; and that all animals living on the produce of the earth should become peaceable, and in harmony with each, being subject to men with all subjection.' Now these things *Papias*, a hearer of John and a companion of Polycarp, an ancient, testifies in the fourth of his books, for there are five books composed by him. And he added, saying, 'Now these things are credible to believers,' ('hæc autem credibilia sunt credentibus.') And when Judas the traitor, he said, not believing, asked, 'But how shall the Lord bring such things to pass?' the Lord said, 'They shall see who shall come to them.'"[8]

Such is a fair and ample specimen of Irenaeus's principles of prophetic interpretation. Observe, next, his view of Jewish restoration:—

"Ezekiel says, . . . 'Thus saith the Lord, I will gather Israel from all nations where they are dispersed; and they shall dwell on the land which I gave to my servant Jacob, and they shall inhabit it in hope, and they shall build houses and plant vines.' . . . . But we have shewn a little ago, that *the Church is the seed of Abraham*. . . . . And Isaiah says, 'And there shall be upon every high mountain streams of water, in that day when . . . . He bindeth up the breach of His people, and healeth the smart of their wound.' Now the smart of the wound by which disobedient man was struck at the beginning in Adam is death,

[8]Adv. Hær., 1. v. c. xxxiii.

which God will heal when He raises us from the dead and *restores us to the heritage of the fathers*, (. . . 'mors, quam sanabit Deus resuscitans nos a mortuis, et restituens in patrum hæreditatem;')[9] as Isaiah says again, 'And thou shalt trust in the Lord; and He shall make thee to possess the earth, and feed thee with the heritage of Jacob thy father.' . . . . Jeremiah says, ... 'God, who scattered Israel, shall gather him as a shepherd doth his flock, ... and they shall come and rejoice in Mount Zion, and shall come to the good things, and into the land of corn, and wine, and fruits, and beasts, and sheep, and . . . . they shall not hunger any more; . . . . and I will satiate the souls of the priests, the sons of Levi; and my people shall be satisfied with my good things.' But we have shewn in a former book, that *the Levites and priests are all the disciples of the Lord*, who profaned the Sabbath in the temple and were guiltless. *Such promises, therefore, most manifestly denote the feasting of the just in the kingdom, upon that creature which God has promised to provide for them.*"—("Tales itaque promissiones manifestissime in regno justorum istius creaturæ epulationem significant," &c.)[10]

3. But I must now come back for a moment to an earlier father, JUSTIN MARTYR, who obtained the crown of martyrdom about the year 163, six years before Irenæus was settled at Lyons. Of his scheme it has been accurately remarked, in a recent work, that he "held the mean between the gross materialism with which the Ebionites—Papias, Irenæus, and Lactantius—explained the millennial hope, and the spiritualising in which Barnabas and Tertullian indulged."[11] Had he believed the literal restoration of the Jews, it could scarcely have failed to come out in his "Dialogue with Trypho the Jew," in which he discusses between those fulfilled at the first advent and those which await the second advent for their accomplishment, (for example, c. 32, 33, 52, 53, 110, 111,) and opens up his millennial system. But in all its 142 chapters, I have not found a trace of this opinion. With all the fathers, he understood the prophecies of Israel's restoration simply of *the Christian Church*; and, with Irenæus and other millenarians, he applies them generally to the resurrection state, though in a higher style of conception than Irenæus. When

---

[9]Here Whitby makes another of his mistakes. "In the times," says he, "of that [millennial] kingdom, Jerusalem shall be built, saith Irenæus, and *the Jews shall be restored to the land He gave to their fathers*," (p. 692.) In support of this statement, Whitby quotes the *half line* which I have marked in the text with italics. How hastily he has read the passage, and how entirely he has missed the sense of it, the reader will be able, from the above full quotation, to see for himself.

[10]Adv. Hær., 1. v. c. xxxiv.

[11]Justin Martyr: his Life, Writings, and Opinions. By Rev. C. Semisch. Pp. 374, 375.—(Clark.)

Trypho, for example, asks him, "Do you really believe that that local Jerusalem will be rebuilt, and do you expect that *your people* [Christians] will be collected there, and rejoice with Christ, together with the patriarchs and prophets, and those of our nation, or even those who became proselytes before the coming of your Christ? Or do you resort to these acknowledgements merely that you may seem to have the better of us in controversy?"[12] Justin replies, "I am not so pitiful, Trypho, as to say one thing and think another. I have before confessed to you that I and many others are of that opinion. . . . I and such Christians as think rightly on all points are persuaded that there will be *a resurrection of the flesh, and a thousand years* IN JERUSALEM, REBUILT, ADORNED, AND ENLARGED, and Ezekiel, Isaiah, and other prophets acknowledge."[13]

From this passage it is perfectly plain that, according to Justin's scheme, the "rebuilt, adorned, and enlarged Jerusalem" was to be, not for the restored Israelites after the flesh, but for all who should partake of the "resurrection of the flesh."

Elsewhere he says—"As Joshua introduced the people into the Holy Land, and distributed it by lot to those who entered with him, so Jesus Christ will turn the dispersion of the people, [this is Justin's *restoration of the Jews,*] and divide to each the good land, but not at all in the same way. For the one gave them the temporary inheritance, not being Christ [who is] God, nor the Son of God; but the other, after the holy resurrection, will give us the eternal possession."[14]

And again—"Christ came, in the power of the omnipotent Father given to Him, calling unto friendship [with God], and blessing, and repentance, and fellowship; and He promised, as has been already

---

[12]*Αληθῶς ὑμεῖς ἀνοικοδομηθῆναι τὸν τόπον Ἱερουσαλὴμ τοῦτον ὁμολογεῖτε, κὰι συναχθήσεσθαι τὸν λαὸν υμῶν καὶ εὐφρανθῆναι σὺν τῷ Χριστῷ, ἅμα τοῖς πατριάρχαις καὶ τοῖς πθοφήταις καὶ τοῖς ἀπὸ τοῦ ἡμετέρου γένους ἤ καὶ τῶν προσηλύτων γενομένων πρὶν ἐλθεῖν ὑμῶν τὸν Χριστόν, προσδοκᾶτε, ἤ, ἵνα δόξῃς περικρατεῖν ἡμῶν ἐν ταῖς ζητήσεσι,πρὸς τό ταῦτα ὁμολογεῖν ἐχώρησας;*

[13]. . . .*'Εγὼ δέ, καὶ εἴ τινές εισιν ὀρθογνωμονες κατὰ πάντα Χριστιανοί, καὶ σάρκος ἀνάστασιν γενήσεσθαι ἐπιστάμεθα καὶ χίλια ἔτη ἐν Ἱερουσαλὴμ οἰκοδομηθείσῃ καὶ κοσμηθείσῃ πλατυνθείσῃ, κ. τ. λ.* —*Cap* . 80.

[14]. . . . *οὕτως καὶ Ιησοῦς ὁ Χριστὸς τὴν διασπορὰν τοῦ λαοῦ επιστρέψει, καὶ διαμεριεῖ τὴν ἀγαθὴν γῆν ἑκάστῳ, οὐκέτι δὲ κατὰ ταὐτά. Ὁ μὲν γὰρ πρόσκαιρον ἔδωκεν αὐτοῖς τὴν κληρονομίαν, ἅτε οὐ Χριστὸς ὁ Θεὸσ ὢν οὐδὲ ὑιὸσ Θεοῦ, ὁ δὲ μετὰ τὴν ἁγίαν ἀνάστασιν αἰώιον ἡμῖν τὴν κατάσχεσιν δωσει.* —*Cap* . 113.

shewn, that the possession of all the saints should be *in that same land*"[15]

4. The same remarks are applicable to TERTULLIAN. Born somewhere about the time of Justin's martyrdom, he reached nearly to the middle of the following century. He was the first Latin writer in the Church; and being a man of iron mould and fervid though rugged eloquence, having taken a prominent part in all the questions of the day and occupied a peculiar position in reference to some of them, his writings, most of which are extant, though depreciated by Milner, are full of interest, and invaluable for reference. Though he frequently discusses the prophecies, and states his millennial expectations, he never includes among them the restoration of the Jews. Like Justin, he has a tract expressly "against the Jews," in which it could hardly have failed to come out; nor could he well have avoided it in some of his other tracts, if it had formed part of his scheme. But I have not been able to find it. Dr. Kaye, indeed, (Bishop, first of Bristol, afterwards of Lincoln,) in his "Ecclesiastical History of the Second and Third Centuries, illustrated from the Writings of Tertullian," says that, in the tract *De Pudicitia*, "he connects the hope of Christians with the Restoration of the Jews;"[16] but the passage which he quotes is too general to prove the point. (It occurs, not in chapter x., as he gives it, but in chapter viii.) Tertullian is commenting on the parable of the Prodigal Son, whom he takes to represent the *Jews* who have forsaken the Lord, and provoked the Holy one of Israel to anger. The elder brother answers best, he thinks, to the *Christian*. "For it is fit," he says, "that the Christian should rejoice and not grieve at the recovery of the Jew, since our whole hope is bound up with the remaining expectation of Israel."—("Christianum enim de restitutione Judæi gaudere, et non dolere, conveniet; siquidem tota spes nostra cum reliqua Israelis expectatione conjuncta est.") This is the passage quoted by Dr. Kaye; and did we know that Tertullian expected the territorial Restoration, we might well enough give such a turn to it. But as we shall presently see that he did not, it is clear that *the general conversion of the Jews to Christ* is all that is meant. Similar phraseology is employed in another place, (Adv. Marc., l. iii. c. 24,) which goes to confirm our interpretation. *Jerome*, indeed, in his numerous allusions to the expectation of "the Jews and of *our*

---

15 *'Ο Χριστὸς κατὰ τὴν τοῦ παντοκράτορος πατρὸς δύναμιν δοθεῖσαν αὐτῷ παραγένετο, εἰς φιλίαν καὶ εὐλογίαν καὶ μετάνοιαν καὶ συνοικίαν καλῶν, τὴν ἐν τῇ αὐτῇ γ: τῶν ἁγίων πάντων μέλλουσαν γίνεσθαι, ὡς προαποδέδεικται, διακατάσχεσιν ἐπηγγελται.—Cap*. 139.

16 Page 363. Camb. 1826.

Judaisers," as he usually calls the millenarian Christians, seems to speak as if they expected the whole temple service to be restored; in which case, one would imagine it to be for none but literal Israelites. But in one of these passages, (on Zech. xiv. 10,) he says, that on that system, instead of the Jews becoming Christians, the "*Christians would become Jews;*" which seems to shew that Jerome did not understand them as assigning those Jewish services to the literal Israel as a distinct people, but rather that Christianity itself would assume a Judaised form, and be characterised by Judaical services during the millennium. One passage will suffice to shew Tertullian's principle of interpretation as it relates to the Jews, and from this the reader may judge for himself. In the Tract "On the Resurrection of the Flesh," reasoning against those who denied it, he says—"So when it is said in Isaiah, 'Ye shall eat the good things of the earth,' ['the good of the land,' as we have it,] we are to understand the good things of the flesh, which await it [the flesh], renewed and angelified,[17] in the kingdom of God—things which eye hath not seen, nor ear heard, nor hath entered into the heart of man. Otherwise, it were vain enough for God to invite to obedience by the fruits of the field and the meats of this life, which He bestows indiscriminately upon the holy and the profane, sending rain upon the evil and the good, and making the sun to shine upon the just and unjust. Happy faith, indeed, if its portion is to consist of those things which the enemies of God and of Christ not only use, but abuse, worshipping their very mercies in opposition to the Creator of them. In 'the good things of the earth,' you think of roots and tubers, while the Lord says that man shall not live by bread only. It is thus that the Jews, by looking for earthly things, lose the heavenly; ignorant at once of the promised bread from heaven, and the oil of Divine unction, and the wine of the Spirit, the water of life flowing from Christ the vine. It *is thus that they take the Holy Land itself to mean* THE PROPER JEWISH SOIL, *which is rather to be understood of the Lord's flesh, which henceforward,* and in all who have put on Christ, IS THE HOLY LAND,—truly holy by the indwelling of the Spirit, truly flowing with milk and honey through the sweetness of its hope, THE TRUE JUDEA in virtue of God's nearness. *For he is not a Jew who is one outwardly, but who is one in the hidden man of the heart.* The same, too, is the temple of God, and Jerusalem, which is thus addressed by Isaiah,—'Awake, awake, O Jerusalem, put on the strength of thine arm, as in the dawn of the

---

[17]"Reformatam et *angelificatam.*" This last is a favourite term of Tertullian's, alluding to our Lord's saying, that "the children of the resurrection" shall be "as the angels of God." In a subsequent chapter, he guards against the abuse of the term by those who denied the identity of the risen body.—See cap. lxii.

day,' to wit, in that integrity which was before the fall. For how could language of this sort be properly applied to that Jerusalem which killed the prophets, and stoned them that were sent unto it, and at length pierced its own Lord? NOR, INDEED, IS SALVATION PROMISED TO ANY LAND AT ALL WHICH MUST, WITH THE FASHION OF THE WHOLE WORLD, PASS AWAY."[18]

He goes on, in the following chapters, to express his faith in the resurrection-state, and comments on Ezekiel's vision of the dry bones, and on the parallel passages in Isaiah as an allegorical prediction of it, which it were "temerity" to apply to "Jewish affairs."

It is impossible to imagine that he who reasoned and wrote thus, believed in the territorial restoration of the literal Israel.

5. CYPRIAN, made Bishop of Carthage about the year 248, and beheaded for Christ in 258, need not detain us. In his treatise "Against the Jews," he does little more than abridge the arguments of Justin and Tertullian; and the very headings of his chapters are enough to shew that he went the whole length of our extract from Tertullian.

In the light of these extracts, the following statement of a respected author, given on the authority of "Lorinus the Jesuit"—that "Cyprian, Jerome, Chrysostom, Theophilus, Alexandrinus, Augustine, and Bede, understood Acts i. 6 to refer to that *literal restoration of the Jews* mentioned in Scripture, though these fathers are either neutral or opposed, as regards other (millenarian) tenets"[19]—will be seen to be quite inaccurate. The truth is exactly the reverse of this Jesuit's statement. *Not one* of these fathers held the literal restoration of the Jews.

6. LACTANTIUS, who flourished in the early part of the fourth century, and died about 330, is the only other millenarian father of any consequence whose writings are extant. In the following passage he gives a pretty full outline of his scheme, similar to that given by

---

[18]. . . "*Sicut et ipsam terram sanctam* JUDAICUM PROPRIE SOLUM *reputant, carnem potius Domini interpretandam, quce exinde et in omnibus Christum indutis* SANCTA SIT TERRA, *vere sancta per incolatum Spiritus Sancti, vere lacte et melle manans per suavitatem spei ipsius*, VERE JUDEA *per Dei familiaritatem.* Non enim qui in manifesto Judæus, sed qui in occulto. Ut et templum Dei eadem sit et Hierusalem, audiens ab Esaia, Exsurge, exsurge Hierusalem, induere fortitudinem brachii Tue: Exsurge, sicut in primordio diei, scilicet in illa integritate quæ fuerat ante delictum transgressionis. Quæ enim in eam Hierusalem voces ejusmodi competent exhortationis et advocationis, quæ occidit prophetas et lapidavit ad se missos, et ipsum postremo Dominum suum confixit? SED NEC ULLI OMNINO TERRÆ SALUS REPROMITTITUR, QUAM OPORTET CUM TOTIUS MUNDI HABITU PRÆTERIRE."—Cap. xxvi.

[19]Brooks' Elements of Prophetical Interpretation, p. 80.

Irenæus; but though we find a metropolitan city in it, and a confluence of all nations to this favoured spot—this seat of the Eternal King—the Jews, as such, are not there, nor has a restored Jewish nationality any place in the system:—"The Son of the Most High and Great God shall come to judge the living and the dead, as saith the Sibvi. . . . . Then those who shall be alive in their bodies shall not die, but shall throughout the same thousand years beget an infinite multitude, and of them shall be a holy offspring and dear to God. But as for those who shall be raised from the dead, they shall be over the living as judges.—('Qui autem ab inferis suscitabuntur, ii præerunt viventibus velut judices.') The [unbelieving] nations, however, shall not be wholly extinguished, but certain shall be left for divine victory, to be triumphed over by the just and subjected to perpetual servitude. About that time, also, the prince of the devils, who is the contriver of all evils, shall be bound with chains, and be in custody during the thousand years of celestial rule, when righteousness shall rule in the world, that no evil may stir against the people of God. After His Advent the just shall be congregated from all the earth, and the judgment being finished, the holy city shall be erected in the midst of the earth, in which God himself, the builder of it, shall dwell with the ruling just, ('cum justis dominantibus commoretur,' *i.e.*, with the raised, who rule over the living, saints.) . . . . Then shall be removed from the world that darkness by which it was overspread, and by which the heavens were obscured, and the moon shall acquire the brightness of the sun, never more to wane. The sun also shall be seven times brighter than it now is. Then the earth shall disclose its fertility, and bring forth of its own accord the most abundant fruits; honey shall ooze out of the rocks, wines shall flow in streams, and rivers shall run over with milk. In fine, the world itself shall rejoice, and all creation, rescued and liberated from the dominion of evil and impiety and crime and error, shall be glad. . . . . Thus shall men live a most tranquil and abundant life, and reign along with God; and the kings of the nations shall come from the ends of the earth with gifts and presents and adore and honour the Great King, whose name shall be renowned and venerable among all the nations that shall be under heaven, and the kings that shall rule in the earth."[20]

We have thus seen that the millenarian fathers, without exception, interpreted the Old Testament prophecies regarding the Jews on the same principles as their opponents; that both parties agreed with those who in subsequent times have denied the territorial

---

[20]Divv. Instt., l. vii. c. 24.

Restoration; and that, while differing widely in their conceptions of the future glory of the Church upon earth, they were at one in excluding the literal Israel from any distinctive standing or special promises under the Gospel.

Before proceeding to another period, I may be permitted to make one general remark on the facts submitted. If the advocates of the Premillennial Advent are entitled to claim the primitive Fathers in support of their system, the opponents of Jewish Restoration have a stronger claim to them. For in the former case they were confessedly divided; in the latter, I think it will now appear that they were unanimous. All parties, however, would do well to sit pretty loose to the Fathers in such matters. For myself, I am disposed to set small store by their support in either of the cases to which I refer. Whatever may be their value in some departments, it is vain to go to them for enlightened and consistent principles of Scripture interpretation, and above all on prophetic subjects. The interpretation of prophecy—besides involving difficulties peculiar to itself, with which the fathers were ill able to grapple—is aided by nothing so much as *time*, that great unfolder of the Divine purposes, and commentator on the inspired oracles. In this particular department, therefore, those who lived *earliest* were, on that very account, under the greatest disadvantage as interpreters, and, in the presence of ripe and judicious students of the Bible in our own days, scarce worthy of being listened to.

CHAPTER II

THE POST-REFORMATION PERIOD

On the fall of Paganism, the interests and studies of the Church took a new direction—not the happiest, certainly, in some respects at least; and prophecy, with the exception of an apocalyptic treatise now and then, dropped out of sight till the Reformation. Nor did our question even then excite any interest. *Not one of the Reformers held* —so far as known *the literal Restoration of the Jews.* It may be thought that the extravagances of the Anabaptists prejudiced them against it. But there is no evidence of this. Their general principles of interpretation are sufficient to explain it. I may refer, in proof of this statement, to *Luther's* and *Calvin's* Commentaries on Prophets (*passim*); and to *Melancthon*, (Aug. Conf.) *Bullinger*, who identifies the literal restoration with *Chiliasm* (or millenarianism), says, "There is a threefold restoration of Israel: one literal, by Cyrus; the next, from Christ to Antichrist, in which many of the prophecies have been fulfilled, as is testified by the evangelists and apostles; and the third, from the restoration of the Gospel and the last judgment [which the Reformers regarded as the next great event to come after the 'restoration of the Gospel' at the Reformation] onwards through eternity."—(Conciones in Apoc., Basil., 1570, p. 99.) *Chytræus*, in the following year, repeated the same statement in a more systematic form. "The first corporal restoration of Israel," says he, "was when they returned under Cyrus and Darius out of all the countries of the earth into their own land, and restored the city and temple of Jerusalem. But much more sublime and glorious is the spiritual restoration by Christ, the King and Shepherd of the dispersed sheep of the house of Israel, who extends the bounds of the Mount Zion, or the kingdom of David, over the whole world, and by the preaching of the Gospel builds the new and eternal city and temple, to wit, the Church of God, in which He Himself reigns and dwells, and having abolished sin and death, hell and all enemies, commences that new and eternal righteousness and life which is consummated in the third and perfect restoration of Israel—in the new and heavenly Jerusalem after the resurrection."—(Explic. Apoc., Witteb., 1571, p. 392.) It was not till about the beginning of the following century—the *post-*

reformation period, as I have called it—that the standing and prospects of the Jews under the Gospel began to attract special attention and became matter of controversy.

1. In 1615, THOMAS BRIGHTMAN published at Amsterdam his once well-known "Revelation of the Revelation" in English, and in 1618 issued in Latin a second edition.[1] On the words, (ch. xvi. 12,) "The sixth angel poured out his vial upon the great river Euphrates; and the water thereof was dried up, that the way of the kings of the east might be prepared"—he gives reasons why these kings of the east must mean *the Jews*, and then says: "But what need have they to have a way prepared for them? What! shall they return to Jerusalem again? There is nothing more certain: the prophets do everywhere confirme it and beate upon it. *Yet they shall not come thither to have their ceremoniall worship restored*, but to make the goodness of God shine forth to all the world, when they shall see Him to geve to that nation (which is now and hath been for many ages scattered thorough out the whole world, and inhabiteth nowhere but by leave and entreaty,) there owne habitations where their fathers dwelt, wherein they shall worship Christ purely and sincerely, according to His will and commandement alone. . . . But what! are the Jews kings? Why not? seing all Christians bee Kings. . . . But the Holy Ghost gives the Jews this magnificall name, because, &c. . . . And besides all this, *the whole east shall be in obedience and subjection unto them*, so that this people are not called kings unworthily, in regard of their large and wide jurisdiction and empire. I have sett downe these things with more store of words, because I would geve our Divines an occasion of thinking more seriously of these things.[2]

2. In 1621, JOHN PRIDEAUX, regius professor of divinity at Oxford—afterwards Bishop of York[3] —delivered a Latin discourse before the university, "On the Calling of the Jews," in which he speaks of the questions which had been raised on this subject as quite recent: and as this discourse was often referred to in the subsequent

---

[1]Mr Elliott says it "appears to have been written and first published in the year 1600 or 1601, before the death of Queen Elizabeth," and for proof says, in a note, "See *e.g*., p. 525, also the second page of the preface." But the original edition, which I have before me, with the date above mentioned, has no preface, nor is there the least indication that I can find of so early a date. "My edition," he adds, "is the fourth, London, 1644;" and this, no doubt, was what misled him.—*Horoæ Apoc*., iv. 452, fourth edition.

[2]Pp. 549-551.

[3]Not *Dean* Prideaux, the author of the "Connection," with whom, though he lived a century later, he is confounded in the work of Mr. Brooks already referred to. The estimable author could not have seen the discourse he refers to, for he says it advocates the Restoration of the Jews—just the reverse of what it does.

discussion of the question, and is the next to the earliest statement that I have lighted on of the system which was then beginning to be advocated, and is in contemptuous opposition to it, I extract from it the following sentences:—

"It is known," says he, "to nearly all, how, amidst our other calamities, *Judaism* has lately prevailed, to the disgrace of divines and the scandal of the weak. Three opinions are flying about on this subject: That of the *madmen*, who think that the legal ceremonies are to be recalled; that of the *dreamers*, in whose brains a Jewish monarchic throne and the frame of a temple are floating; and that of the *zealots*, who are looking shortly for I know not what sublimated doctrine, and doctors more than *angelical* and *seraphic* from them [the Jews] when converted. . . . . With regard to the *ceremonies*, though there were slight skirmishes between Peter and Paul, Jerome and Augustin, Aquinas and Scotus, regarding their honourable burial, the apostolic practice, and the time of their abrogation, there was no difference about the thing itself, and the truth only shone more clearly from the conflict. . . . . The chiliastic [or millenarian] school were ashamed to urge the ceremonies. . . . . Whether any Christians go the length of the Jews [whose expectations of a third temple, and a throne at Jerusalem, and an army to be sumptuously entertained, he details,] I know not. But observe how near they come. For they hold a stupendous conversion of the Jews after the end of the Turkish kingdom, to commence in precisely 350 years. Then they bring them, converted, out of I know not what countries of the East, and expect the Euphrates to be miraculously dried up to open for them a passage. After this they engage them with the Turkish army, not far from Jerusalem, where the Sultan himself falls first, and then his army. . . . . Then shall be established that most glorious kingdom at Jerusalem, under which all tribes shall be united. The earth shall be more fertile than when of old it flowed with milk and honey. So ample shall be their dominion, that not only the Egyptians, Assyrians, and the most extensive countries of the East, converted by their example, but even in the West, the Christians shall of their own accord submit themselves and acknowledge their primacy. Such *Hebrew roots* have been swallowed by some without a grain of salt,"—among whom the worthy professor is grieved to find some men "otherwise *learned* and *orthodox*."[4]

The reader may perhaps observe how closely the expectations here sketched resembles the scheme of Lactantius; only substituting a

[4]Viginti-Duæ Lectiones de totidem Religionis capitibus præcipue hoc tempore controversis, &c., per Joannem Prideaux, &c. Oxon. 1648.

Jewish supremacy over Christians for his *Christian* supremacy over the nations spared at Christ's coming to be brought under subjection.

But after discarding Jewish *restoration* as part of the scheme of Jewish *supremacy* Prideaux finds the remaining ground far from undisputed. Though himself disposed to stop here, others, it seems, thought themselves bound to go a step farther—discarding even Jewish CONVERSION in any *general* and *national* sense. I pray the reader's special attention to this point. When I come to discuss the question, it will be seen how much hinges on this. Meantime, it is interesting to observe how the opponents of the Restoration fell out among themselves about even the Conversion of the Jews. They were unanimous in holding, that under the Gospel the Jews are on a level, in all respects, with other men; from which one section of them argued, that their conversion could be no *national* affair, but that, like the Gentiles, they would sooner or later, from time to time, come individually over to the Christian faith. "There are," says Prideaux, "who take 'Israel' in our text [Rom. xi. 25, 26, 'And so all Israel shall be saved,'] allegorically, for the people of God collected from amongst Jews and Gentiles, and who think it suffices, for the fulfilment of the apostle's prediction, if *some* from among the Jews are from time to time, in any age, converted to the faith. So *Bucer, Melancthon, Faber, Œcolampadius, Calvin, and nearly all the Lutherans. Selneccer* treats those who think otherwise as fanatics." How they could interpret the 11th chapter of the Epistle to the Romans on their principle, may be matter of wonder. But having taken up their ground, as to the standing of the Jews under the Gospel, they seem to have thought it incumbent upon them to carry it into this and every similar passage of Scripture.

3. Contemporary with Prideaux was the celebrated JOSEPH MEDE, whose writings on the prophecies have contributed so largely to mould the views of subsequent writers. Though he wrote nothing expressly on this subject, he speaks once and again of the restoration of the Jews to Palestine as certain from Scripture.

4. The admirable JAMES DURHAM, minister of the Outer-High Church, Glasgow, in the middle of the seventeenth century, whose Commentary on the Revelation is known less than it deserves, (being just his pulpit expositions with some additional matter,) not only held the Restoration of the Jews to their own land, but gives, in short compass and in modest spirit, solid reasons for his belief. To some of these I shall by and by refer.

Most of the English writers on prophecy during this century appear to have been of the same opinion; although the majority of divines whose attention had not been directed to prophetical subjects, were probably opposed to it. Greenhill, one of the Westminister divines, whose large Exposition of Ezekiel was some time ago replublished, and who himself held it, thus laconically states the general opinion in his day: "The Jews' return to their own land is denied by some, questioned by many, and doubted by most."[5] In Powell's Concordance (1673) the return and re-establishment of the Jews, with many miraculous and peculiar circumstances, is laid down with abundant references to prophetic Scripture.

But though in England the question seems not to have attracted much attention, it was otherwise in Holland, where, during nearly this whole century, not only the Restoration, but even the Conversion of the Jews seems to have been matter of pretty keen disputation; the able theologians of that country perceiving that the two questions were closely bound up with each other. A few examples will be required to carry on the history.

5. In 1636, the well-known VOETIUS, (De Voet,) professor of divinity at Utrecht, held a Disputation "on the General Conversion of the Jews," (from Rom. xi. 25-29,) in which he says, "A doubt has here been raised, whether the text is to be understood of any general and future conversion of the Jews; or whether the 'mystery' which is here opened from the prophets is merely the conversion of the spiritual Israel of God, (Gal. vi. 16,) that is, of that fulness of Gentiles and the remnant of the Jews, who were partly then converted by the apostles, and partly will be converted from time to time, even to the end of the world, however few they may be. The latter opinion is espoused, among the fathers, by *Theodoret, Augustin, Jerome, Coesarius* (in Gregory Nazianzen); among the moderns, by *Melancthon, Calvin, Osiander, Hyperion*, and lately by *Wollebius*." The advocates of the former opinion—of a general future Conversion—which the author himself espouses, fill a quarto page of his works, and cannot be given here. When he comes to the *Restoration*, he speaks in measured and cautious terms. After adverting to the "fable," as he calls it, of a drying up of the Euphrates, to afford the Israelites a passage, (from Isa. xi. 15,) and to the victory of the Jews over the Turks, (Mic. v. 6, Isa. xi. 15,) and over Antichrist, (Zech. xiv. 14,) which, he says, is "equally uncertain," he adds, "The occupation of their own land, which *Brightman* considers most certain, cannot certainly be yielded on his grounds. That the Jews will remain in a state of splendour to the end of the world, and as a separate and unmixed people, is not probable, at least uncertain. In fine, a millennial kingdom is a dream." In his disputation on this latter subject,

[5]Greenhill's Ezekiel, Sherman's Edition, p. 828. London, 1889.

"the millennial kingdom," in the same volume—after referring to the notion of a restored temple, together with the ceremonies, "at least some of them," which he says some imagined to themselves, though they had published nothing upon it—he adds, "Nor do they recede far enough from these who cleave too much to a corporal and peculiar restoration of the converted *Jews, and of their separate polity, as well ecclesiastical as civil.*"[6]

6. WALŒUS, professor of theology at Leyden, at the same time, in his "Manual of the Reformed Religion," discusses this subject under the head of "the opinion of the Chiliasts," [millenarians.] "This opinion," he says, (of the Jews' restoration,) "if it does not bring Christ from heaven, *as there are some who do not*, appears to hurt no article of faith; for a spiritual conversion does not conflict with a secular kingdom, as may be seen in the conversion of the emperors of Gentile kingdoms; and it has some advocates, as *Brightman*, among the orthodox. But there are scriptures which solidly refute this opinion of the corporal restoration of the Jews *and their polity*," which he adduces at length.[7]

7. In the year 1670, one of the Dutch pastors had published a treatise advocating the restoration not only of the Jews, but of their ceremonies, with a ritual separation of Jew and Gentile, and the subjection of the latter to the former. In the following year appeared another treatise to much the same effect. This roused the indignation of MARESIUS, (Des Marets,) professor of divinity at Groningen—against such *semi-Jewish* and *Ebionitish* opinions, as he styles them. The sentiments of *Altingius*, (James Alting,) professor of divinity in the same university, and apparently at the same time, having been quoted against him, he appeals to several passages in a work of his, "from which it might be gathered, that he neither expected the erection of a third temple, nor the restoration of the Jewish polity or worship, nor the recall of the twelve tribes of Israel to Palestine, nor a temporal kingdom of Christ upon earth, nor any other advent of His but the second, to judge the world, *nor any conversion of the Jews to take place towards the end of the world than their junction to the Gentile Christians, by whose instrumentality they will be converted.* If any doctor," he adds, "can reconcile this with the modern semi-Judaism, he shall be my *magnus Apollo.*"[8]

I think there is something instructive here. While those who held a future general *Conversion* of the Jews found themselves constrained

---

[6]Gisb. Voetii Selectarum Disputationum, pars secunda, pp. 136, 137, and 159. Ultraj. 1655.

[7]Anton. Walœi Opera Omnia, tom. i. p. 547.

[8]Sam. Maresii. System. Theolog., pp. 300, 362, 804, 805. Gron. 1673.

to speak of their *Restoration* as a thing not easily disproved—such was *Voetius*—those, on the other hand, who were prepared to speak strongly against their *Restoration* found themselves obliged to give up, along with it, their national *Conversion*—as did *Maresius*. I request the reader to bear this important fact in mind. But,

8. The sentiments of ALTINGIUS are not fairly represented by his colleague. He may not have spoken out explicitly on the subject when he wrote the treatise to which Maresius refers—I have not the volume at hand to see—but, as an appendix to his Sermons on the Eleventh of Romans, he gives a discourse "On the Restoration of Israel to his own Land," delivered before his university in 1672, in which the affirmative of the question is maintained at length.[9] For this he suffered no little reproach, being held up, he tells us in the preface to his Sermons, as half a Jew, and such alike. But if the opponents of Jewish Restoration expected to bear down that opinion by confounding it with the restoration of the ceremonies, and raising a prejudice against its advocates as *Judaisers*, they failed in their object. Maresius himself had pupils who could distinguish things that differ; one in particular, who soon outshone his teachers, and on this question took up the opposite position from his master.

9. I refer to the distinguished WITSIUS, who, in his choice tractate "On the Ten Tribes of Israel,"[10] maintained the restoration to Palestine with such cautious and judicious distinctions between what he regarded as infringing on the spirituality and catholicity of the Gospel dispensation, and what seemed in no way to touch these, that though the opinion might be opposed, it could not well be disparaged and calumniated. Accordingly,

10. Though we find MARCKIUS (professor of divinity at Groningen towards the end of the century) reasoning against it in his "Compendium of Christian Theology," it is as a *complex* restoration, *with distinctive peculiarities*, rather than as a simple restoration, that he opposes it.[11]

11. In this sense DE MOOR understood him, who filled the divinity chair at Leyden in the middle of the last century. Commenting on this part of Marck's "Compendium," which he used as his textbook, he thus guardedly expresses himself, in his voluminous "Perpetual Commentary on Marck"—"This question (of the Restoration) is debated with great probability on both sides. With regard to the *negative* side, which the author (Marck) takes, the terms of the

---

[9]Jac. Altingii Opera, tom. quart. Amst. 1686.

[10]*Δεκάφυλον*, sive de Decem Tribubus Israel. Witsii Opera, tom. sec. Amst. 1683.

[11]Joh. Marckii Compend. Theol. Christ., cap. xxxii. 24. Amst. 1690.

question must be well attended to. For the controversy is not about the liberty of the converted Jews to return to the land of Canaan, or the occupation of it along with other Christians, but about the restoration of the land of Canaan to the Jews for a peculiar possession, to the exclusion of other nations, *and about the setting up of the Jewish polity*. The question is not about the building of a city somewhere on the site of the ancient Jerusalem, but about the rebuilding of Jerusalem as the metropolis of the restored Jewish nation."[12] In other words, it was only as mixed up with the restoration of *religious distinctions* or *ritual peculiarities*, that either the author or his commentator saw anything requiring to be opposed in the territorial Restoration.

Other advocates of the literal Restoration besides those named by us are referred to by De Moor. But the Dutchmen have detained us long enough, and before closing this period, and without particularising the great BENGEL and his followers in Germany, the eloquent JURIEU of the French Reformed Church, and some others, we must cross the Atlantic for a moment, to meet with

12. INCREASE MATHER, (father of Cotton Mather,) whose treatise on "The Mystery of Israel's Salvation—Glorious, Wonderful, Spiritual, *Temporal*," 1669, thus notices the opinions on this subject:—

"The light of those truths which do concern the Jews is wonderfully broken forth of late. Not long since, it seemed very paradoxical to affirm that ever there should be a *general conversion* of the Jewish nation. But that truth of late hath gained much ground throughout the world. And albeit there have ever been some amongst the orthodox that have in the general thesis concurred, that such a thing shall be in the appointed season; yet as to the glory of this day, and the happy time which then shall come and continue in the Church, [he means the *Reign on earth*, which he believed in,] there hath been little known in many ages during the reign of Antichrist; only in these late days these things have obtained credit much more universally than heretofore, and that's a sign that the time of the end draweth on apace." (Pp. 43, 44.)

About the middle of last century, not only the Church everywhere, but society at large, seemed to experience a deep decline. Yet showers of blessing fell on some favoured spots, and men like *President Edwards*, whom God at that dead period made the instrument of a glorious revival in America, were led to search the prophetic

---

[12]Bern. De Moor Comment. Perpet. in J. Marckii Compend. Theol. Christ. Pars Sexta, cap. xxxii., (XX) 24, p. 130. Lugd. Bat. 1771.

Scriptures for light as to the prospects of the Church and of the world. See his very interesting remarks on this subject in his "Call to United Extraordinary Prayer," and in the latter part of his "History of Redemption," in which he expresses his expectation of a glorious conversion of the Jews to Christ, but is silent upon their restoration, and probably did not believe in it. A variety of publications, too, more or less bearing on the illustration of prophecy, contributed to keep alive attention to this subject, and to prepare thoughtful minds for that new era which, in this as in so many other respects, opened upon the Church at the close of the last century.[13]

---

[13]The following are some of the publications to which I allude:—*Vitringa's* Works (on Prophecy generally, 1708; on Isaiah, 1714 and 1720; on the Apocalypse, 1719); *Fleming's* "Fulfilling of the Scriptures," 1726; *Daubuz* and *Lowman* on the Revelation, 1730 and 1745; the valuable "Commentary on the Prophets" by *Prebendary Lowth*, (the bishop's father, first published about the middle of the century,) in which the Restoration, along with the Conversion of the Jews, is brought prominently forward; *Bengel's* "Gnomon" of the New Testament, which first appeared about the same time, and apocalyptic part of which was apeedily translated into English; *Bishop Newton's* "Dissertations on the Prophecies," 1759, which, by their popularity, contributed to interest the general public in the subject: *Whitby's* "Treatise of the True Millennium," appended to his "Paraphrase and Commentary on the New Testament"—"shewing that it is not a reign of persons raised from the dead, but of the Church flourishing gloriously for a thousand years after the conversion of the Jews, and the flowing in of all nations to them thus converted to the Christian faith." With regard to our question, he says, "Though I dare not absolutely deny what they [millenarians] all positively affirm, that the city of Jerusalem shall be then rebuilt, and the converted Jews shall return to it, because this probably may be collected from those words of Christ, 'Jerusalem shall be trodden down till the time of the Gentiles is coming in,' (Luke xxi. 24.) and all the prophets seem to declare the Jews shall then return to their own land (Jer. xxxi. 38-40;) yet do I confidently deny what *Barnabas* and others of them do contend for,—viz., that the temple of Jerusalem shall be then built again." (Page 696.) This is a repetition of his former mistake about Barnabas (see p. 17, above.) About this time an immense impulse was given to the critical study of the Prophecies by the publication of *Kennicott's* "Researches on the State of the Hebrew Text," 1753-59, and subsequently of his Hebrew Bible, 1776-80, and *De Rossi's*, 1784-88,—the fruit of which was seen in such works as *Dr. Blaney's* "Jeremiah," 1784; *Bishop Lowth's* "Isaiah," 1778; *Archbishop Newcome's* "Minor Prophets," 1785, and "Ezekiel," 1788; *Blaney's* "Zechariah," 1797: and subsequently *Bishop Horsley's* "Biblical Criticism on the First Nine Prophetical Books,"—the chief portion of which, however, was not published till after his death. Horsley adopted the premillennial view, and the restoration of the Jews occupied a prominent place in his scheme. It is a pity that his excessive rage for *mending* the text, and his extravagant literalism, render this part of his writings unsafe—I had almost said useless. In Scotland such subjects seem to have excited small interest. There appeared, however, a sensible "Commentary on the Revelation," by *Dr. Bryce Johnstone*, 1794; in 1795, *Fraser's* (Kirkhill) "Key to the Prophecies," a work of great merit; in 1800, a "Commentary on Isaiah," by the same—a less useful work (the author finds the millennium and the restoration of the Jews in almost every chapter); and in 1799, *Snodgrass* on the Revelation.

And now, in reviewing this second period, the reader will observe, that though, in the first century of the Reformation, not one orthodox theologian appears to have held the Restoration of the Jews, and some not to have looked even for any general Conversion of them, yet with the opening of the next century—the era of systematic theology—it began to attract attention, and, as the century advanced, divided the soundest and most accomplished divines. It will be admitted, then, that to represent this opinion as bound up with the expectation of a restored Judaism, as some now do, is to take a view of it, which, to say the least, is not evident, which some of the ablest continental divines did not take of it, and with which very few of them ventured to charge it. Nor should the reader forget the difficulty which was felt by the deniers of the *Restoration*, in maintaining along with this any national Conversion of the Jews. It was maintained by the majority of them, but at the expense of their consistency, in the opinion of those who denied both.

A few paragraphs will suffice to bring down the history of our own day.

CHAPTER III

THE PRESENT PERIOD

The close of the last century was distinguished by two events of which it is difficult to say which has exercised, and is yet destined to exercise, the greater influence—the *French Revolution*, and the institution of *Bible and Missionary Societies*. The former contributed to awaken the spirit which gave birth to the latter; and civil and religious society, acted on simultaneously by new and mighty influences, entered together on a new era, which, after the lapse of more than half-a-century, is to all appearance but in its infancy. It were foreign to my present purpose to advert to the general features of this era, even in its religious aspect. One feature of it, however, cannot be omitted—the impulse which has been given to the investigation of prophecy, and more particularly the expectations which have been awakened respecting the Jews. In the French Revolution, and the events which succeeded it, many thought they saw the fulfilment of some of the principal apocalyptic predictions—the close of the mystic 1260 days, the death and resurrection of the witnesses, the effusion of the greater number of the vials of wrath upon the Antichristian interest, and preparation making for the great decisive conflict between the kingdoms of Christ and of Belial. Others, not so much addicted to this kind of study, thought that in the gigantic efforts and unparalleled success of our evangelistic associations might at least be discerned the "angel flying through the midst of heaven, having the everlasting Gospel to preach to them that dwell on the earth, and to every nation, and kindred, and tongue, and people," preparatory to the latter day. Even those who were averse to connecting the events of the time with any specific predictions, were ready to admit that they involved something more decisive in the history of Christianity than any turn that things had taken since the Reformation. With such impressions abroad, the multitude of treatises on prophetic subjects soon exceeded all precedent; and almost every such treatise, if it did not devote considerable space to the inbringing and restoration of the Jews, proceeded on the supposition that the time of their general conversion was approaching, and that either before or after that event they would be restored to their father-land.

It is a curious fact, that, in the midst of the French Revolution, the celebrated philosopher and eccentric Socinian preacher, *Dr. Priestley*, preached and published a Fast Sermon on "The Present State of Europe compared with Ancient Prophecies," (1794,) which went through three editions almost immediately. The author holds it evident that the second coming of Christ will be coincident with the commencement of the millennium, or the future peaceable and happy state of the world, which, according to all the prophecies, will take place after the restoration of the Jews "to their own country, to be at the head of all the nations of the earth." (Pp. 3, 19.) In the later editions of *Scott's* widely-circulated Commentary, the restoration of the Jews occupies a prominent place in the notes on the prophets. *Faber, Cunninghame*, (Lainshaw,) *Frere, Irving, Fry, M'Neile, Bickersteth, Burgh, Brooks, Birks, Elliott, Bonars, Wood, Molyneux, Auberlen*, and others, all make the conversion and restoration of the Jews one of the main turning-points in the transition of the world from its present to its millennial state. *Faber* is the only writer of any note who, while contending against the *Personal Presence*, is not disinclined to admit of a *Shechinah-glory* of Christ, during the millennium, in a restored *temple* at Jerusalem.

A considerable time ago, when the disputes between Egypt and Turkey drew all eyes towards *Syria* as the battle-field, and the European Cabinets seemed at a loss to know what to do with it, it was gravely proposed to give *Palestine* to the Jews, erecting it into an independent kingdom, under the protection of "the Powers." Some suggested that such moneyed Jews as Sir Moses Montefiore, who had gone to Syria expressly in behalf of his nation, should *buy up* the country, and invite his countrymen to settle in it on advantageous terms. Nay, in an article which appeared in a London newspaper, (if I remember rightly,) it was suggested whether subscriptions might not be entered into for enabling the Jews to set about the rebuilding of their temple at Jerusalem. Perhaps the yet fresh massacre of the Christians by the Druses—more or less aided by the Mohammedans—of Syria, with the difficulty of a satisfactory settlement of that country, may give rise to similar proposals, and result in steps which will pave the way for more extensive changes.

Dr. Urwick, in his work on the Second Advent, without discussing the question, affirms the restoration of the Jews to be inconsistent with right principles of Scripture interpretation. *Dr. Henderson*, in his critical Commentary on Isaiah, (1845,) thinks it impossible to give an unforced interpretation to many passages of that prophet on any principle which shall exclude the Restoration of the Jews; while the late lamented *Professor Alexander* of Princeton, in his critical work on the same prophet, (1846-7,) is equally strenuous on the other side. And *Dr. Fairbairn*, in an appendix to the first volume of his "Typology," (first edition, 1845,) has a long and able Dissertation on this subject, maintaining the Restoration to be contrary to sound principles of Scripture typology, and consistent only with out-and-out literalism, and a complete reestablishment of the Mosaic institutions. In the second and enlarged edition of this valuable work that appendix is not given; but the "Exposition of Ezekiel" by the same author, proceeds throughout on the non-restoration principle, while his more recent work on "Prophecy"—which regards the expectation of a literal Restoration as "semi-Jewish"—goes at some length into the argument in support of the negative view. In the American *Bibliotheca Sacra*, for May and August 1847, there are two able and temperate articles on this subject, in which the negative is maintained.

I might have adverted to the modern *Delitzch* School, in Lutheran Germany, which takes *Bengel* as its model, but deviates from him in several things, and to occasional references to this subject in more recent but not important publications.

But the facts already adduced suffice to shew, that although the affirmative side of the question of Restoration has been espoused by a majority of those who have made prophecy a subject of special study, there is weight enough of authority on the negative side to require, from all, the candid admission that neither side is free from difficulties. For myself, I make no pretensions in this treatise to the removal of all difficulties on the side on which I think the truth lies; nor will the tone which I assume be by some considered decided enough. As for those who talk of the evidence in favour of the restoration of the Jews as equal to that for the truth of the Bible—I am sorry to say the case is not hypothetical—my advocacy of their opinion will, in their eyes, go for little. But I write for those who would rather have two or three good arguments than a score of bad ones—who would not have even a good argument unduly pressed, and who, in regard to doubtful ground, desire only to know how the case stands in the living oracles.

For if the casting away of them be the reconciling of the world, what shall the receiving of them be, but life from the dead? (Romans 11:15).

Concluding the parenthesis of verses 13 and 14 in his present ministry with its hope of saving 'some of them' Paul reverts to the prospect already envisaged in verse 12. According to the view we are here opposing, the prediction of verses 12 and 15 has to do with the aggregate of individual Jews saved through the ages and not a future national conversion. But the verses cannot bear that meaning for it ignores a vital part of Paul's argument, namely that the parallel drawn between the 'casting away' and 'the receiving of them' requires the subject to be the same in both instances. The people who were rejected are to be readmitted.

The remnant of believers never fell nor were cut off, and it cannot therefore be of them that Paul says they will be 'received' and grafted in again (v. 23). Thus Elnathan Parr, answering those who denied that 'any other calling of the Jews to be expected than in these days, now and then one', asserts: 'the very reading of the words of the 11, 12 and this verse, make the contrary manifest: **If the casting away of them:** ***of whom? Of the nation, say the learned men:*** **What shall the receiving of them?** ***Of whom? Of them which are cast away; that is the nation: or else we make the Apostle say he knows not what: not that the same individuals of the nation which are cast away shall be received, but the body of the people to be understood.'***

The sense of verses 12 and 15, according to the common Puritan interpretation, points to a vast addition to the Church by Israel's conversion with resulting wider blessing for the world. There is a great revival predicted here!*

---

*Iain Murray, *The Puritan Hope: Revival and the Interpretation of Prophecy* (Edinburgh, Scotland: Banner of Truth, 1984), p. 66.

PART SECOND

THE PRINCIPLES OF THE QUESTION

CHAPTER I

THE GROUND CLEARED

Here let me state at once in what sense I propose to advocate the Restoration of the Jews.

Not a shred of Judaism do I expect to be restored. For no temple at Jerusalem do I look. Circumcision, priesthood, sacrifices, ritual separations and peculiarities, I hold to have been all done away in Christ, never more to be revived. If the Restoration of the Jews cannot be maintained without one or more of these Judaisms, I shall give it up; for not one of these things can I make consistent with the explicit testimony of Scripture, and the catholic character and spiritual genius of Christianity. But it is because I think the Restoration of the Jews is unjustly mixed up with them—because I think it has a ground of its own, and solid ground, to stand upon, when all these are swept off the stage of the Gospel economy and our system of divinity—and because, as it seems to me, the denial of it involves principles of interpretation which cannot be gone through with, puts a forced in place of a natural sense upon many passages, and leaves some things unexplained, which, on the opposite view, are clear and satisfying; it is because I take this view of the Restoration of the Jews that I am not able to give it up, and am, on the contrary, constrained to hold it fast.

That the Restoration of the Jews, from all the places of their dispersion, is predicted clearly, repeatedly, and circumstantially in Scripture, is admitted on all hands. The only question is how this is to be understood—whether *literally* or *figuratively*; and, if literally, whether of a *past* or of a *future* restoration. On the literal view, there are two opposite extremes, some applying it nearly all to a *past* restoration, while others understand it all, in its full and proper sense, of a restoration yet *future*. To the latter class belong the Jews themselves, who look for a rebuilt temple, a re-established priesthood, the restoration of their bloody sacrifices, and an Israelitish supremacy, at once religious and civil, over all the nations of the earth. Strange to say there are Christian interpreters who deduce the same conclusions from the prophecies in question, in connexion, of course, with evangelical truth, and the Christ as King of the Jews, and Lord of the whole earth.

For example:—"Zion and Jerusalem," says *Mr. Fry*, Rector of Desford, "are to be the great source of spiritual blessedness to the whole world. This 'city of Jehovah' is represented as the grand centre and emporium of civil and religious power, whither all nations resort for their laws and government. 'He shall reign in Jerusalem unto the ends of the earth.'" "But what most surprises us is, that a ritual of worship, so like the Mosaic ceremonial, should again be restored by Divine appointment, rather than institutions more analogous to those of the Gospel Church, and especially that the sacrifices of animal victims should be again enjoined. For we read of all the various offerings of the Levitical economy, not only 'peace-offering' and 'meat-offering,' but 'burnt-offerings,' 'trespass-offerings,' and 'sin-offerings.' We can only reply, such is the Divine pleasure. It is not for us to judge what would be best for Israel, and for the world at large, in this future age." "However averse to our preconceived notions may be the restitution of ceremonial sacrifices, that restitution exactly corresponds with the prediction in the close of the 51st Psalm, where a reference is clear to Israel of the last times—'Do good in thy good pleasure unto Zion; build the walls of Jerusalem: then wilt thou desire the right sacrifices, an offering and a holocaust; then shall they offer steers upon thine altars.'"[1]

Mr. Molyneux, in his recent Lectures on "Israel's Future," not only contends for the restoration of the Mosaic sacrifices, but assigns the following as the probable reasons and objects of it:—"The law [sacrificial] must yet peradventure point back to Christ, and teach them *retrospectively* what it was intended to teach *prospectively*—the sacrificial and expiatory nature of Christ's work. . . . . Thus the sacrifices themselves—*presenting, however, the object in a stronger light*—may *virtually* be to them what the sacrament of the 'Supper' is *actually* to us; and they, in the former, may continually shew forth

[1]The Second Advent, &c., by the Rev. John Fry, Rector of Desford, Leicestershire; 2 vols., 1822: vol. i., pp. 129, 583, 585, 586. Compare Freemantle's "Glory of Israel after the Advent," in Twelve Lectures, by Clergymen of the Church of England, on the Second Coming, &c.; 1844: pp. 273-278.

the Lord's death when He *shall have* come, as we continually, in the latter, do shew forth the Lord's death *till He come.*"[2]

One more example of this school of interpretation, and the most recent, may be added, from the able work of *Professor Auberlen* of Basle, on "The Prophecies of Daniel and the Revelation of St John:"—

"Israel is again to be at the head of all humanity. . . . . In the Old Testament, the whole Jewish national life was religious; but only in an external legal manner: . . . . in the millennial kingdom, all spheres of life will be truly Christianised from within outwardly. From this point of view, it will not be offensive to say that the Mosaic ceremonial law corresponds to the priestly office of Israel—the civil law to its kingly office. The Gentile Church could only adopt the moral law; in like manner, her sole influence is by the word working inwardly, by exercising the prophetic office. But *when the royal and the priestly office shall be revived*, then—the principles of the Epistle to the Hebrews remaining as true and immovable as ever—the *ceremonial* and civil law of Moses also will develop its spiritual depths *in the Divine worship, and in the constitution of the millennial kingdom*," &c.[3]

Of the opposite extreme to this, which applies nearly all the prophecies to *past* events, the late lamented *Professor Alexander* of Princeton thus speaks:—"It is an ancient and still current doctrine, that the main subject of his (Isaiah's) prophecies throughout is the restoration from the Babylonish exile. While this hypothesis has been assumed as undeniable by many Christian writers, it affords the whole foundation of the modern neological criticism and exegesis."[4] Strong language this, but scarcely too strong. Among the Christian writers here alluded to, may be classed a countryman of his own, the writer of the two fore-mentioned articles in the *Bibliotheca Sacra*, who seems to regard this event as the burden of a great part of the prophetic writings; and how many critics of our own country during last century took the same view is well known. Few, however, deny that there *are* prophecies of Israel's restoration which belong to Christian times—prophecies which have received no literal fulfilment, either in the return from Babylon or in any other past events. How, then, are these disposed of by those who deny the future

---

[2]Israel's Future: Lectures delivered in the Lock Chapel in Lent, 1852. By Rev. Capel Molyneux. Fourth Thousand, 1853. Pp. 257, 258.

[3]The Prophecies, &c. Translated by the Rev. Adolph Saphir. Edinburgh: Clark. Pp. 340, 348, 349.

[4]The Later Prophecies of Isaiah. By Joseph Addison Alexander, Professor in the Theological Seminary, Princeton, New Jersey: 1847. Introd., p.14.

Restoration? They are viewed as the *Jewish dress* of *Christian events.* The restoration itself, and the "Israel" to be restored, are held to be alike spiritual; the ideas and language of an extinct economy being employed to depict a dispensation in which there is neither Jew nor Gentile, dispersion nor restoration. That Christian events are predicted in Jewish language by the prophets, it is impossible to deny. If this be overlooked, we shall be ready to put our Christianity into bondage to a restored Judaism, as some have actually done, and to draw from the prophets the crudest representations of millennial religion. But the question is, whether the principle is *kept within its just limits* by those who use it to disprove the future restoration of the Jews.

But let us hear it as enunciated by themselves:—"Where prophecy," says the writer in the *Bibliotheca Sacra,* "thus runs into the present dispensation—a spiritual dispensation—is it not to be interpreted spiritually, according to the nature of the dispensation to which it refers? The dress may be ancient, but the truth refers to those latter times. He (Ezekiel) spoke of a restoration, but it was a restoration *then* to take place. He glanced occasionally, as others had done, to the Messiah's time; but his utterances of the Messiah's time are to be understood according to the nature of the Messiah's dispensation, to which they relate. Whatever be the dress of his thought, it is a grand and glorious spiritual reality into which the germ is to unfold. This we believe to be the economy of ancient prophecy in relation to these latter times."[5]

Those who have written against the territorial restoration of the natural Israel insist strongly on the necessity of abiding by some *uniform* principle of interpretation. If "Israel" in the Old Testament is held to mean Israel literally, then "David," it is alleged, must be held to mean simply David; but if Christ is held to have come in the room of David, under the Gospel, then Christ's people must be held to have come in the room of David's subjects. Plausible reasoning certainly. But whether, according to this mode of reasoning, it would be possible for God to predict even the *conversion* of His ancient people; whether, if God should think fit to foretell their submission to Christ, as a submission to "David their king," our friends would not hasten to put them out of court, insisting that, since David in the supposed prediction does not mean David, it would be a mongrel species of interpretation to make Israel mean Israel—that as a literal Israel *cannot* be connected in the same prophecy with an antitypical David, the thing meant in the prophecy *cannot* be the conversion of his

---

[5]*Biblioth, Sacra.* for Aug. 1847, pp. 475,476.

ancient people, but simply the *Church's submission* to Christ—whether, I say, this would not legitimately follow from the foregoing way of reasoning, we shall have to consider by and by. At present I am merely stating the different ways in which the prophecies in question are disposed of.

The late *Dr. Arnold* carried this spiritual principle to its extreme verge. Prophecy, according to him, is no "anticipation of history," as it has been termed:—

"History, in our common sense of the term, is busy with particular *nations, times, places, actions*, and even *persons*. Prophecy fixes our attention on *principles*, on good and evil, on truth and falsehood, on God and on His enemy. Prophecy, then, is God's voice speaking to us respecting the issue, in all time, of that great struggle which is the real interest of human life, the struggle between good and evil. Beset as we are by evil within us and without, it is the natural and earnest question of the human mind, What shall be the end at last? And the answer is given by prophecy, that it shall be well at last; that there shall be a time when good shall perfectly triumph. But the answer declares also, that the struggle shall be long and hard; that there will be much to suffer before the victory be complete. The Seed of the woman shall bruise the serpent's head, but the serpent, notwithstanding, shall first bruise His heel. So completely is the earliest prophecy recorded in Scripture, the sum and substance, so to speak, of the whole language of prophecy, however diversified soever in its particular forms."[6]

It is easy to see whither this will lead us. If there be no historical fulfilments of prophecy if *facts* are never predicted, but only *principles*, which find their development, to a greater or less extent, in the facts of history, profane as well as sacred, and only their concentrated and most perfect development in Christ and His Church—it will follow that *Christ's Person and Work*, historically considered, are nowhere the subject of *direct* prediction in the Old Testament; that all which the apostles applied to Him, and which we have been accustomed to regard as referring to the *historical Christ*, "do not," to use Dr. Arnold's own words, "relate to the Jewish or to Christian times, but are either the expressions of religious affections generally, such as submission, hope, love, &c, or else refer to some particular circumstances in the life and condition of the writer, or of the Jewish nation, and do not at all shew that anything more remote, or any events of a more universal and spiritual character, were designed to

---

[6]Two Sermons on the Interpretation of Prophecy. By Thomas Arnold, D.D.: Oxford, 1839. Pp. 3-5.

be prophesied."—(Preface, p. i.) And lest the reader should fail to see how far this principle was intended to carry him, the ingenious author refers, among a number of other passages, to the *fifty-third chapter of Isaiah.* (whose proper subject he conceives to be, not the sufferings of Christ and the following glory, but "the return of the Jews from captivity, and its accompanying blessings,") to the *twenty-second* and *hundred and tenth* Psalms, to Isa. 1xi. 1-3, and to Zech. xiii. 7. To these, and every other Old Testament prediction, the pregnant remark is made to apply, that "the true subject of pure prophecy, as distinct from *history*, is not any human *person or persons, fact or facts*, but *ideas and principles*, which in no merely human persons or actions have ever been embodied perfectly." Thus *Christ and His Church*, historically considered, are not the subject-matter of prophecy at all. They are but *ideally* in the Old Testament, embodying the great general religious ideas which are the proper burden of prophecy.

Had such views been confined to the learned and ingenious author of them, I should not have taken the trouble to present them so explicitly to the reader. But who that knows the influence which Dr. Arnold's writings are exercising in England—who that observes the fascination which an idealised, unbiblical Christianity is exercising on our young men, and the frightful extent to which a rationalistic Christianity is diffusing itself among the more pretentious of the English clergy—who that observes how Hengstenberg, and even Dr. J. A. Alexander, in their Commentaries on the Psalms, deal with the *sixteenth* and *twenty-second* Psalms, and Tholuck's leanings in the same direction[7] —who, in short, that has himself felt the difficulties of the subject, the measure of truth that there is in the views here referred to, and the ability with which they are brought forward, can but warn his readers of their unsettling tendency? And when I state that one chief purpose which Dr. Arnold expected his system to serve was to get rid of the *restoration of the Jews*, as matter of prophecy—that the notes, at least, to his two sermons, which occupy thrice as much space as the text, are chiefly taken up with shewing how his principle bears upon that question, the reader will see why I have dwelt upon it, and may possibly be led to suspect, that it is difficult to get any principle which will serve out-and-out for the extrusion of the Jew from the prophecies of the Redeemer's kingdom which would not go a good deal further than that—further, indeed, than most are prepared to follow.

---

[7]Comment. on Hebrews, vol. ii., Appendix i. Clark's Biblical Cabinet: 1842.

Before leaving Dr. Arnold, and by way of shewing how extremes meet, I cannot resist quoting a passage in which he concedes even the literal restoration of the Jews as a thing perfectly possible, though not capable of antecedent proof from the prophecies, and not necessary to their proper fulfilment:—

"But," says he, "although the full and real completion of the prophecies relating to Israel belongs neither to the First historical Israel, nor yet to the second, the visible Church of Christ, but to those only who shall be found to have been true Israelites, children of God in the Spirit, whether they belonged to the Jewish or to the Christian Israel according to the flesh; yet if any one urges that, over and above this real and adequate fulfilment, there may be also a lower fulfilment again vouchsafed, even to the old historical Israel, whenever he shall turn to the Lord, then I will not attempt to deny this position, provided it be allowed that such a fulfilment is by no means necessary to the truth of prophecy; that it is given *ex abundanti*; and that as in no case we have a right to expect it, so, if it be withheld, we ought neither to feel surprise nor perplexity. Instances of such a fulfilment of prophecy are certainly to be met with in Scripture."

After quoting and commenting on John xviii. 8, 9; Isa. 1iii. 4, and Matt. viii. 16, 17; Ps. xxii. 16, 18, and John xix. 24, 37, as examples of this kind of fulfilment, he continues,—"With these examples before us, I would not dare to say that God may not be pleased to vouchsafe some great and special blessings to the remnant of the historical Israel, when they shall again be grafted into the Israel of God. But even if none such are granted to them, the prophecies relating to the future and final blessing of Israel seem, to my mind, to have their abundant fulfilment in the rest reserved for the people of God. If God's people should live in His presence for ever in perfect safety, and crowned with glory, I cannot conceive what more can be wanting to the adequate fulfilment of the most magnificent language of prophecy relative to the future triumphs of Israel."—(Note 4, pp. 36-38.)

To the principle of *ex abundanti* fulfilments of prophecy—that is to say, fulfilments over and above what is necessary to the essence of the thing, and not to be anticipated with certainty till they occur—I have no objection: it is a sound and important principle; But I am afraid that, on Dr. Arnold's views, *historical* fulfilment must be regarded as all *ex abundanti* together.

From the above remarks, the reader will see that, what with erroneous principles, and sound principles which appear to be pushed too far, the subject is involved in no little difficulty. A few propositions, based on New Testament intimations—the surest of all footing—will comprise the materials of what I regard as a scriptural settlement of this interesting question. Our first two propositions will be of the nature of *concessions* to those who *deny* the restoration of the Jews; after which I shall endeavour to shew that, notwithstanding these concessions, due to truth, there remain sufficient grounds for believing that this restoration is matter of Divine prediction.

CHAPTER II.

CONCESSIONS TO THOSE WHO DENY THE RESTORATION OF THE JEWS—FIRST CONCESSION

PROPOSITION I.—*The "wall of partition" between Jew and Gentile has been broken down, never more to be rebuilt.*

The passages on this point are familiar to all; but I quote some of them for the sake of a remark or two which I mean to make on them.

"He is our peace, who hath made both [Jew and Gentile] one, and hath broken down the middle wall of partition between us; having abolished in his flesh the enmity, even the law of commandments contained in ordinances. . . . Now therefore ye [Gentiles] are no more strangers and foreigners, but fellow-citizens with the saints, and of the household of God." (Eph. ii. 14, 15, 19.)

It is impossible for language more clearly to intimate that Jews and Gentiles are placed, by the work of Christ, *on a footing of perfect equality* before God, not only in point of acceptance, but *as members of the Church visible*. Those who contend for the restoration of Jewish peculiarities during the millennium would have the apostle to mean, merely that Gentiles have now access to Christ and salvation as well as Jews. But Christ and salvation were never inaccessible to Gentiles. The ceremonial barriers placed them in a more disadvantageous position, in this respect, than the Jews; but that was all. And it is just these ritual disadvantages which the apostle says have been taken out of the way, to make room for a new incorporation of both into one fellowship, having all things common, as pertaining to the "city" and "house" of God. The ceremonial sacredness of places, persons, times, vessels—all typical institutions and observances—have yielded to the spiritualities and simplicities of the New Testament, to the genius of which all such distinctions are utterly foreign.

But our Lord's announcements to the woman of Samaria are, if possible, still more explicit. Having consulted Him in the dispute between the Jews and the Samaritans about the proper place of (central) worship, she received this information:—

"Woman, believe me, the hour cometh when ye shall *neither in this mountain nor yet at Jerusalem* worship the Father"—that is, of course, in the sense in which He was then actually worshipped at Jerusalem; for He takes care to tell her, that the Jews were right in the dispute between them and the Samaritans:—"Ye worship ye know not what: we know that we worship; for salvation is of the Jews." But, He adds, the dispute is soon to be at an end, by privilege which has hitherto belonged to Jerusalem being extended to all places alike:—"But the hour cometh, and now is, when the true worshippers shall worship the Father in spirit and in truth; for the father seeketh such to worship him." (John iv. 21-23.)

Now does this mean that, under the new economy, the worship of Gentiles *out of* Jerusalem would be as acceptable as the worship of the Jews *in it*,—that the *central and sacred* character of Jerusalem would continue unchanged, but that believing Gentiles, though as much "strangers and foreigners" as ever, as truly "aliens from the commonwealth of Israel" as ever, in respect of ceremonies, and church-officers, and modes of worship, would nevertheless get access to *Christ* and *salvation* as truly as the Jews? Could such a construction by possibility be put upon the Saviour's language, we could listen to the arguments for a millennial Judaism. But as, beyond all doubt, the Saviour meant to announce that Jerusalem was going to lose its peculiar character—that it would cease to be, even to the Jews themselves, "the city of their solemnities, whither the tribes should go up"—that, in fact, it would possess not a whit more of a distinctive religious character than the mountain of Samaria about which the woman consulted him, I cannot but wonder that Christian men and dear brethern, sitting at the Redeemer's feet to receive the law at His mouth, should dream of a revived Judaism, and picture to themselves "believing nations frequenting the" restored "temple, in order to get understanding in the types and shadows; looking on the sons of Zadok ministering in that peculiar sanctuary, to learn portions of truth with new impressiveness and fulness." But, it is said, "The account of this [restored] temple, which occupies chapters xl. to xlviii. of Exekiel. is embedded in literalities on either side. Here, then, lies the difficulty. All seems literal on either side; and is there to arise in the midst of this a great spiritual building, possessing nothing in common with the literalities around it? The point of difficulty lies *there*." To this I unhesitatingly reply, *Let the literalities go*, if they cannot stand with the naked and unmistakeable announcements of the Lord of the temple. I do not quite see, indeed, that we are shut up to the alternative of losing all literalities, or making every thing literal; but I am perfectly prepared to part with whatever may be demanded by a firm adherence to the announcements of Christ. True, "there are many dark things in the Word;" but they will become darker still if, instead of explaining the dark things by the clear, *we explain the clear things by the dark, making the Old Testament the key to the New.* It is this unnatural method which lies at the foundation of all the *Jewish* expectations of Christians; and never till we reverse the process are we safe from the danger to which we found *Jerome* alluding, of *Judaizing our Christianity*, instead of Christianizing the adherents of Judaism.

As a last refuge, we sometimes hear it said, that though an Aaronic priesthood, and bloody sacrifices, and circumcision, and a metropolitan ceremonial at Jerusalem, may be unsuitable to the genius of the *present* economy, they may, for aught that we know, be consistent enough with *one to come.* This surely, is a desperate argument. Nor should I allude to it, but to ask my readers whether this be the impression which they gather from the apostle's reasonings on the subject of the ceremonies, in the Epistles to the *Galatians, Colossians*, and *Hebrews*? Was it only the *abuse* of them against which he wrote? Or was it only their *temporary* removal which he contemplated, in the view of their ultimate restoration? Does he not characterise them as, in their own nature, "worldly rudiments," 'beggarly elements," the mere discipline of minors, as a "bondage" unsuited to the liberty of Christ's freemen? (Gal. iv.) Are they not represented as "a shadow," of which "the body is Christ," for the entire neglect and abandonment of which Christians ought not to allow themselves to be "judged" by Judaizing zealots, who were swarming in some of the infant churches, and whose policy was to sap and mine whatever was spiritual, and free, and catholic in the new economy? (Col. ii.) Is not the priesthood said to be "changed," and the ceremonial institute to be "disannulled," expressly "*because of the weakness and unprofitableness thereof?*" Now, to what order did those "sons of Zadok" belong, the "ministrations" of whose descendants in the restored temple are expected to give "new impressiveness and fulness to certain portions of truth?" They belonged, as every one knows, to that very Aaronic order which the apostle says has been swept off the stage of the Church, with all that appertained to it, as a weak and useless thing after Christ's coming. Yet further; is not the co-existence of two priesthoods regarded as a thing incongruous, and does not the apostle represent the whole ritual system as in a "decaying, antiquated, and evanescent" state when he wrote? (Heb. viii.) Now, is it conceivable that such language would have been used of a system only temporarily set aside, to be brought back, with a few changes, to more than its pristine splendour? If such expectations, or anything like them, are not directly in the teeth of all that the apostle says on the subject of the temple-service, he has used language which it was next to impossible not to misunderstand, and which the whole Church, with hardly an exception, has been misinterpreting to this hour. Yet Professor Auberlen says, "the principles of the Epistle to the Hebrews remain [on this theory] as true and immoveable as ever"! I confidently reply, they do not, and cannot.

On the strength of these remarks, we might turn our proposition into the following

RULE:

WHEREVER JEWISH PECULIARITIES OCCUR IN THE PROPHETIC PICTURES OF MESSIAH'S KINGDOM, THEY ARE TO BE UNDERSTOOD OF THE CORRESPONDING REALITIES UNDER THE GOSPEL.

The *principle* of this rule cannot be questioned. Every one proceeds upon it, more or less, in interpreting prophecies, *translating* the old phraseology into the new—substituting Christian ideas for Jewish. He would be a bold interpreter who would affirm that *in no case* are the events of the new economy predicted in the language of the old. Take but one example, Mal. i. 11—"From the rising of the sun unto the going down of the same my name shall be great among the Gentiles; and in every place incense shall be offered unto my name, and a pure offering; for my name shall be great among the heathen, saith the Lord of hosts." Are there any, except *Romanists* and *Romanizers*, who take "incense" here, and the "pure offering" *literally*? Is not the prediction understood to mean simply this, that not at Jerusalem only, but everywhere, and not by Jews only, but by all nations without distinction, from one end of the world to the other, *acceptable worship* shall ascend to God? Well, but how is it that there is so general an understanding that this is the sense of it? Clearly because "incense" and "offering," in the Jewish sense, having given place under the Gospel to "spiritual sacrifices, acceptable to God by Jesus Christ," *there is no other kind of worship* of which we can understand the prediction. Now all that our rule means is, that we must carry this principle of prophetic interpretation through all cases of like nature.

But the example now adduced illustrates our rule in another way. The Jewish idea, under which the prediction is couched, is not merely that "incense and a pure offering" shall be offered to God by all nations, but "in every place"—as if they would have the temple-service at home, and not need to go to Jerusalem for it. But in other places the reverse of this is expressly predicted. In Isaiah and Ezekiel, the catholicity of the Church's worship is expressed by all nations flowing to Jerusalem, and going up to the mountain of the Lord, to the house of the God of Jacob; whereas in Malachi, instead of them *going to the temple*, the temple is represented as *coming to them*. If, then, we would not make the prophets contradict themselves, we must understand both representations as designed to announce one and the same idea, the catholicity and spirituality of the Gospel worship.

There is one class of prophecies to which I must particularly advert, which come under the same law of interpretation, though not quite so manifestly, as the former—those, I mean, in which "Zion" and "Jerusalem" are the subject of evangelical prediction. If the Israelites are to be nationally restored to Palestine, there can be nothing surprising in *Jerusalem* becoming again the capital of the kingdom, and the seat of government; nor will any one who believes in the future restoration of the Jews, hesitate to admit that Jerusalem *is* so spoken of in the prophecies as either the actual future metropolis of the reconstituted nation, or at least as an historic symbol of its restored nationality. But Jerusalem of old was something more than the capital of a political kingdom, and the seat of a civil government. It was "the city of the great King"—the place of Jehovah's special presence, power, grace, and glory, in connexion with the ceremonial worship established there. "*In Salem was his tabernacle, and his dwelling-place in Zion.*" (Ps. lxxvi. 2.) But we have seen that these localities have been, by the work of Christ, divested for ever of all their peculiar sacredness, and that in respect of acceptable worship, "Zion" and "Jerusalem" are "in every place" where God is "worshipped in spirit and in truth." It is this very change, beyond all doubt, which the apostle designed to express, when he said to the Hebrews, who were clinging to the local Jerusalem and the literal Zion, after all their glory had passed away, "*But ye are come unto Mount Zion, and unto the city of the living God, the heavenly Jerusalem.*" (Heb. xii. 22.) To say, in the face of this most naked statement, that the *religious peculiarities* of the local Jerusalem and the literal Mount Zion are either not abolished at all, or abolished only for a time, to be again restored, is, if it may be said without offence, intolerable. To all the evangelical prophecies which represent Zion and Jerusalem in terms of their ancient peculiarities, we must unhesitatingly apply the rule we have laid down. Does any one hold up to us this prophecy and that, exclaiming, There, surely, is Jerusalem reinstated in its ancient sacredness, and Zion once more "the mountain of the Lord's house?"—I calmly reply in the apostle's words, "YE ARE COME unto Mount Zion, and unto the city of the living God, the heavenly Jerusalem:" Ye are come to the Zion and Jerusalem of *a catholic and spiritual Israel*—to the only Zion and Jerusalem that will ever, in any *religious* sense, exist upon earth.

Of this use of the terms in question, let one example suffice for all—from the fourth chapter of Isaiah. In the preceding chapter and the first verse of this one, the ruin of the Jewish commonwealth had been foretold. This is immediately followed up by a delightful prediction of a purified remnant of that devoted people to be gathered under Messiah, in whom the Church's identity in its passage from the old to the new economy would be preserved, and who should constitute the nucleus of a catholic Israel, purer in character, and more acceptable in its worship than ever before. "In that day," says the prophet, "shall the Branch of Jehovah [Messiah, as Son of God] be beautiful and glorious, and the Fruit of the earth [the same Messiah, as Son of man] shall be excellent and comely to the escaped of Israel."—(See Alexander, *in loc.*) On the day of Pentecost, three thousand Jews, added to the hundred and twenty that had been gathered in the days of the Redeemer's flesh, constituted the Church of God. To these "escaped of Israel" Messiah was "beautiful and glorious, excellent and comely." Then this prophecy began to receive its proper fulfilment.[1]

Now, observe what follows:—"And it shall be that he that is left *in Zion*, and he that remaineth [or is spared] *in Jerusalem*, shall be called holy: every one that is written to life *in Jerusalem*." (Ver. 3.) To take "Jerusalem" and "Zion" here in the sense of mere *localities* where Israelites shall happen to be found when these events are fulfilled, would be absurd. Nor are they here employed metaphorically to denote the *people* of Israel, for that would be to make "the escaped" to be the same with the places where they remain. Clearly, these localities are here referred to in their *church signification*. And what is that? In Old Testament language to be "in Zion," is to be under the religious ordinances of which Zion was the centre and the soul—to be Jehovah's worshippers. To be indifferent or undisturbed under such precious means, is to be "at ease in Zion;" to continue unrenewed, and live a life of sin, in spite of such means, is to be

[1]Should any one say, Nay, but it points to the millennial state, and to the Jewish remnant then to be restored to Palestine—it matters nothing to my object in quoting it. I think this is *not* the sense of it, and that violence must be done both to the connexion and the contents of the chapter to bring out this result. But such a view of it would only strengthen my argument from its *language*, which is all I have to do with here.

"sinners in Zion;" whereas, when they have stamped their own holy image upon those placed under them, such are said to have been "born in Zion," and are called "the children of Zion." This phraseology, so familiar under the old economy, furnishes an easy key to the expressions before us—"the left in Zion," and "the spared in Jerusalem," who, in their new character, as attracted to Messiah's beauty and glory, excellence and comeliness, should be called holy; or, in New Testament language, "the remnant [of the old Israel] according to the election of grace;" of whom it is said that "as many as were ordained to eternal life, believed."

In the next verse the figure is slightly modified, while its general sense remains unchanged:—"When the Lord shall have washed away the filth of the daughters of Zion, and shall have purged the blood of Jerusalem from the midst thereof, by the spirit of judgement, and by the spirit of burning," pointing to the purifying effect of those trying events which were to attend the transition of the Church from the old to the new economy.

But the verse which follows is still more important:—"And the Lord will create upon every dwelling-place" (or, "over the whole extent")[2] "of Mount Zion, and upon her assemblies, a cloud and smoke by day, and the shining of a flaming fire by night: for upon all the glory shall be a defence." (Ver. 5.) "The Church is not only," says Professor Alexander on this verse, "to be purified by God's judgements, but glorified by His manifested presence, and in the state of glory kept secure by His protection. The presence of God is here denoted by the ancient symbol of a fiery cloud, and is promised to the Church in its whole extent, and to its several assemblies, as distinguished from the one indivisible congregation, and its own exclusive place of meeting, under the old economy." If this be a correct view of the prediction—and the unanimous voice of Christian expositors pronounces in favour of it—what view does it give us of "Mount Zion?" Does it celebrate the honours of the literal mountain of that name, and of the temple on it, as a point of religious attraction for the whole world? It does just the reverse. It represents Mount Zion as *coextensive with the purified Church under Messiah, and particularly with her public "assemblies."* That Divine presence, protection and glory, which, after being enjoyed by the ancient Church all through the wilderness, took up its fixed abode on Zion as the place of their assemblies, shall burst its cerements under the

---

[2]Literally, "upon all the place of Mount Zion," that is, in its extended sense. When the idea of "dwelling" is to be expressed, as in our version, the full form, מָכוֹן לְשִׁבְתְּךָ, "place for dwelling," is used. See Exod. xv. 17; 1 Kings viii. 13, 39, 43; 2 Chron. vi. 33, 39; Ps. xxxiii. 14.

Gospel, spread its wings of love over the whole amplitude of Messiah's kingdom, and hover, cloud-like, over every Christian assembly, making a "Mount Zion" of every spot where New Testament worship is offered "in spirit and in truth." Such a picture of the new economy is intelligible on the apostle's principle, *"Ye are come unto Mount Zion;"* but if we are to expect a material temple yet to be erected on the literal Mount Zion for all nations, with all its carnal and bloody accompaniments, it is *not* intelligible.

In a word, on the obvious principle of interpretation embodied in our rule, there is no real difficulty in disposing of whatever Judaisms we may find in the prophetic pictures of Messiah's kingdom. Being all buried in the grave of Christ, and the system of them being adapted only to an immature and preparatory state, we must of necessity substitute for them the spiritualities that have taken their place.

CHAPTER III

CONCESSIONS TO THE OPPONENTS OF TERRITORIAL RESTORATION—SECOND CONCESSION

Our next proposition may be regarded as falling under the first, and has been partly anticipated by the foregoing exposition; but it is important enough to be taken by itself.

PROPOSITION II.—*The Gospel Church is not a different Church from that which existed before, but the same Church of God—formerly confined to the Jews, and now, under a new form, embracing all nations.*

The natural Israel were in possession of the Church when Christ came. Such of them as believed were its last representatives under the old, and its first members under the new economy. In them its identity was preserved, and they were the proper heirs of the "blessing of Abraham." On the wall of partition being broken down, the Jews are not said to have *gone out* to the Gentiles, but the Gentiles are said to have *come in* to the Jews. This is an important distinction. "Aliens from the commonwealth of Israel, and strangers from the covenants of promise," those who were in this sense "far off" are said to have been "made nigh by the blood of Christ," and now to be "no more strangers and foreigners, but FELLOW-CITIZENS WITH THE SAINTS, [the believing Jews,] and of the household of God." The great mystery, for the first time clearly revealed "unto the holy apostles and prophets by the Spirit," was, "that the Gentiles should be FELLOW-HEIRS, and of the same body" with the Jews, who were the proper heirs, and only to be *disinherited* by unbelief. In striking confirmation of this view of the standing of the Jews is the following language of the apostle, in that remarkable chapter where he treats formally of this point:—"If some of the branches be broken off, and thou [Gentile], being a wild olive-tree, wert GRAFFED IN AMONG THEM, and WITH THEM partakest of the root and fatness of the olive-tree, boast not against the branches; but if thou boast, THOU BEAREST NOT THE ROOT, BUT THE ROOT THEE. . . . If thou wert cut out of the olive-tree which is wild by nature, and wert graffed, contrary to nature, into a good olive-tree, how much more should these, which be THE NATURAL BRANCHES, be graffed into their own olive-tree?" (Rom. xi. 17, 18, 24.) In short, the Gospel Church is historically and lineally "THE ISRAEL OF GOD" (Gal. vi. 16); not another, but the same Israel which came out of the loins of Jacob, and which—after going down into Egypt, and coming out with a high hand, wandering for forty years in the wilderness, obtaining possession of the promised land and at length in the fulness of time giving birth to Messiah—opened its bosom to receive its outcast brother the Gentile to the fellowship of its own *name*, and all its own *nearness to God*. The believing Jew has gone out from nothing, but the believing Gentile has come in to everything. True, they are now incorporated into one; but it is one "Israel of God." This Israel may, in point of fact, be nearly all Gentiles, and the "remnant" of the natural Israel, "according to the election of grace," may be reduced to the very lowest. But even if there were but *one*—as if just "that the purpose of God, according to election, might stand"—*that one would be* THE ROOT, *and all the rest but* THE BRANCHES.

If this be correct, we may expect to find the prophetic language framed in correspondence with it. If it be true that God's "Israel," under the Gospel, though *radically the same* as before, *comprehends all believing Gentiles*, it is incredible that the prophets, when depicting the new economy, should have always used this and similar terms in their *old* and *restricted* sense. This is what the extreme literalists hold.[1] By "Israel," "Jacob," "Judah," "the people" of the covenant, and such like terms in the prophecies, they insist that we are to understand the Jews as *contradistinguished from the Gentiles*. The consequence of this it is easy to see. What is foretold of the *Church of God*, under one or other of these names, as distinguished from the uncovenanted world without, its enemies and persecutors, is applied to the Jewish *nation*, as distinguished from other nations as near to God under the Gospel as themselves; and the most extravagant expectations of Jewish NATIONAL superiority and glory are spun out of the prophetic intimations of the elevation of *the Lord's people* to their proper rule over the world. This is the necessary result of a false principle of interpretation; and it would lead further astray than most Christians allow themselves to be drawn by it. None but the

---

[1]Even Dr. Henderson is too often led astray in this direction. Ascribing to "Israel," in its old sense, what is meant of it in its Evangelical amplitude as the Gospel Church, he carries his ideas of Jewish supremacy, and even of a restored temple and a metropolitan worship, to an extent which, with his other views, is utterly incongruous.

Jewish interpreters probably go through with it, nor do even they go all the length of the naked letter.

Doubtless there are places where Jews and Gentiles are expressly distinguished from each other; and in these places the former, of course, are to be taken in their restricted sense. Such are the following:—"I will give thee [Messiah] for a covenant of the *people* (עָם), for a light of the *Gentiles*" (גוים)—"It is a light thing that thou shouldest be my Servant, to raise up the tribes of *Jacob*, and to restore the preserved of *Israel*: I also will give thee for a Light of the *Gentiles*, that thou mayest be my Salvation unto the end of the earth." (Isa. xlii. 6, xlix. 6.) But in other places the terms, descriptive of God's ancient people, are most manifestly used in their *catholic* sense to set forth the blessed privileges and character of God's people, or the Church of Christ, composed of Jews and Gentiles, as "one body by the Cross."

Take one example from the *fifty-fourth* chapter of Isaiah. The evangelical prophet having in the preceding chapter predicted the "sufferings of Christ," and generally, also, "the following glories,"[2] expatiates here on this latter theme. Of this chapter, Dr. Henderson says, "Some consider it to be exclusively applicable to the Jews as a people; but the interpretation put upon verse first by the apostle, (Gal. iv. 27,) and the facts of history, militate against such application. Though Isaiah does not lose sight of that people as originally constituting the Church, yet having his eye upon the spiritual seed of the Messiah, to be chiefly collected from the heathen world, he merged for a time the peculiar interests of Judaism in those of the universal Church." (Page 388.) The only objection I have to this statement is, that it gives a prominence to "the peculiar interests of Judaism," or rather "the Jews," which this prophet does not give to them, at least in this last portion of his book. But now observe the strain of the chapter. "Enlarge the place of thy tent" —says the rapt prophet, addressing the Israelitish Church, or the believing portion of it—"and let them stretch forth the curtains of thine habitations; for thou shalt break forth on the right hand and on the left, and thy seed shall inherit the Gentiles." Messiah's sufferings have opened the door of faith to the Gentiles—God is about to persuade Japhet to dwell in the tents of Shem. (Gen. ix. 27) Now shall be fulfilled the promise to Abraham, that he should be "the father of many nations," who, walking in the steps of his faith, shall be verily "Abraham's seed, and heirs according to the promise." But the prophet goes on to say, that such a surprising enlargement would make them "forget the

---

[2]*Τὰς μετὰ ταῦτα δόξας.* (1 Pet. i. 11.)

shame of their youth, [in Egypt,] and not remember the reproach of their widowhood [in Babylon] any more. For," he adds, "thy Maker is thine Husband; the Lord of hosts is His name; and thy Redeemer the Holy One of Israel; The God of the whole earth shall He be called." Instead of losing her old name and her rightful honours under this influx of strangers, she would find all intact, discerning "her own Husband" in the Head of the new economy, and "the Holy One of Israel" in "the God of the whole earth." When He "forsook her" before, it was "for a small moment;" but now that He has had mercy on her, (in the blood of the covenant) it is "with everlasting kindness, nor shall the covenant of His peace be ever removed from her." "Afflicted, tossed with tempest, and not comforted," was her former lot; now "her foundations shall be laid with sapphires, and all her borders be of pleasant stones. All her children shall be taught of the Lord, and great shall be the peace of her children. In righteousness shall she be established; she shall be far from oppression: her enemies shall gather together against her, but they shall fall for her sake." In short, "no weapon formed against her shall prosper; and every tongue that riseth against her in judgment she shall condemn. *This is the heritage of the servants of the Lord; and their righteousness is of me, saith the Lord.*"

Now, what will those make of this chapter who contend that Israel, in the prophecies, always means Israel in the same restricted sense in every place? Certainly the Israel addressed at the opening of it consisted of the *natural seed* of Abraham—the believing portion of them; for they are bidden open their doors to the Gentiles as a thing that till then had never been done. But immediately *this is regarded as done*; in virtue of which, *though the same party continues to be addressed, it is under an entirely new aspect*—all its ancient peculiarities merged in those catholic glories which distinguish the new economy. To apply the contents of this and similar chapters—for it is but a specimen of many—to the Jewish *nation*, in contradistinction from believing Gentiles, is as extravagant in itself as it is opposed to the internal evidence of the chapter, and to the general strain of evangelical prophecy. On such a principle the Church of God, even under the Gospel, would be resolved into the *Jewish people*. Those who in the prophecies are held forth as the enemies and persecutors of Israel, will in that case be not simply the irreligious, but all of every nation who are not *Jews;* and *Gentile* Christianity will disappear from the prophetic page, save as it may be regarded as given anew to the world by the restored Jews. Whether there be not a considerable advance towards this in the writings of some extreme futurising literalists, and whether it be not the power of Gospel truth which alone prevents this tendency from shewing itself in others, let the intelligent readers of their writings decide.

I shall not attempt to turn this second proposition into a rule, as I did the first, because I know of no summary method for determining whether a prophecy regarding Israel in Messiah's times is to be understood of *the Israel of God* in its catholic sense—the *Church* under the Gospel—or of the *Jews* distinctively as a people. "The question," says Professor Alexander, "whether any prophecy is general or particular, literal or figurative, can only be determined by a thorough independent scrutiny of each case by itself, in reference, form, and substance, text and context, without regard to arbitrary and exclusive theories, but with a due regard to the analogy of Scripture in general, and of other prophecies in particular, especially of such as belong to the same writer, or at least to the same period, and apparently relate to the same subject. This is far from being so attractive or so easy as the sweeping application of a comprehensive canon to all cases, like or unlike; but it seems to be the only process likely to afford a satisfactory result."[3]

Such, then, are the concessions which, at the bidding of truth, I am prepared right willingly to make to the negative side of this question. On any other principles than those laid down in the two preceding propositions, I could not maintain the Restoration of the Jews. That it cannot in that case be maintained at all, will very likely be the opinion both of the extreme spiritualists who deny, and of the extreme literalists who affirm the Restoration. But as we proceed with our propositions, it will appear, I think, that there are still grounds for the affirmative side of the question, which it will not be very easy to shake.

---

[3]Earlier Prophecies of Isaiah, Introd. pp. xlvi. xlvii.

CHAPTER IV

POSITIVE EVIDENCE FOR THE TERRITORIAL RESTORATION—PRELIMINARY REMARKS

All that is written against the future restoration of the Jews goes on the supposition that, *as a people*, they are at an end; that the Divine purposes towards them as a nation were accomplished and exhausted when their peculiar economy passed away; and that now they are to be regarded in no other light than as sinners of mankind needing salvation, and blessed, on their believing, like other believers, with all spiritual blessings in Christ. One cannot take up a treatise on the negative side of this question without perceiving that this is the fundamental idea on which all rests. It is not denied that their restoration *may* take place, and that it *may* be predicted, though they think it is not. But when a view of their original destination is taken up which makes it in the last degree improbable that they should be restored, and in the last degree improbable that their restoration should be predicted, no wonder that the evidence for it in the prophecies is not seen. How, indeed, can we expect it?

Professor Alexander, for example, in the preface to his second volume on Isaiah, seems to leave the question so far open; but he only seems to do it. "As to the question in dispute," he says, meaning the one before us, "the ground which I have taken and endeavoured to maintain is the negative position, that the truth of these 'exceeding great and precious promises' is not suspended on the future restoration of the Jews to Palestine, *without denying such a restoration to be possible, or promised elsewhere*." I say this concession is more apparent than real, for the author has precluded himself from admitting that *any specific events* belonging to the new economy are predicted in the Old Testament. In his very able Introduction he lays down this sweeping principle, that all the predictions which relate to the old economy "are described by individual specific strokes," whereas the new economy is represented "as a definite, yet *undivided* whole." "Beyond the great turning-point between the two dispensations, *all is taken in at a single glance*." (Page xxix.) Of course, if this be true, it is vain to look for such a "specific stroke" as the Jews' Restoration to Palestine; nor need I tell the reader that he does not find it within the limits of his prophet—Isaiah. On his principles, he might take up book after book of the Old Testament, and, in the preface to his exposition of each, might concede such a restoration to be "possible or promised *elsewhere*;" but till he allow that "specific strokes" are admissible in Old Testament prophecies of Gospel times, to concede that it may be promised *anywhere* in the Old Testament amounts to nothing.

But is not even the *conversion* of the Jews a pretty specific stroke? Yet that is admitted by Professor Alexander to be predicted by Isaiah. (On chap. xi.) How he manages to explain this, I do not know; but I can imagine no way of reconciling his Introduction with the treatment of this particular prophecy.

Similar admissions are made by other able writers, that *possibly* the restoration of the Jews may be in the Divine purposes, and, consequently, may be in the Divine predictions, *though not involved in the original connexion with Canaan.* But I need not tell the reader that such writers never find them. The plain truth is, that if the natural seed of Abraham was chosen for merely preparatory and temporary purposes—purposes limited to their peculiar and now abolished economy—the question is ended. Till we have sifted and settled this point, then, in vain do we plunge into the prophecies. We may ply one another with texts enough, but it is only when we have disposed of the preliminary question that we have sure footing in the prophetic Scriptures. After that, however, the process will be short and simple; and to this accordingly I now address myself.

CHAPTER V

POSITIVE EVIDENCE FOR THE TERRITORIAL RESTORATION

Two propositions, it will be borne in mind, have been laid down, of the nature of *concessions* to the negative side of this question. In making these concessions, I was merely disencumbering myself of useless armour—of weapons which would have been hurtful only to myself. But now I come to the positive evidence for the Restoration of the Jews to their own land. And whereas the New Testament is supposed to give no countenance to such an expectation, and this forms with many the whole argument against it, I shall entrench myself in the New Testament first of all.

PROPOSITION III.—*The national conversion of the Israelitish people is explicitly predicted in the New Testament.*

The five following texts I simply note at the outset, without commenting upon them, as indirectly and generally bearing on this expectation:—

Matt. xxiii. 39—"I say unto you, Ye shall not see me henceforth, till *ye shall say, Blessed is he that cometh in the name of the Lord.*"

Luke xxi. 24—"Jerusalem shall be trodden down of the Gentiles, UNTIL *the times of the Gentiles be fulfilled.*"

"And certainly," says *Durham,* in his modest way, "some words of Christ's—Matt. xxiii. [39]; Luke xxi. 24—limiting their outward desolation, and the desolation of their house and land, to the time they should say Hosanna to Him and acknowledge Him, and to the time of the fulness of the Gentiles—do also speak for this."[1]

Acts i. 6, 7—"When they therefore were come together, they asked of him, saying, Lord, wilt thou *at this time* restore again the kingdom to Israel? And he said unto them, It is not for you to know *the times or the seasons,* which the father hath put in his own power."

---

[1]Commentary upon the Book of Revelation (on chap. xvi. 12).

"The apostles," says *Bengel* on this passage, "presupposing the *thing*, (i.e., the restoration of the kingdom to Israel,) inquired about the *time;* and the reply which follows has the like reference. 'The times and the seasons, which the Father hath put in His own power.' *Therefore the thing itself is sure; else it would have not time at all.*"

Acts iii. 19—"Repent therefore, and be converted, unto the blotting out of your sins (*ὅπως ἂν ἔλθωσι*), in order that *times of refreshing may come* from the presence of the Lord." (Compare Zech. iii. 9, 10.)

2 Cor. iii. 15, 16—"Even unto this day, when Moses is read, the vail is upon their heart. Nevertheless, *when it* [the heart of the Jewish nation] shall *turn to the Lord*, the vail shall be taken away."

To some of these passages I may recur under a subsequent head. But it is in the eleventh of the Romans that the present standing and predicted future of the Jewish nation is formally and largely handled; and the information there contained leaves nothing to be desired. The substance of it is this: that the rejection of God's ancient people under the Gospel is to be taken with two limitations—first, "*that even at this present time* [the period of rejection] *there is a remnant according to the election of grace*;" and second, *that the nation at large, as contradistinguished from this elect remnant, shall yet be brought in.* As "they were broken off for unbelief," and the Gentiles "stand by faith," so if the Gentiles be found faithless, they also shall be cut off, while the body of the Jewish nation, "if they abide not still in unbelief, shall be graffed in; for God is able to graff them in again." In fact, the "blindness" that "has happened to Israel is but 'in part'"—that is, partial and temporary[2]—"until the fulness of the Gentiles be come in;" after which "*all Israel shall be saved.*" Much needless criticism has been bestowed upon this last statement, to shew that "all" to be saved is neither to be taken numerically and absolutely on the one hand, nor yet, on the other, to be confounded with the elect remnant, which there ever is, of believing and saved Israelites. The contrast which runs through the whole chapter shews, beyond all reasonable doubt, what is meant, namely, that whereas it is but a handful of Israelites who at any time, during the period of rejection, are in the Church—the great body of the nation being in an outcast and excommunicated state—the time is coming when not a remnant only, as now, but "all" shall be saved; meaning, the bulk and body of the nation, as contradistinguished from this remnant.

---

2 *'Απὸ μέρους, partly, in a sort.* Compare chap. xv. 15, "in some sort;" ver. 24, "somewhat;" 2 Cor. i. 14, ii. 5, "in part."

This is so very evident, that the only wonder is how it should ever have been otherwise understood. And yet we have seen that a considerable number of able divines, when the *Restoration* of the Jews came to be discussed—holding that the national destinies of the seed of Abraham were all accomplished long ago—felt that even a general *Conversion* of them was rather *in the way*, and, to get rid of it, adopted the violent expedient of identifying the two parties whom the apostle expressly contrasts—the "all Israel" to be saved at a definite future period, and the "elect remnant" saved all along since the rejection of the nation. Unnatural as was such a view of the chapter, we can hardly wonder at it. For on their hypothesis—that the nationality of the Jews had exhausted its original purposes long ago—how can the facts of their history since the destruction of Jerusalem be accounted for? Why did not the nation, by little and little, melt away after the extinction of their polity by the Romans, or become absorbed in the various places of their dispersion? Why has a special providence counterworked, in their case, all the laws by which nations are affected, in respect of acknowledged identity, numbers, and prosperity? On supposition that the national destination of the Israelites was bound up with their restricted and now extinct economy, why all this profusion, so to speak, of special care *to preserve their nationality unbroken,* their identity indisputable? We know what will *now* be said by some in reply to this. God, it will be said, has reserved them for a national conversion to the faith of Christ; and it is with a view to this that such care has been taken of them. But this though true, does not meet the difficulty. The wonder is, that such a destiny as a *national* conversion *should,* on their principles, be in store for them—no *other* nationalities being expected, or even tolerated, in connexion with and as the sequel of this most signal one. *Individual conversion* from time to time, and *ultimate absorption,* would seem to suit best with the hypothesis we are controverting.

Accordingly, we find the chapter before us nearly as much in the way now as formerly with those who deny the restoration of the Jews. There is, at least, very much the same tendency to throw obscurity over this exceedingly clear chapter. We have an example of this in *Archbishop Whately.* In a volume entitled, "A View of the Scripture Revelations concerning a Future State, laid before his Parishioners by a Country Pastor," (known to be the learned prelate,) and in the lecture headed, "The Expected Restoration of the Jews and the Millennium," we find the following short sentence:—"The passage (Rom. xi.) is one that is generally confessed to be obscure and of doubtful interpretation." On this there is a note, the first paragraph of which is as follows:—"The principal obscurity, perhaps, consists in this, that where the apostle is apparently holding out a hope of the ultimate conversion and salvation of 'all Israel,' it is not clear in what sense, or with what modification, the word 'all' is to be taken. He could not, one would suppose, mean it to include all the Jews who were at the time living, nor all those many millions of them who through more than fifty generations, since have lived and died in unbelief."[3] All that follows is about the comfort of knowing, that no such obscurities rest on anything essential to salvation, and with these very poor remarks the subject is dismissed.

But, it will be said, "We concede the general conversion of the Jewish nation, in terms of Proposition III.; resting it, however, not on Old Testament prophecy, nor on the terms of the Abrahamic covenant, but solely on the New Testament evidence, which, being decisive, we of course accept, but whose silence on the subject of a territorial restoration ought to decide that question in the negative."

This is intelligible ground; but that it is untenable, I shall now endeavour to shew.

PROPOSITION IV.—*The New Testament sends us back to the Old, and specially to the terms of the Abrahamic covenant, as our primary warrant for expecting the recovery of "all Israel."*

Continuing our comments on the eleventh of Romans, let the following passage be carefully observed:—"And so all Israel shall be saved: as it is written, There shall come out of Sion the Deliverer, and shall turn away ungodliness from Jacob: for this is my covenant unto them, when I shall take away their sins. As concerning the gospel, they are enemies for your sakes; but *as touching the election, they are beloved for the fathers' sakes. For the gifts and calling of God are without repentance.*" (Rom. xi. 26-29.)

Here the apostle, instead of giving it out on his own proper authority that "all Israel shall be saved," carries his appeal to two of the prophets—to Isaiah (chap. lix. 20), and to Jeremiah (chap. xxxi. 31-34); giving the substance rather than the very words of their prophecies. *Professor Alexander* would undermine the authority of the apostle's first reference, considered as a proof passage, holding it to be no Old Testament prediction of Israel's future conversion, but merely convenient phraseology for expressing *his own* prophecy of that event. "It seems to me"—says the learned Professor, on Isa. lix. 20—"that the variation in Paul's words, not only from the Hebrew but the Septuagint, together with the use which the apostle makes of

[3]A view, &c., p. 191. Sixth Edit. Fellowes, 1847.

this citation, warrant the conclusion that he is not there *interpreting* Isaiah, but employing the familiar language of an ancient prophecy as the vehicle for *a new one*. Other examples of this practice have occurred before, nor is there anything unworthy or unreasonable in it, when the context in both cases clearly shows the author's drift, as in the case before us, where it seems no less clear that Paul employs the language to predict the future restoration of the Jews (to the Divine favour, he means, not to their own land) than that Isaiah uses it to foretell the deliverance of God's people from their enemies in case of their repentance, without any reference to local, temporal, or national distinctions. This hypothesis in reference to Paul's quotation has the advantage of accounting for his change of the original expression, which may then be regarded as a kind of caution against that very error into which interpreters have generally fallen."[4] "A manifestly untenable view," says *Dr. Fairbairn*; "for how could we, in that case, have vindicated the apostle from the want of godly simplicity, using, as he must then have done, his accustomed formula for prophetical quotations ('as it is written') only to disguise and recommend an announcement properly his own? We repudiate any such solution of the difficulty, which would represent the apostle as sailing under false colours."[5] This is strong language, but the case almost demanded it. It is needless, however, to linger upon this, since the apostle carries us farther back than Isaiah and Jeremiah—back to the Abrahamic covenant itself, on our view of which will depend the interpretation of all the prophecies bearing on the subject, and, if I am not greatly mistaken, the whole question.

When the apostle says, "As touching the *election,* they are beloved for the fathers' sake," he means, of course, not that "election of grace" by which individual Jews are from time to time called, but the original "election" of Abraham and his seed. And when he says, in respect of that election, "*they* are beloved for *the fathers' sake,*" he means that the bulk and body of the nation, now out of covenant, are "beloved" because of their ancestral connexions—their lineal descent from and oneness in covenant with "the fathers," with whom God originally established His covenant. I do not see how it is possible to put any other sense upon the apostle's words. And if this be the meaning of them, they give us a view of the Abrahamic covenant very different, as respects the natural Israel, from that of our opponents in this question, and many others. In their view, Abraham and his natural seed were chosen for purely *temporary* purposes—

---

[4]Later Prophecies of Isaiah, p. 367.

[5]Prophecy, &c., p. 278.

purposes which received their full accomplishment on the completion of Christ's work, and the opening of the new economy. In connexion with these temporary purposes, *the land* was conferred upon them; and as without it those ends could not have been attained, so when the object was gained, the grant was virtually withdrawn—it *ipso facto* ceased and determined—the *grace* of the covenant, of which Abraham and his seed after the flesh were but the depositaries and trustees, alone remaining, to flow from age to age, through the blood of the covenant, to all the *spiritual* seed of Abraham,—to Jew and Gentile alike.

I cannot better convey this view of the Abrahamic covenant, whose untenableness I propose to show, than in the words of the great *Dr. Owen,* which I rather select as being, for sobriety, fulness, and precision, all that my opponents would probably desire.

"Although"—says he, speaking of the promised land—"it is called an 'everlasting inheritance,' yet it was so only on two accounts:—1. That it was typical of that heavenly inheritance which is eternal. 2. Because, as unto right and title, it was to be continued unto the end of that limited perpetuity which God granted unto the Church-state in that land; that is, unto the coming of the promised Seed, in whom all nations should be blessed, which the call of Abraham did principally regard. Until that time was expired, although many incursions were made into and upon this inheritance, yet were they all that made them oppressors, and were punished for their usurpation. But when the grant of it to them expired, and those wicked tenants of God's vineyard forfeited their right unto it by their unbelief and their murdering the true Heir, God disinherited them, dispossessed them, and left them neither right nor title to, nor any interest in, this inheritance, as it is this day. It is no more the inheritance of Abraham; but in Christ he is become 'heir of the world,' and his spiritual posterity enjoy all the privileges of it. Wherefore the grant of this land for an inheritance unto Abraham in his posterity had a season limited unto it. Upon the expiration of that term, their right and title unto it were cancelled and disannulled. And thereon God in His providence sent the armies of the Romans to dispossess them, which they accordingly did, unto this day. Nor have the present Jews any more or better title unto the land of Canaan than unto any other country in the world. Nor shall their title be renewed thereunto upon their conversion unto God. For the limitation of their right was unto that time wherein it was typical of the heavenly inheritance: that now ceasing forever, there can be no especial title to it revived."[6]

---

[6]Owen on the Hebrews; exposition of ch. xi. 8.

The drift of all this is, that the natural Israel, *as such,* have nothing to do now with the Abrahamic covenant. The interest they had in it as a people terminated with their peculiar economy. What interest they have in it now is common to them with ourselves, the interest which the elect of every nation have in the grace of the everlasting covenant. True, it is of the *land,* not the *people,* that Dr. Owen is speaking. But as we shall by and by more fully see that the choice of the people and the grant of the land went together, and stand on precisely the same footing—as articles of the Abrahamic covenant, yet distinct from the *grace* of it—they must stand or fall together; the same arguments proving them both to have terminated with the Jewish economy, or both to be in force still. Now, my argument is this that *one* of these inseparable things is explicitly declared by the apostle to be as much in force now as it was at the beginning; and, consequently, *the other* must be viewed in the same light. The *people*—not the remnant of them, according to the election of grace, but the *nation,* considered as the natural descendants of Abraham—are still an elect people, and, as such, "beloved." In other words, the very same love which chose "the fathers," and rested on them as the parent stem of the nation, yearns over their descendants, and will yet recover them from unbelief.

There is only one way of meeting this, and it seems to me feeble enough. *Dr. Arnold,* at a loss apparently to account, on his principle, for the continuance of the Jewish nationality under the Gospel, and the special promises regarding them in the New Testament, speaks as if the whole explanation of it lay in that principle of affection which leads one to be kind to the descendants of a friend for that friend's sake. On this principle, when Paul says, "They are beloved *for the fathers' sake,*" the meaning would simply be, that the present Jews were dear to God from (if I may so express it) ancestral recollections—that though all covenant *connexion* with them is entirely at an end, and all covenant *obligations* to them as a people have been long ago exhausted, yet the blood of "the fathers" flowing in their veins will make the nation ever dear to God. It is a beautiful thought; nor are such ideas altogether foreign to Scripture, particularly in reference to the seed of Abraham.[7] But in this case its application is unfortunate; for the apostle explains, in the very next clause, what he means by their being, "as touching the election, beloved for the

[7]"Art not thou," cried Jehoshaphat, "our God, who didst drive out the inhabitants of this land before thy people Israel, and gavest it to the seed of Abraham THY FRIEND for ever?" (2 Chron. xx. 7.) Compare with this the following: "But thou, Israel, art my servant, Jacob whom I have chosen, the seed of Abraham MY FRIEND." (Isa. xli. 8.)

fathers' sakes:" "for," adds he, "THE GIFTS AND THE CALLING OF GOD ARE WITHOUT REPENTANCE." This cannot mean the gifts and calling of the *elect;* for how can the irrevocableness of these prove that the *Israelitish nation* at this day, and abiding still in unbelief, is dear to God for their fathers' sakes? No; it is the IRREVOCABLENESS OF THE ABRAHAMIC COVENANT, IN ALL ITS ARTICLES, on which the apostle is reasoning—those articles which relate to the *choice of the people* and the *grant of the land* to them, as well as those which are common to them with all who believe. True, it is the people only of whom the apostle is directly speaking. But the one is, *in principle,* inseparable from the other. The argument from the perpetuity of the *people* carries with it the irrevocableness of their *land*; just as, if the argument had been built upon the *land,* it would have carried with it the perpetuity of its *people.*

Should this be disputed—should any one say, "We admit the perpetuity of the *people,* and are willing to allow that the original covenant of their separation was meant to stretch through all time; but we cannot see that this applies to the *land,* or, at least, that the apostle's argument goes that length"—I am ready to meet this too. Leave the apostle now out of the question, and let us go to the Old Testament, taking with us merely this apostolic doctrine, *that the covenant choice of Abraham and his natural seed was made in perpetuity.* I ask nothing more.

SUPPLEMENTARY NOTE.

In the foregoing remarks on the eleventh of Romans, I have quoted only so much of the chapter as was necessary to my purpose. But as this does scanty justice to the teaching of so pregnant a portion of Scripture on the present standing and future prospects of the Jewish nation, I take the liberty of inserting here so much of additional comment on this chapter, from a recent work of my own on the entire Epistle, as may enable the reader somewhat better to apprehend the general strain and progress of the apostle's thought.

Rom. xi. 1—I say then, Hath God cast away his people? God forbid. Our Lord did indeed announce that "the kingdom of God should be *taken from* Israel" (Matt. xxi. 41); and when asked by the eleven, after His resurrection, if He would at that time "*restore* the kingdom to Israel," His reply is in some sense a virtual admission that Israel was, in some sense, already out of the covenant. (Acts i. 6-8.) Yet there the apostle teaches that, in two respects, Israel was *not* "cast away:" First, Not *totally*; Second, Not *finally*. FIRST, Israel is not *wholly* cast away. **for I also am an Israelite**—and so a living witness to the contrary.

5. Even so at this present time—'in this present season;' this period of Israel's rejection. (See Acts i. 7, *Gr.*) **there is a remnant according to the election of grace**—*q.d.,* 'As in Elijah's time the apostasy of Israel was not so universal as it seemed to be, and as he in his despondency concluded it to be, so now the rejection of Christ by Israel is not so appalling in extent as one would be apt to think: There is now, as there was then, a faithful remnant; not, however, of persons naturally better than the unbelieving mass, but of persons graciously chosen to salvation.' **7-10. What then?**—How stands the fact? **Israel hath not obtained that which he seeketh for** (*i.e.,* Justification, or acceptance with God, chap. ix. 31); but the election (the elect remnant of Israel) 'found it, and the rest were hardened,' or 'judicially given over to the hardness of their own hearts.' **as it is written,** (Isa. xxix. 10 and Deut. xxix. 4,) **God hath given them the spirit of slumber** ('stupor') . . . .**unto this** ('this present') **day. And David saith,**—(Ps. lxix. 23,) which in such a Messianic psalm must be meant of the rejectors of Christ. **Let their table,** &c.,—*i.e.*, 'Let their very blessings prove a curse to them, and their enjoyments only sting and take vengeance on them.' **let their eyes be darkened, ... and bow down their back alway.** The apostle's object in making these quotations is to shew that what he had been compelled to say of the then condition and prospects of his nation was more than borne out by their own Scriptures. But, SECONDLY, God hath not cast away His people *finally*. The illustration of this point extends from ver. 11 to ver. 31.

11. I say then, Have they stumbled that they should fall? God forbid; but through their fall salvation is come to the Gentiles, to provoke them to jealousy. 12. Now if the fall of them be the riches of the (Gentile) **world.**—as being the occasion of their accession to Christ. **and the diminishing of them** (*i.e.*, the reduction of the *true* Israel to so small a remnant) **the riches of the Gentiles; how much more their fulness!**—*i.e.*, their full recovery (see on ver. 26); *q.d.*, 'If an event so untoward as Israel's fall was the occasion of such unspeakable good to the Gentile world, of how much greater good may we expect an event so blessed as their full recovery to be productive?' **15. For if the casting away of them**—The apostle had denied that they were cast away (ver. 1); here he affirms it. But both are true: they *were* cast away, though neither totally nor finally, and it is of this partial and temporary rejection that the apostle here speaks. **be the reconciling of**

the (Gentile) **world, what shall the receiving of them be, but life from the dead?**—It is surely very strained to explain this of the literal resurrection, as most modern critics, following some of the fathers, do; but to take it as a mere proverbial expression for the highest felicity, [*Grotius,* &c.,] is too loose. The meaning seems to be, that the reception of the whole family of Israel, scattered, as they are, among all nations under heaven, and the most inveterate enemies of the Lord Jesus, will be such a stupendous manifestation of the power of God upon the spirits of men, and of His glorious presence with the heralds of the Cross, as will not only kindly devout astonishment far and wide, but so change the dominant mode of thinking and feeling on all spiritual things, as to seem like a *resurrection from the dead.*

16. For ('But') **if the first-fruit be holy, the lump is also [holy]; and if the root, so the branches.**—As the separation unto God of Abraham, Isaac, and Jacob from the rest of mankind, as the parent stem of their race, was as real an offering of first-fruit as that which hallowed the produce of the earth, so, in the Divine estimation, it was as real a separation of the mass or "lump" of that nation in all time to God. The figure of the "root" and its "branches" is of like import—the consecration of the one of them extending to the other. **17, 18. And if** (notwithstanding this consecration of Abraham's race to God) **some of the branches**—The mass of the unbelieving and rejected Israelites are here called "some," not, as before, to meet Jewish prejudice, but with the opposite view of checking Gentile pride. **and thou, being a wild olive, wert** ('wast') **graffed in among them**—Though it is more usual to graft the superior cutting upon the inferior stem, the opposite method, which is intended here, is not without example. **and with them partakest** (along with the branches left, the believing remnant) **of the root and fatness of the olive tree** (the rich grace secured by covenant to the true seed of Abraham); **boast not against the** (rejected) **branches. But if thou** (do) **boast,** (remember that) **thou bearest not** ('it is not thou that bearest') **the root, but the root thee**—*q.d.*, 'If the branches may not boast over the root that bears them, then may not the Gentile boast over the seed of Abraham; for what is thy standing, O Gentile, in relation to Israel, but that of a branch in relation to the root? from Israel hath come all that thou art and hast in the family of God; for "salvation is of the Jews" (John iv. 22).' **19-21. Thou wilt say then** (as a plea for boasting), **The branches were broken off, that I might be graffed in. Well**—(*q.d.*, 'Be it so, but remember that') **because of unbelief they were broken off, and thou standest** (not as a Gentile, but solely) **by faith**—But as faith cannot live in those "whose soul is lifted up," (Hab. ii. 4,) **Be not high-minded, but fear: for if God spared not the natural branches,** (sprung from the parent stem.) **take heed lest he also spare not thee** (a mere wild graft)—The former might, beforehand, have been thought very improbable; but, after that, no one can wonder at the latter. **23. And they also,** ('Yea, and they,') **if they abide not still in unbelief, shall be graffed in: for God is able to graff them in again**—This appeal to the *power* of God to effect the recovery of His ancient people implies the vast difficulty of it—which all who have ever laboured for the conversion of the Jews are made depressingly to feel. That intelligent expositors should think that this was meant of *individual* Jews, re-introduced from time to time into the family of God on their believing on the Lord Jesus, is surprising; and yet those who deny the *national* recovery of Israel must and do so interpret the apostle. But this is to confound the two things which the apostle carefully distinguishes. Individual Jews have been at all times admissible, and have been admitted, to the Church through the gate of faith in the Lord Jesus. This is the "remnant, *even at this present time,* according to the election of grace," of which the apostle, in the first part of the chapter, had cited himself as one. But here he manifestly speaks of something *not* then existing, but to be looked forward to as a great future event in the economy of God, the re-engrafting of *the nation as such*, when they "abide not in unbelief." And though this is here spoken of merely as a supposition (if their unbelief shall cease)—in order to set it over against the other supposition, of what will happen to the Gentiles if they shall not abide in the faith—the supposition is turned into an explicit prediction in the verses following. **24. For if thou wert cut** ('wert cut off') **from the olive tree, which is wild by nature, and wast graffed contrary to nature into a good olive tree; how much more shall these,** &c.—This is just the converse of ver. 21:'As the excision of the merely *engrafted* Gentiles through unbelief is a thing much more to be expected than was the excision of the *natural* Israel, before it happened; so the restoration of Israel, when they shall be brought to believe in Jesus, is a thing far more in the line of what we should expect, than the admission of the Gentiles to a standing which they never before enjoyed.'

25. For I would not, that ye should be ignorant of this mystery—The word "mystery," so often used by our apostle, does not mean (as with us) something incomprehensible, but 'something before kept secret, either wholly or for the most part, and now only fully disclosed,' (*cf.* chapter xvi. 25; 1 Cor. ii. 7-10; Eph. i. 9,10,

iii. 3-6, 9, 10, &c.) **lest ye should be wise in your own conceits**—as if ye alone were in all time coming to be the family of God. **that blindness** ('hardness') **in part is happened to** ('hath come upon') **Israel**—*i.e.*, hath come partially, or upon a portion of Israel. **until the fulness of the Gentiles be** ('have') **come in**—*i.e.*, not the general conversion of the world to Christ, as many take it; for this would seem to contradict the latter part of this chapter, and throw the national recovery of Israel too far into the future: besides, in ver. 15, the apostle seems to speak of the receiving of Israel, not as following, but as contributing largely to bring about the general conversion of the world—but, 'until the Gentiles have had their *full* time of the visible Church all to themselves, while the Jews are out, which the Jews had till the Gentiles were brought in.' See Luke xxi. 24. **26, 27 And so all Israel shall be saved**—To understand this great statement, as some still do, merely of such a gradual inbringing of *individual* Jews, that there shall at length remain none in unbelief, is to do manifest violence both to it and to the whole context. It can only mean the ultimate ingathering of Israel as a *nation*, in contrast with the present 'remnant.' [So *Tholuck, Meyer, De Wette, Philippi, Alford, Hodge.*] Three confirmations of this now follow: two from the prophets, and a third from the Abrahamic covenant itself. *First,* **as it is written, There shall come out of Sion the Deliverer, and shall** (or, according to what seems the true reading, without the 'and'—'He shall') **turn away ungodliness from Jacob**—The apostle, having drawn his illustrations of man's *sinfulness* chiefly from Psalm xiv. and Isa. lix., now seems to combine the language of the same two places regarding Israel's *salvation* from it. [*Bengel.*] In the one place the Psalmist longs to see "the salvation of Israel coming *out of Zion*" (Ps. xiv. 7); in the other, the prophet announces that "the Redeemer (or, 'Deliverer') shall come to (or, *for*) Zion," (Isa. lix. 20.) But as all the glorious manifestations of Israel's God were regarded as issuing out of Zion, as the seat of His manifested glory (Ps. xx. 2, cx. 2; Isa. xxxi. 9), the turn which the apostle gives to the words merely adds to them that familiar idea. And whereas the prophet announces that He "shall come to (or, '*for*') them that turn from transgression in Jacob," while the apostle makes him say that He shall come "to turn away ungodliness *from* Jacob," this is taken from the **LXX** version, and seems to indicate a different reading of the original text. The sense, however, is substantially the same in both. *Second,* **for**—rather, 'and;' introducing a new quotation. **this is my covenant with them** (*lit.*, 'this is the covenant from me unto them') **when I shall take away their sins**—This is rather a brief summary of Jer. xxxi. 31-34, than the express words of any prediction. Those who believe that there are no predictions regarding the literal Israel in the Old Testament, that stretch beyond the end of the Jewish economy, are obliged to view these quotations by the apostle as mere adaptations of Old Testament language, to express his own predictions, [*Alexander* on Isaiah, &c.] But how forced this is, we shall presently see. **28, 29. As concerning the gospel, they are enemies for your sakes**—*i.e.*, they are regarded and treated as enemies (in a state of exclusion through unbelief, from the family of God) for the benefit of you Gentiles; in the sense of ver. 11, 15. **but as touching the election** (of Abraham and his seed), **they are beloved**—*even in their state of exclusion*—**for the fathers' sakes. For the gifts and calling** ('and the calling') **of God are without repentance** ('not to be,' or 'cannot be repented of')—By "the *calling* of God," in this case, is meant that sovereign act by which God, in the exercise of His free choice, 'called' Abraham to be the father of a peculiar people; while "the *gifts* of God" here denote the articles of the covenant which God made with Abraham, and which constituted the real distinction between his and all other families of the earth. Both these, says the apostle, are irrevocable; and as the point for which he refers to this at all is the *final destiny* of the Israelitish nation, it is clear that the *perpetuity through all time of the Abrahamic covenant* is the thing here affirmed. And lest any should say that though Israel, *as a nation,* has no destiny at all under the Gospel, but as a people disappeared from the stage when the middle wall of partition was broken down, yet the Abrahamic covenant still endures in the *spiritual* seed of Abraham, made up of Jews and Gentiles in one undistinguished mass of redeemed men under the Gospel—the apostle, as if to preclude that supposition, expressly states that the very Israel who, as concerning the Gospel, are regarded as "enemies for the Gentiles' sakes," are "*beloved for the fathers' sakes;*" and it is in proof of this that he adds, "For the gifts and the calling of God are without repentance." But in what sense are the now unbelieving and excluded children of Israel "beloved for the fathers' sakes?" Not merely from ancestral *recollections,* according to Dr. Arnold's beautiful idea (see page 126), but from ancestral *connexions* and *obligations,* or their lineal descent from and oneness in covenant with the fathers with whom God originally established it. In other words, the natural Israel—not "the *remnant* of them according to the election of grace," but THE NATION, sprung from Abraham according to the flesh—are still an elect people, and as such, "beloved." The very same love which chose the fathers, and rested on the fathers as a parent stem of the nation, still rests on their descendants at large, and will yet recover them from unbelief, and reinstate them in the family of God. **30, 31. For as ye in times past have not believed** (or, 'obeyed') **God**—that is, yielded not to God 'the obedience of faith,' while strangers to Christ—**yet now have obtained mercy through** (by occasion of) **their unbelief; even so have these** (the Jews) **now not believed** (or, 'now been disobedient'), **that through your mercy** (the mercy shewn to you) **they also may obtain mercy**—Here is an entirely new idea. The apostle has hitherto dwelt upon the unbelief of the Jews as making way for the faith of the Gentiles—the exclusion of the one occasioning the reception of the other; a truth yielding to generous, believing Gentiles but mingled satisfaction. Now, opening a more cheering prospect, he speaks of the mercy shewn to the Gentiles as a means of Israel's recovery; which seems to mean that it will be by the instrumentality of believing Gentiles that Israel as a nation is at length to "look on Him whom they have pierced and mourn for Him" and so to "obtain mercy." (See 2 Cor. iii. 15, 16.) **32. For God hath concluded them all in unbelief** ('hath shut them all up to unbelief') **that he might have mercy upon all**—*i.e.*, those "all" of whom he had been discoursing; the Gentiles first, and after them the Jews. The apostle is here dealing with those great divisions of mankind, Jew and Gentile; and what he here says is, that God's purpose was to shut up each of these divisions of men to the experience first of an unhumbled, condemned state, without Christ, and then to the experience of His mercy in Christ.

33. O the depth, &c.—The apostle now yields himself up to the admiring contemplation of the grandeur of that Divine plan which he had sketched out. **of the riches both of the wisdom and knowledge of God**—The "knowledge" points probably to the vast sweep of Divine comprehension herein displayed; the "wisdom" to that fitness to accomplish the ends intended, which is stamped on all this procedure. **34, 35. For who hath known the mind of the Lord?—or who hath been his counsellor?—or who hath first given to him, and it shall be recompensed to him** ('and shall have recompense made to him') **again?**—God's plans and methods in the dispensation of his grace have a reach of comprehension and wisdom stamped upon them which finite mortals cannot fathom, much less could ever have imagined before they were disclosed. **36. For of him, and through him, and to him, are all things: to whom** ('to Him') **be glory for ever. Amen**—Thus worthily—with a brevity only equalled by its sublimity—does the apostle here sum up this whole matter. "OF Him are all things," as their eternal Source: "THROUGH Him are all things," inasmuch as

He brings all to pass which in His eternal counsels He purposed: "To Him are all things," as being His own last End; the manifestation of the glory of His own perfections being the ultimate, because the highest possible, design of all His procedure from first to last.

On this rich chapter, *Note*. . . . (6.) God's covenant with Abraham and his natural seed is a perpetual covenant, in equal force under the Gospel as before it. Therefore it is, that the Jews as a nation still survive, in spite of all the laws which, in similar circumstances, have either extinguished or destroyed the identity of other nations. And therefore it is that the Jews as a nation will yet be restored to the family of God, through the subjection of their proud hearts to Him whom they have pierced. And as believing Gentiles will be honoured to be the instruments of this stupendous change, so shall the vast Gentile world reap such benefit from it, that it shall be like the communication of life to them from the dead. (7.) Thus has the Christian Church the highest motive to the establishment and vigorous prosecution of *Missions to the Jews*; God having not only promised that there shall be a remnant of them gathered in every age, but pledged Himself to the final ingathering of the whole nation, assigned the honour of that ingathering to the Gentile Church, and assured them that the event, when it does arrive, shall have a life-giving effect upon the whole world. (Ver. 12-16, 26-31.) (8.) Those who think that in all the evangelical prophecies of the Old Testament the terms "Jacob," "Israel," &c., are to be understood solely of *the Christian Church*, would appear to read the Old Testament differently from the apostle, who, from the use of those very terms in Old Testament prophecy, draws arguments to prove that God has mercy in store for *the natural Israel*. (Ver. 26, 27.) (9.) Mere intellectual investigations into Divine truth in general, and the sense of the living oracles in particular, as they have a hardening effect, so they are a great contrast to the spirit of our apostle, whose lengthened sketch of God's majestic procedure towards men in Christ Jesus ends here in a burst of *admiration* , which loses itself in the still higher frame of *adoration*. (Ver. 33-36.)[8]

[8]Commentary on the Epistle to the Romans: Embracing the Latest Results of Criticism. Collins, 1860. Pp. 113-125.

CHAPTER VI

POSITIVE EVIDENCE FOR THE TERRITORIAL RESTORATION CONTINUED

Before proceeding to examine a few of the most pertinent passages of Old Testament Scripture—which I purposely reserved till we should get firm footing in the *New Testament*—it may be well to say down, in another proposition, what I wish to prove.

PROPOSITION V.—*The* PEOPLE *and the* LAND *of Israel are so connected in numerous prophecies of the Old Testament, that whatever* LITERALITY *and* PERPETUITY *are ascribed to the one must, on all strict principles of interpretation, be attributed to the other also.*

A few out of many examples will suffice to illustrate and establish this proposition: first, from the historical; next, from the prophetical books of the Old Testament.

FIRST. Beginning with the historical books,—

1. The Abrahamic covenant itself ought to lead the way. We give it in full, first, as renewed to the patriarch himself, in connexion with its seal—circumcision—and then as renewed to Jacob at Bethel.

"And Abram fell on his face; and God talked with him, saying, As for me, behold, my covenant is with thee, and thou shalt be a father of many nations. Neither shall thy name any more be called Abram, but thy name shall be Abraham: for a father of many nations have I made thee. And I will make thee exceeding fruitful, and I will make nations of thee, and kings shall come out of thee. And I will establish my covenant between me and thee, and thy seed after thee, in their generations, for an everlasting covenant, to be a God unto thee, and to thy seed after thee. And I will give unto thee, and to thy seed after thee, the land wherin thou art a stranger, all the land of Canaan, for an everlasting possession; and I will be their God." (Gen. xvii. 3-8.)

"And Jacob dreamed, and behold a ladder set up on the earth, and the top of it reached to heaven: and behold the angels of God ascending and decending on it. And, behold, the LORD stood above it, and said, I am the LORD God of Abraham thy father, and the God of

Isaac: the land whereon thou liest, to thee will I give it, and to thy seed: and thy seed shall be as the dust of the earth; and thou shalt spread abroad to the west, and to the east, and to the north, and to the south: and in thee, and in thy seed, shall all the families of the earth be blessed. And, behold, I am with thee, and will keep thee in all places whither thou goest, and will bring thee again into this land: for I will not leave thee, until I have done that which I have spoken to thee of." (Gen. xxviii. 12-15.)

In the first four verses of the first passage the promise is, that Abraham "should be the heir of the world," and "the father of all them that believe, though they be not circumcised," who, "being Christ's, are Abraham's seed, and heirs according to the promise," whether they be Jews or Gentiles. It is impossible to doubt this to be the sense of the first article, with the fourth of the Romans before us, in which it is expounded and commented upon at large.

Next follows God's covenant with Abraham, and his seed after him in their generations, for an everlasting covenant, to be a God unto him, and to his seed after him." Whether the word "everlasting" means here the whole duration of the Jewish economy, or of the nation itself—their generations through all time, in perpetuity—depends upon the subject. But that question we have found settled already by the apostle; for it is to this article of the covenant that he refers when he says, that, "as touching the *election,*" the Israelitish nation, *as such,* is as dear to God now, under the Gospel, as ever it was in the time of "the fathers." It is with his eye resting on *this* article of the covenant, (for the first article is common to Jews and Gentiles, and the last relates to the *land,* and there is no other—I say, it is with his eye resting on this article,) that he says, "*The gifts and the calling of God are without repentance*"—that is to say, irrevocable—and so must be yet resting (he argues) on the *natural Israel,* as a body. His whole argument may be thus expressed: 'Jehovah promised to be a God to Abraham, and to his seed, through all their generations, for an everlasting covenant. But just now He is *not* their God, nor are they His people. Because of unbelief they have been broken off, and a long period of blindness is to happen to Israel, during which "the fulness of the Gentiles will be coming in," and Abraham will be becoming the father of many believing nations, according to the first article of the covenant. But hath God cast away His people whom he foreknew? Nay; but He will be "a God" to them yet; for the promise to them is for all their generations to perpetuity. It is as much in force now as ever; "and *so* all Israel shall be saved."' Of course, I am not to be understood as meaning to *restrict* the glorious promise—"I will be a God unto thee, and to thy seed after thee"—to the *natural* Israel. I am only repeating what the apostle says, that this promise contains a security for the final inbringing of the Jewish *nation,* that the promise may not fail to its natural heirs:—"To the Jew *first,* but also to the Gentile."

The remaining article conveys *the land* "to him and to his seed after him, for an everlasting possession,"—the whole concluding with the rich and all inclusive promise, "and I will be their God."

Now, let the reader mark the identity of language in which the *choice of the people* and the *grant of the land* are expressed. As the parties are the same—"Abraham and his seed"—so the duration of the grant runs parallel with that of the choice. Are the *people* chosen by an "everlasting covenant?"—the *land* is guaranteed to them for an "everlasting possession." And as we have seen that the covenant rests on the people *still,* and will yet fetch them home to God, ought we not to conclude that the land is kept for them too, awaiting only the removal of their unbelief, and their restoration to covenant?

The second passage contains six promises. In the first three, Jehovah, in the visions of the night, promulgates afresh to Jacob—in his *public* character as the third trustee of the Abrahamic covenant after Abraham and Isaac—the three great articles of that covenant: the *land,* whereon he lay; the *seed,* countless as the stars; and the *blessing,* to come to all nations through that seed—that is to say, through One[1] to spring from the lonely sleeper's loins—answering to that promise in the other passage, "I will be a God unto thee, and to thy seed after thee:" this *grace* of the covenant we know to have been meant for all believing nations, who, "in Christ, are Abraham's seed, and heirs according to the promise." (Gal. iii. 29.) The other three promises, following these, are to Jacob *personally,* but merely to assure him that, in spite of all appearances to the contrary, not one good thing should fail of all that the Lord had spoken to him.

Now my argument is this: Of the three articles of the covenant, here afresh promulgated, two are pronounced by the apostle to be still in as full force as the day they went out of God's mouth. First, the *seed*—that is, the natural seed of Abraham—"are beloved for the fathers' sakes," because "the gifts and the calling of God are without repentance;" and this even during their present unbelieving and outcast condition. Second, the *grace* or blessing of the covenant is still in store for them against the day when "there shall come out of Sion the Deliverer, and turn away ungodliness from Jacob." Since, then, two of the articles of this Abrahamic covenant are at this day in as full

---

[1]Compare Psalm lxxii. 17—
"Men shall be blessed in Him:
All nations shall call Him blessed."

force as at the first, is it reasonable to say that the only remaining one—the *land*—has lost its force under the Gospel?

Let us hear *Durham* on this point. "What reasons do plead for the Jews' CONVERSION do in some degree plead for a TEMPORAL RESTITUTION. Thus, God's electing them to be His people, and making an everlasting covenant with them. The promise of their dwelling for ever in that land, which peculiarly was given to that race—in a more special manner, and by more singular rights and titles, than any other in the world—is comprehended in that covenant. And if any say that that is not a saving promise, or absolute; so neither was His promise of continuing them a visible church, or His people, absolute—as the events of both alike do clear. Yet is weight laid on His covenant with their fathers, so far as to make them again His people; and why not in this particular also? For it is not simply that He covenanted with them in a covenant of grace—for so hath He done with many others—but in a covenant with special promises, and grounds that make it a singular tie in these things beyond what others have: see Rom. xi. 28."[2]

2. In the *twenty-sixth chapter of Leviticus,* we find Moses giving the people one of those prophetic sketches of their future history, in the way of warning and encouragement, which form the basis, and constitute in fact the substance, of all that is found in the later prophets, as respects the people of Israel. It is true that both the judgments there threatened, and the mercies there promised, are held forth *hypothetically,*—on supposition of their wickedly departing from the Lord, and afterwards repenting,—"*if* they shall confess their iniquity." But since the conditions are turned—as they are in other places—into absolute announcements of what was to take place, the hypothetical forms of expression are to be regarded as merely the fitting mode of conveying warnings against defection and encouragements to repentance. It is thus that Paul speaks in the chapter to which I have so often referred. He says of the rejected Jews, "They, *if* they abide not still in unbelief, shall be graffed in; for God is able to graff them in again." But he is in no doubt whether they *will* cease from their unbelief, and whether God *will* graff them in; for he adds, "And so all Israel *shall be* saved,—There shall come out of Sion the Deliverer, and *shall turn away ungodliness from Jacob."*

With these explanations, then, let us observe some of the closing announcements of this chapter:—

"If they shall confess their iniquity, and the iniquity of their fathers, ... and that I have walked contrary unto them, and have

[2]Comm. on Rev., *ut supra,* (on chap. xvi. 12.)

brought them into the land of their enemies; if then their uncircumcised hearts be humbled, and they then accept the punishment of their iniquity: THEN WILL I REMEMBER MY COVENANT with Jacob, and also my covenant with Isaac, and also my covenant with Abraham will I remember; AND I WILL REMEMBER THE LAND. The land also shall be left of them, and shall enjoy her sabbaths, while she lieth desolate without them: and they shall accept of the punishment of their iniquity; because, even because they despised my judgments, and because their soul abhorred by statutes. And yet for all that, when they be in the land of their enemies, I will not cast them away, neither will I abhor them, to destroy them utterly, and to break my covenant with them; for I am the LORD their God. But I will for their sakes *remember the covenant of their ancestors,* . . . . that I might be their God: I am the LORD." (Lev. xxvi. 40-45.)

It is impossible to deny that the "remembrance of *the covenant* " here, and the "remembrance of *the land,* go together. If, indeed, it be not the natural Israel at all, but *the Church,* which is here spoken of, all is of course figurative, and restoration to the literal Canaan is out of the question. But as this is absurd, the only other way of setting aside this testimony is to allege *either* that no historical sketch was here intended, but merely the inculcation of certain principles of Divine procedure, and, therefore, that no specific events are to be sought for in Israelitish history as the fulfilment of this chapter; *or,* that the defection and the return here alluded to, had their fulfilment in the sins which drove the Israelites to Babylon, and in that restoration from it which was the last great event in their history, ere they ceased, with the termination of their economy, to be the subject of prophecy considered as a distinct people.

The former of these suppositions is such a loose way of dealing with plain narrative predictions, that it is impossible to admit it here without abandoning compass and rudder, and driving before every wind of fancy which may visit the interpreter of prophetic Scripture. It may be applied safely enough to some of the discursive strains of the evangelical prophet; but to employ it here looks too like an expedient for getting rid of unwelcome conclusions. As to the other supposition, having before us the *fact* of a dispersion far more judgment-like in its character, and of far longer continuance than the Babylonish one; and having the apostolic *assurance* that in respect of it God means for their sakes to remember the "covenant of their ancestors," and that in this sense "the gifts and calling of God are without repentance:"—having these before us, is it not a most unnatural and violent restriction of the announcements of this chapter to say, that they go no further down than the return from Babylon—

that while professing, as on the face of it appears plain, to look forward "to their latter end," it should stop short at a comparatively early stage, both of their guilt and of God's mercy to them?

What, then, remains, but that the period definitely pointed to, when "they shall accept of the punishment of their iniquity," is the same of which Paul says, "the Deliverer shall turn away ungodliness from Jacob,"—and that God's then "remembering for their sakes the covenant of their ancestors" corresponds to His remembering that "His gifts and calling are without repentance," and so causing that "all Israel shall be saved." And if the chapter do really extend onward to that period, and conclude with the final recovery of the Jewish nation, in pursuance of His ancient covenant engagements, the question about *the land* would appear to be settled; for the same terms are applied to it as to the people. *They stand or fall together* in the covenant.

"Neither," says *Durham*, "can that promise made to Israel, (Deut. xxx. 2-4, &c.,) that whenever they should repent the Lord would gather them from the nations whither they were scattered, and return them to their own land, be thought void and null after Christ's coming, especially considering the general repentance and mourning which is to accompany their conversion. Therefore it would seem by that promise they may expect their own land, *it being a part of* God's engagement to the natural seed of Abraham."[3]

3. The *thirty-second of Deuteronomy* is another of those prophetic sketches of the fortunes of Israel, poured forth in the form of song. I shall refer only to the last verse of the song, and the rather because its sense, though clear enough of itself, is fixed beyond dispute by the use which our apostle makes of it.

"Rejoice, O ye nations, [גוֹיִם, Gentiles,] with his people [עַמּוֹ]; for he will avenge the blood of his servants, and will render vengeance to his adversaries, and will be merciful *unto his land, and to his people*." (Deut. xxxii. 43.) The first clause of this verse is the second of the apostle's four quotations from the Old Testament, in the fifteenth of the Romans, to prove the union of Jews and Gentiles in Christ under the Gospel:—"And again he saith, [namely, in this place of Deuteronomy,] Rejoice, ye Gentiles, with his people." To Gospel times, then, Moses points in this closing call to Jews and Gentiles to rejoice together in a common redeeming God; and what are the words with which the song dies away? "He will be merciful to *his land*, and to *his people*" (עַמּוֹ). What people? Surely the same people

---

[3]Comm. *ut supra*.

who are expressly distinguished from the Gentiles in the first part of the verse.

Here, then, we have all the three things which we found in the Abrahamic covenant; there is "the common *salvation,*" there is "the *people* beloved for the fathers' sakes," and there is "the *land* "—"the Lord's land"—all appertaining to Gospel times.

And now, in the light of these specimens from the historical books, I venture to appeal to the reader whether it be true that "the restoration of the Jews to their ancient territory *is not involved in their original connexion with Canaan;*" whether, rather, the very reverse has not been solidly established.

SECONDLY. In advancing to the prophets, we may now lay it down as an established principle, that *the extinction of the Jewish economy has not brought to and end the "gifts and the calling of God" with respect to the natural Israel*; that although the body of the nation was broken off because of unbelief, yet God hath not cast away His people whom He foreknew; that they are not only capable of recovery, like other sinners of mankind, and have furnished to the company of the redeemed in every age a remnant according to the "election of grace," but, "as touching the election" of the race in the person of Abraham, "they are beloved for the fathers' sakes" *as a nation,* and, in virtue of this ancient covenant-love, are to be nationally brought in again. In carrying this important principle with us into the examination of the prophetical books, I am far from intending to forestall the conclusions to which a sober investigation of each passage by itself may bring us. I wish merely to neutralise, by means of it, the antecedent presumption which some would persuade us there is against our finding the future destinies of the Jews made the subject of prophecy. After what has been established, I confidently ask if the antecedent probabilities do not lie all in the opposite direction. Let the reader, then, only come prepared to look without prejudice at whatever, on the fair rules of interpretation, may be found to point to the natural Israel, and I have little doubt that he will find himself constrained to allow, that not only *a national conversion,* but in connexion with it their *restoration to the land of their fathers,* is the subject of numerous prophecies.

1. The *eleventh of Isaiah* is, I think, decisive. The general subject of the first ten verses is the Person, Character, and Kingdom of Messiah. The tenth verse announces Him as "a root of Jesse"—to spring from the loins of Jesse's son—"who should stand as an ensign

of *the people* [meaning Israel[4]]; to which *the Gentiles* also should seek; and whose rest," in the midst of these associated families of the earth, all blessed in Him and calling Him blessed, "should be glorious." From this the prophet passes on to announce, as a distinct and specific event, a glorious recovery of "the remnant of His people"—the remnent body of the Israelitish nation—in the latter day:—

"And it shall come to pass in that day, that the Lord shall set his hand again the second time to recover the remnant of his people, which shall be left, from Assyria, and from Egypt, and from Pathros, and from Cush, and from Elam, and from Shinar, and from Hamath, and from the islands of the sea. And he shall set up an ensign for the nations, and shall assemble the outcasts of Israel, and gather together the dispersed of Judah from the four corners of the earth. The envy also of Ephraim shall depart, and the adversaries of Judah shall be cut off: Ephraim shall not envy Judah, and Judah shall not vex Ephraim. But they shall fly upon the shoulders of the Philistines toward the west; they shall spoil them of the east together: they shall lay their hand upon Edom and Moab; and the children of Ammon shall obey them. And the LORD shall utterly destroy the tongue of the Egyptian sea; and with his mighty wind shall he shake his hand over the river, and shall smite it in the seven streams, and make men go over dryshod. And there shall be an highway for the remnant of his people, which shall be left, from Assyria; like as it was to Israel in the day that he came up out of the land of Egypt." (Isaiah xi. 11-16.)

Rejecting, as altogether unnatural and inadmissible, the *Babylonish* reference which Henderson gives to this remarkable prophecy, and agreeing with Alexander in holding that not only "its complete," but its only proper fulfilment, "is to be expected *when all Israel shall be saved,*" there remains but one question: Are we to take the prediction *figuratively*—as Calvin, Vitringa, Hengstenberg, and Alexander do—as denoting "the admission of the Jews to Christ's kingdom on repentance and reception of the Christian faith;" or, are we to take it as a prophecy of their literal return to the land of their fathers in a converted state? The reasons for taking it figuratively appear to me to be very weak. "It *must* be taken figuratively," says Alexander, "because the nations mentioned in the 11th verse have long ceased to exist." Yet in his exposition of the nineteenth chapter, to which we

---

[4]Though the plural (עַמִּים) is here used, instead of the ordinary singular, the meaning cannot be mistaken. In Ps. xlvii. 13 [12], Hos. x. 14, and elsewhere, we have the same usage. Possibly the plural may be here employed to denote the different *divisions* of the nation who are, sooner or later, to be gathered under the red banner of the slain Lamb.

shall come presently, and on verse 23, the same author says, "The ancestral names, *Mizraim* and *Asshur*, are put not only for their descendants, but for the countries which they occupied." (Page 364.) And who would say that any violence is done to the prophecy before us, by understanding those ancient countries and peoples, whither the dispersed Jews went of old, to denote all the places and peoples whence they are to return at the time here predicted? Nay, in the author's exposition of the 14th verse of this very chapter, he grants in principle all that I require to justify my view of the countries named in the 11th verse. "The nations here named," says he—Philistines, Edom, Moab, Ammon—"are put for enemies in general, or the heathen world; this method of description being rendered more emphatic by the historical associations which the names awaken." (Page 235.)

But is not the *language* so figurative that we are constrained to view the *event* couched under it in the same light? Why so? May not the setting up of an ensign to the nations for the assembling of the outcasts of Israel and gathering together the dispersed of Judah from the four corners of the earth, may not their flying on the shoulders of the Philistines, and so forth, be as fitting a way of expressing their safe and auspicious return to their ancient inheritance, as for expressing the facilities which those nations will afford for their *conversion to God?* If the only question be, whether the language more suitably expresses their spiritual conversion or their territorial restoration, I, for my part, have no hesitation in giving my vote in favour of the latter. And if this be the only reason—and there is positively no other—for taking the predicted restoration figuratively, I cannot but hold that a glorious restoration of the Jewish nation to their own land is the manifest subject of this prophecy, as the foregoing verse (the 10th) holds forth their union in one Church with the Gentiles under Christ.

Does any one still ask, whether this would not require us to understand the 15th verse of a miraculous dividing of the Red Sea and the Euphrates to afford the Israelites a passage home? I answer that Alexander's exposition of this verse suits just as well with my view of the prophecy as his own. "All obstacles," says he, "even the most formidable, shall be overcome or taken away by His almighty power. This idea is naturally expressed by the dividing of the Red Sea and the Euphrates, because Egypt and Assyria are the two great powers from which Israel suffered," &c. (Page 235.) No one who considers attentively such passages as Isaiah li. 10, 11, and xliii. 16-20, will doubt that they are just expressions of the same power which formerly dried up seas and rivers, to be again put forth in behalf of

His people, in *analogous* and higher ways. Whether it be the turning of seas and rivers into dry land, or making rivers in the desert, all is for His people, and just means, causing all things to minister them.

2. The *nineteenth of Isaiah* furnishes another striking prediction, as I think, of Israel's restoration. It occurs in the two last verses of the chapter. The first seventeen verses consist of threatenings; the last eight of promises to the land. "In verses 18-21, the Egyptians are described as acknowledging the true God in consequence of what they had suffered at His hand, and the deliverance which He had granted them. In verses 22-25, the same cause is described as leading to an intimate union between Egypt, Assyria, and Israel, in the service of Jehovah and the enjoyment of His favour."[5]

"In that day shall there be a highway out of Egypt to Assyria, and the Assyrian shall come into Egypt, and the Egyptian into Assyria; and the Egyptians shall serve [God] with the Assyrians. In that day shall Israel be the third with Egypt and with Assyria, even a blessing in the midst of the land: whom the LORD of hosts shall bless, saying, Blessed be Egypt my people, and Assyria the work of my hands, and Israel mine inheritance." (Isa. xix. 23-25.)

"The meaning," says Alexander, "obviously is, that Israel shall be one of three, or a party to a triple union; the ancestral names, *Mizraim* and *Asshur,* being put not only for their descendants, but for the countries which they occupied. This perfect union of those three great powers in the service of God and the enjoyment of His favour, is expressed in the last verse by a solemn benediction on the three, in which language commonly applied to Israel exclusively is extended to Egypt and Assyria."[6] The only question then is, whether this be merely a figurative way of expressing the breaking down of the middle wall of partition between Jew and Gentile, and the peace and friendship between powers once the most hostile to each other which the gospel shall bring about; or whether it be designed literally to predict *one remarkable exemplification* of this, in the case of Egypt, Assyria, and Israel. That the latter is the correct view of the prophecy, I take to be almost demonstrable from the scope of the chapter. It is headed, "The burden of Egypt." It is occupied with the *history* of Egypt, the judgments which were to reduce it, and the

---

[5]Alexander on the chapter.

[6]By one of those caprices of interpretation observable in Henderson, by which he makes some things all *future* which are not so, he throws this and the eleventh, and other chapters, all into the *past,* without reason. This obliges him to understand the last verse of this chapter as still making a distinction in favour of Israel, in direct opposition to the manifest object of the prophecy, which was to predict the perfect equality of *Egypt, Assyria,* and *Israel*.

beneficial effects which would result from this, in its conversion to the true God; and the verses before us (the last three in the chapter) wind up the sketch of Egypt's fortunes by picturing to us its perfect and delightful union in the service of God with those who used to be its sworn enemies. To represent this final stage of Egypt's fortunes as merely pictorial, while all the previous stages are viewed as literal history, seems to me to do violence to all the rules of sober interpretation. But if we take it literally in the case of *Egypt,* can it possibly be figurative in the case of *Assyria* and *Israel?* Undoubtedly not.

Here, then, we have Israel *geographically* described as embosomed securely in the latter day between Assyria and Egypt, in equal enjoyment of the Divine favour, and exhibiting to the world the refreshing spectacle of a "brotherly covenant." On any other view than that of their territorial restoration, I do not see how the latter part of this chapter is to be tolerably explained.[7]

3. In the *twenty-third chapter of Jeremiah,* we have the following well-known evangelical promise:—

"Behold, the days come, saith the LORD, that I will raise unto David a righteous Branch, and a King shall reign and prosper, and shall execute judgment and justice in the earth. In his days Judah shall be saved, and Israel shall dwell safely: and this is his name whereby he shall be called, THE LORD OUR RIGHTEOUSNESS. Therefore, behold, the days come, saith the LORD, that they shall no more say, The LORD liveth, which brought up the children of Israel out of the land of Egypt; but, The LORD liveth, which brought up and which led the seed of the house of Israel out of the north country, and from all countries whither I had driven them; and they shall dwell in their own land." (Jer. xxiii. 5-8.)

---

[7]Before leaving Isaiah, I had intended to make some remarks on the famous lix. 20, which the apostle quotes in the eleventh of the Romans, in confirmation of his announcement that "all Israel shall be saved"—("And the Redeemer shall come to Zion, and unto them that turn from transgression in Jacob, saith the Lord")—in order to point out the objections which appear to me to lie against Professor Alexander's view of the passage (given above, pp. 120, 121), and at the same time, to shew that even on his own view of the chapter—admitting that it is the *first* Jewish converts to whom the Redeemer is represented as coming, at the introduction of the new economy—that interpretation would be sufficient to justify the apostle's application of it to the *whole nation*, when at length converted—on the important principle (too little adverted to by interpreters), that "if the *first-fruit* be holy, the *lump* is also holy; and if the root be holy, so are the branches" (Rom. xi. 16); and consequently that the "making of the new covenant with the house of Israel and with the house of Judah" (Jer. xxxi. 31), of whom there were but an handful of faithful representatives, when "the blood of the covenant" first opened it up to the Church, shall yet be realized in the whole nation (so the apostle reasons, Rom. xi. 27). But as this does not immediately involve our question of *restoration*, of which I have yet one or two examples to give, I shall pass from it.

The force of the argument for the restoration promised in the latter part of this passage being yet *future*, arises from its immediate connexion with the foregoing promise of Christ. To say that in the two former verses, we have a prediction of Christ and His kingdom, and the two latter of the return of Israel merely from the *Babylonish captivity*, is certainly harsh. But, it may be said, supposing it conceded that the whole passage relates to Gospel times, may it not be a figurative description of the happiness of the Church under Christ; and all the rather, because "Judah's being saved, and Israel's dwelling safely" under Christ, cannot be restricted to the Jews, on the principles of this treatise, without identifying the Gospel Church with the Jewish nation? I think the principles which have been laid down furnish a complete answer to this objection. Of "Judah and Israel," when Christ, "the righteous Branch of David," presented Himself to the nation, there were found only a handful of faithful representatives. This very handful, however, constituted the Church, along with all "who from among the Gentiles were turned to God," who thus became "Abraham's seed, and heirs according to the promise"— "fellow-citizens with the saints, and of the household of God." This compound body constituted the "Judah saved," the "Israel dwelling safely" under Christ's shadow, as it is this day. But are no more of the literal "Judah and Israel" to be saved, and dwell safely under Christ? Hath God cast away His people whom He foreknew? God forbid. For if the *first-fruit* be holy, the *lump* is also holy; and if the root be holy, so are the branches. And so all Israel shall be saved. Then shall be brought to pass, in its amplest sense, the saying of our passage, "In his days Judah shall be saved, and Israel shall dwell safely." And it is as a sequel to this exhilarating announcement, that the territorial restoration of the converted nation, blessed in Christ, is introduced. Let the reader now say whether this view of the whole passage is not perfectly self-consistent, and in harmony with all that we have hitherto found on the subject.

4. I give but one more example, from the *thirty-seventh of Ezekiel*—the vision of the dry bones. The whole chapter is important, but I quote only the concluding verses:—

"Thus saith the Lord GOD, Behold, I will take the children of Israel from among the heathen, whither they be gone, and will gather them on every side, and bring them into their own land: and I will make them one nation in the land, upon the mountains of Israel, and one king shall be king to them all: and they shall be no more two nations, neither shall they be divided into two kingdoms any more at all: neither shall they defile themselves anymore with their idols, nor with their detestable things, nor with any of their transgressions: but

I will save them out of all their dwelling-places, wherein they have sinned, and will cleanse them: so shall they be my people, and I will be their God. And David my servant shall be king over them; and they all shall have one shepherd: they shall also walk in my judgments, and observe my statutes, and do them. And they shall dwell in the land that I have given unto Jacob my servant, wherein your fathers have dwelt; and they shall dwell therein, even they, and their children, and their children's children for ever: and my servant David shall be their prince for ever. Moreover, I will make a covenant of peace with them; it shall be an everlasting covenant with them: and I will place them, and multiply them, and will set my sanctuary in the midst of them for evermore. My tabernacle also shall be with them: yea, I will be their God, and they shall be my People. And the heathen shall know that I the LORD do sanctify Israel, when my sanctuary shall be in the midst of them for evermore." (Ezek. xxxvii. 21-28.)

Although I have no doubt that this was intended to assure the captives of Babylon of their restoration from *that* captivity, it does not follow from this admission, as many seem to think, that the return from Babylon is the *proper subject* of this prophecy. For just as the promise of Immanuel, to spring from the nation *many centuries* after it was threatened with extinction by the kings of Israel and Syria, was sufficient to assure the heart of Ahaz that he had no reason to be afraid of those kings (Isa. vii.); so the promise here of the final resettlement of the whole nation in their own land, under Christ, as their King, was enough to assure the poor captives of Ezekiel's day that they were in no danger of rotting in Babylon, and that even if they did, a resurrection of their nationality would take place, "that the scripture might not be broken."

The grand objection to applying this version to the return from *Babylon* is, not merely the language in which their re-settlement in Palestine, never more to be plucked up, is expressed, and the extent of spiritual renovation ascribed to them—so exceedingly hyperbolical if understood of anything then realised—but the explicit mention of *Messiah* as their Shepherd and King, the life of their restored state. To say that this means no more than that the nation, restored from Babylon, would ultimately give birth to Messiah the King, who even then was over them as the Angel of the Covenant, is surely a very tame exposition of the language. That the headship of Christ over them here relates to Gospel times, I think there can be no reasonable doubt. The only doubt of this which could suggest itself I have removed in the preceding paragraph.

If this prophecy, then, relates to Gospel times, its testimony to the final restoration of all Israel to their own land, under Christ, appears decisive. For it can hardly relate to any other than the *literal Israel.* I should think this must be admitted, whatever difference may exist as to the *time* of fulfilment. Neither can it relate to a "remnant," as contradistinguished from "all Israel." It is the *nation* converted to God—"*one nation* in the land, upon the mountains of Israel."[8] And if any one should ask whether the restoration here promised may not be a figurative representation of their spiritual conversion, the answer is obvious. *That is predicted, too,* and quite distinctly from their restoration. The two together constitute one complete picture. As their sins were the *cause,* and their dispersion the *effect,* so their conversion, removing the cause of their present dispersion, shall be accompanied by their return, under the Divine favour, to their father-land. The covenant-*favour* and the covenant-*land* go hand in hand.

Before leaving this passage, and concluding my series of examples, I request the reader's attention for a moment to the sweeping yet plausible principle already alluded to, which the passage before us is, I think, sufficient to overthrow. If "Jews" means Jew, it is insisted that "David" must mean David; but if Christ comes in the room of David, Christ's people must come in the room of David's subjects. Let us then apply this principle to the passage before us, and see what comes out. It is of no consequence to this particular point whether the prophecy be understood of the return from Babylon, or from the present dispersion. Our present question is, who are meant by "Israel" and "David?" Now it is admitted on all hands that "David" here means *Christ.* But if so, then, on the above principle, "Israel" must mean *the Christian Church*; which surely is harsh. Those who understand the prophecy of the return from Babylon, and the moral reformation which followed that event, may deem the Christian Church under Christ the fullest exemplification of the principles partially brought out in Israel after their return home. I can understand this. Dr. M'Crie's Sermons on the Unity of the Church, founded on a verse of this chapter, are an example of this way of using the truths which it conveys. Nor have I any quarrel with it. All that I affirm is, that, historically and strictly, "Israel" here means Israel, whether in time past or in time future. If this be

---

[8]I do not expect a separate restoration of the ten tribes. I think Dr. Robinson has shewn, in reply to Dr. Grant's "Nestorians," that the amalgamation of the two divisions has already taken place, and when they return and are settled as one undivided nation upon the mountains of Israel, the prophecy will be sufficiently fulfilled. See also *Witsius, ut supra,* p. 52.

granted, it will follow, on the principle in question, that "David" must mean David, not Christ; which is absurd. This principle, then, is more plausible than solid. If God means yet to turn the heart of Israel to Himself (2 Cor. iii. 16), there can be no more fitting language in which to announce it than that which Ezekiel here employs: "So shall they be my people, and I will be their God; and David my servant shall be king over them." It cannot be said that this would be an incongruous mode of announcing what we know is yet to take place. But supposing such language were found in any passage at all, as an announcement of the literal Israel's conversion, we should be obliged—if all must be sacrificed to uniformity in the narrow sense of the term insisted on—to *thrust one of the parties out of the passage;* and either understand the word "Israel" to be spiritual or the word "David" to be literal: in other words, we should be obliged by strict principles of interpretation to misunderstand the Divine mind in that prediction.

These specimens may suffice. It is hardly necessary to say that many others might be given. But as I should scarcely hope to carry conviction, by a multiplication of passages, to any who may be yet unconvinced, I leave these, in connexion with the important *principles* which I endeavoured first of all to establish, with the intelligent reader, requesting him to weigh all in the balances of the sanctuary.

CHAPTER VII

POSITIVE EVIDENCE FOR THE TERRITORIAL RESTORATION CONCLUDED

ONE other proposition will embody all the remaining evidence in favour of a territorial restoration: nor will it require more than a sentence or two of illustration.

PROPOSITION VI.—*The connexion uniformly held forth in Scripture, in the case of the Jews, between* DEFECTION *and* DISPERSION, *and between* RECONCILIATION *and* RESTORATION, *constitutes strong ground for expecting that their final* CONVERSION *will be accompanied by a final* RESTORATION *to their fatherland*.

Let the reader observe this connexion in the following passages:—

"Lord, thou hast been *favourable unto* THY LAND: thou hast *brought back the captivity of Jacob.* Thou hast *forgiven the iniquity of* THY PEOPLE: thou hast *covered all their sin.*" (Ps. lxxxv. 1, 2)

"And I will *bring* ISRAEL *again to his* HABITATION, and he shall feed on Carmel and Bashan, and his soul shall be satisfied upon mount Ephraim and Gilead. *In those days, and in that time,* saith the Lord, *the iniquity of Israel shall be sought for, and there shall be none;* and the sins of Judah, and they shall not be found: *for I will pardon them whom I reserve.*" (Jer. l. 19, 20.)

"*And I will remove the iniquity of that land in one day. In that day,* saith the Lord of hosts, *shall ye call every man his neighbour under the vine and under the fig-tree.*" (Zech. iii. 9, 10.)

The thing to be noticed here is not the *time* of fulfilment. It is the connexion which obtains in all of these passages—and other examples of the same connexion might be given—between *pardon* of the sin for which they were driven away, and *restoration* to the covenant-land. Now, will any one say that the *present* dispersion of the Jews is not expressly connected by our Lord with God's wrath against them to the uttermost? It is impossible to doubt this with His prophecy of the destruction of Jerusalem before us. And if this be granted, how can it well be doubted, from the unity of the Divine procedure, that their final conversion to God, and submission to His Christ, will be marked by the ancient token of reconciliation—their return to the delightsome land? Able writers on the other side, in noticing the leading considerations in favour of the restoration, have overlooked this one, which I deem one of the strongest of all, especially when connected with the perpetuity of the Abrahamic covenant, in respect both of the people and the land.

CHAPTER VIII

OBJECTIONS TO THE TERRITORIAL RESTORATION ANSWERED

THE objections and difficulties to which a territorial restoration of the Jews is liable are not slight, and a candid consideration of them, in a treatise which professes to survey the question on all sides, is indispensable. I am the more ready to investigate these difficulties, as from this point of view the whole subject admits of fresh illustrations, and the positions which I have endeavoured to establish—if I do not deceive myself—will receive important confirmation.

OBJECTION I.—'Admitting the difficulty of refuting the argument from the 11th of Romans, for the perpetuity of the Abrahamic covenant, in respect of the promised *land* as well as the promised *seed*, we are still at a loss to understand how no allusion to the *land* should have been dropt by the apostle, and not a trace of it should be found in the New Testament, as the future inheritance of converted Israel, if any such prospect awaits the natural seed of Abraham.'

Answer.—This objection would sweep away more things than those who urge it would like to part with. Take the case of the *Sabbath*. On the principle of this objection, its perpetuity cannot well be maintained. For there is no positive enactment of it in the New Testament; nay, so emphatically is the freedom of the Gospel Church from all legal bondage, even in respect to the observance of days, proclaimed in the New Testament, that some are at a loss to understand how its cessation under the Gospel can be reasonably doubted. How is this to be met? I turn, for example, to those words of Christ, "THE SON OF MAN IS LORD ALSO OF THE SABBATH-DAY," (Matt. xii. 8,) and ask, To what purpose is He Lord of the Sabbath? To abolish it? That were a strange kind of lordship? Nay, surely, but to own it, to interpret it, to ennoble it, by merging it in "THE LORD'S DAY," (Rev. i. 10,) and thus—breathing the new life into it, by which its law is converted into life and love—to preside over it. He found it when He came; he served Himself Heir to it and Lord of it, and the new Economy which He came to introduce, and which could not leave this alone unaffected, penetrated and transfigured it.

So with respect to *Infant Baptism*. On the principle of this objection, it cannot well be vindicated. For not only does the New Testament contain no positive injunction to baptize infants, but by requiring faith as the indispensable qualification for baptism, seems even to exclude it. How do we meet this? By referring, for example, to the comprehension of the infant seed within the Abrahamic covenant, and the law which required the visible "seal" of that covenant to be put upon the children of Abraham in their infancy; thus proclaiming the standing of the Church's infant seed in perpetuity, as being not like the heathen *without the covenant*, and so "common and unclean," but *within the covenant*, and so "holy," and, *as such*, having a right to the visible seal of that standing. And when I find the apostle enjoining the believing husband not to put away his unbelieving wife, if willing to stay with him, and the believing wife not to leave her unbelieving husband, if willing to dwell with her, because "the unbelieving husband is *sanctified* by the wife, and the unbelieving wife is *sanctified* by the husband, *else were their children unclean, but now are they holy*" (1 Cor. vii. 14)—that is to say, that if either of the parents is a believer, *the children are regarded as within the covenant;* "otherwise they would be UNCLEAN, but now (or in the case supposed) they are HOLY," or within the sacred enclosure of the covenant, with all its promises—I say, when I find this, I perceive clearly that the apostle held the standing of the children of believing parents in the Church of God to be the same with that of Abraham's infant seed, a standing *within* the covenant of grace, a holy standing. I do not find him formally announcing this as a new principle, but, what is of far more force, just alluding to it, as a fixed and recognised principle in the Church of God; and I find him expressing it in the well-known phraseology of the ancient Church, as if thereby designing to teach the Gentile Christians of Corinth that they had come into a Church of long standing, whose fundamental principles, amidst all changes of life and form, continued unchanged. And I am the more confirmed in this view of things when I find the same apostle, in another place, addressing the very children of believers as being themselves within the circle of Christian influences, and as such accessible to Christian considerations: "*Children, obey your parents* IN THE LORD; *for this is right. Honour thy father and mother; which is the first commandment with promise; that it may be well with thee, and that thou mayest live long on the earth.*" (Eph. vi. 1-3.)

Such is the view which I take of all the cases that fall under the objection we are considering. To express it comprehensively:—

What is permanent in the kingdom of God under the Old Testament is PRESUMED *in the New; our Lord and His apostles occupying themselves only with such questions and cases as emerged at the time, and the principles applicable to them.*

Were this principle sufficiently observed, it would not be so hastily presumed that if a territorial restoration be in reserve for the natural Israel, it must needs be explicitly mentioned in the New Testament. The two articles of the Abrahamic covenant about which alone there was any difficulty or dispute at that time are expressly treated of, and the perpetuity of the covenant in respect of both is explicitly and emphatically affirmed—the perpetuity of the natural SEED of the covenant, and the perpetuity of the GRACE of the covenant, as being primarily designed for the natural seed, and accordingly kept in store for them against the day of their national conversion: and the only remaining article of the covenant—the LAND—being confessedly subordinate to the other two, and a point about which all questions at the time are checked, as being impertinent and unseasonable, (Acts i. 6-8,) was left to be covered by the two primary articles.

OBJECTION II.—'The idea of any particular territory having a special destination under the Gospel seems inconsistent with the genius of the new Economy, as a *spiritual* dispensation.'

Answer.—I am afraid that this objection would land us in conclusions not very palatable to those who advance it. On what pleas do such able advocates of the Society of Friends as Joseph John Gurney vindicate their disuse of *Baptism and the Lord's Supper?* He is too candid to deny the force of those injunctions to observe them which were given both by our Lord himself and by the apostle of the Gentiles; nor does he question the validity of the evidence, furnished by the Acts and the Epistles, that they were actually observed by the primitive Christians. But he thinks that the entire spirituality of the Church of Christ is so strongly and emphatically taught in the New Testament, and is such a characteristic and vital feature of it, that he cannot persuade himself that the preservation of these externalities, or their being kept up as permanent institutions of the Church of Christ, is consistent with the genius of the Gospel; and he finds himself accordingly shut up to the conclusion, that they were designed only for temporary use, to wean by degrees the people of the Lord from those outward ceremonies which they would find it hard to give up all at once. When, however, this weaning process should in course of time be complete, the Church would, of its own accord, cease from such observances.[1]

---

[1]Observations on the Distinguishing Views and Practices of the Society of Friends. By Joseph John Gurney. Chap. IV., On the Disuse of all Typical Rites in the Worship of God. Pp. 99-177. Second Edit., 8 vo, 1834.

The only use which I make of these facts is to impress upon my Christian brethren the danger of allowing our minds to be swayed by *antecedent presumptions* on questions of this nature. To what extent, or in what particulars, *externalities* of any kind have been abolished under the Gospel, for men yet in the body, is not to be determined by any presumptions of ours; or, at least, we must hold all such presumptions subject to correction and modification by the testimony of Scripture.

CHAPTER IX

OBJECTIONS CONTINUED

OBJECTION III.— 'Upon the principles of this treatise, we must apply to the natural seed of Abraham a number of passages of the Old Testament, some of which are expressly applied in the New Testament to Gentile believers. Thus Hos. i. 9-11:[1] "Then said God, Call his name, Lo-ammi [Not my people]: for ye are not my people, and I will not be your *God*. Yet the number of the children of Israel shall be as the sand of the sea, which is not measured nor numbered; and it shall come to pass, that in the place where it was said unto them, not my people [are] ye, [there] it shall be said unto them, Sons of the living God! Then shall the children of Judah and the children of Israel be gathered [or assemble themselves] together, and appoint themselves one Head, and they shall come up out of the land: for great shall be the day of Jezreel." Also chap. ii. 23:[2] "And I will say to Lo-ammi [to the Not my people], Ammi [My people] thou! and they shall say, My God!" Now observe how plainly both of these passages, which seem to refer exclusively to *the natural Israel*, are applied to *the Gentiles* by the apostle Paul, and the latter passage by the apostle Peter also: "And that he might make known the riches of his glory on the vessels of mercy, which he had afore prepared unto glory even us, whom he hath called, *not of the Jews only, but also of the Gentiles: as he saith also in Hosea, I will call them my people, which were not my people; and her beloved, which was not beloved.* And it shall come to pass, that in the place where it was said unto them, Not my people, there shall they be called the children of the living God." (Rom. ix. 23-26. See also 1 Pet. ii. 10.)'

Answer.—I have given these passages in full, because they are considered decisive specimens of a class which are thought to settle our question in the negative. Nor am I insensible to their force. But their plausibility—as evidence against the restoration of the natural Israel—lies in taking it for granted that the *real* sense of these passages is their *whole* sense. I perfectly admit the former: I entirely

[1]Or, in the Hebrew, chap. i. 9, and ii. 1, 2.

[2]In the Hebrew, chap. ii. 25.

deny the latter. Nothing can be more admirable, up to a certain point, than *Hengstenberg's* commentary on the above portion of Hosea; beyond this, however, I shall shew it to be fallacious. The following extract from his invaluable work on the "Christology of the Old Testament,"[3] though long, will, by shewing the reader how he deals with the *people*, best illustrate the fallacy of his reasoning on the subject of the *land*. And I am the rather induced to give this extract, long as it is, with my own comments, as his school of prophetic interpretation has able representatives in this country.

"The first point requiring to be settled is the subject of the verse—'The children of Israel shall be as the sand,' &c. Every other reference except that to the Ten Tribes is here out of the question; since it is the same party who in the preceding verse were called 'Lo-ammi,' that are now to be called 'Sons of the living God.' Several of the ancient expositors assume here a sudden transition to *the Christian Church*; but this would be a fatal leap. Nor are we to understand by 'the children of Israel,' all the descendants of Jacob; for 'the children of Judah' are distinguished from them in verse 2. Substantially, however, those two are included, as appears from this very verse; for both are then to form one nation of brethern. . . . The reference in the first part of this verse to the promise in Genesis cannot be at all mistaken: 'I will multiply thy seed as the stars of heaven, and as the sand which is on the sea-shore,' &c. (Gen. xxii. 17, xxxii. 12, &c., and compare Jer. xxxiii. 22.) . . . If now we seek for the historical reference of such announcements, we must go back to the sense of them in Genesis. By many they are referred merely to the *bodily* descendants of the patriarch: by many also to their spiritual descendants, their successors in the faith. But the latter reference is quite arbitrary, and the former could only be well founded if the congregation of the Lord had been destined solely for the natural descendants, and the Gentiles had all been refused admittance into it. But that such is not the case, is evident from the command to circumcise every bond-servant; for by circumcision a man was received among the people of God. . . . According to the constant doctrine of the Old as well as the New Testament, *there is only one Church of God from Abraham to the end of the days—only one House under two dispensations*. John the Baptist proceeds upon the supposition that the members of the New Testament Church must be children of Abraham, else the covenant and promise of God would come to nought. But since the bodily descent from Abraham is no security against the danger of exclusion from his posterity; . . . so, on the other hand,

[3]Second Edition, English Translation, (Clark, Edinburgh, 1854,) pp. 209, &c.

God, in the exercise of His sovereign liberty, may give to Abraham, in the room of His degenerate children after the flesh, adopted children innumerable, who shall sit down with him, and Isaac, and Jacob in the kingdom of God, whilst the children of the kingdom are cast out. After these remarks on the promise to the patriarchs, there can be no longer any difficulty in stating the historical reference to the announcement before us. It cannot refer to the bodily descendants of Abraham, *as such.*"

Here begin the fallacies which I wish to point out. Up to the last two words, all is solid and admirable; and if by "as such" the learned author had merely meant "the bodily descendants of Abraham" *without his faith*, I should have assented to that too. And it does look—but only look—as if that were his meaning. "Degenerate sons" he adds, "are not a blessing; they are no objects of promise, no sons in the full sense. Every one is a son of Abraham only in so far as he is a son of God. For this reason, the phrases 'sons of Israel,' and 'sons of the living God' are in the passage before us *connected with each other.*" True, they are connected; but how? Not as meaning one and the same thing; for the contrary is taught in this very verse. The prediction is, that the children of Israel after the flesh, though for long ages "degenerate sons," shall one day *become* "sons of the living God." So that "degenerate sons"—though they be "no blessing," and are "no sons in the full sense"—may be and are "objects of promise."

But even this seems afterwards to be admitted; for it is added: "Not as though the corporeal descent were altogether a matter of indifference. The corporeal descendants of the patriarchs had the nearest claims to their becoming their children in the full sense. It was to them that the means of becoming so were first granted. (Rom. ix. 4.) But all these advantages were unavailing to them *while they allowed them to remain unused.* In these circumstances, neither the promise to Abraham, nor the announcement of Hosea, had any reference to them. Both of them would have remained to this day unfulfilled, although the unconverted children of Israel had increased so as to have become the most populous nation on the face of the whole earth. It thus appears that the announcement before us was first truly realised in the time of the Messiah, at which time the family of the patriarchs was so mightily increased; and that it will be yet more fully realised, partly by the reception of an innumerable multitude of *adopted* sons [believing Gentiles], and partly by the elevation of those who were sons, only in a lower sense [the children of Abraham only after the flesh], to be sons in the *highest* sense [partakers of Abraham's faith]."

I have nothing whatever to object to this statement. I object only to its completeness. It considers the prophet's announcement as fulfilled *generally in Messianic times*, and nothing more; whereas, I think—from the whole strain and context of the prophecy itself, as interpreted by the apostolic announcements regarding the Future of Israel—that it points specifically to that period in the history of the natural seed of Abraham, when "all Israel shall be saved," and when, with all nations "walking in the steps of Abraham's faith," "THE ISRAEL OF GOD" shall, in its widest sense, be manifested, and "fill the face of the world with fruit."

But my agreement with the learned author, and the point at which I diverge from him, will still better appear from his admirable comment on ch. i. 11 (*Heb.*, ch. ii. 1). After shewing that the union among the tribes of Israel here predicted is such as "has for its foundation the return of Israel to the true God, and to the Davidic dynasty" (see ch. iii. 5); that *Christ* is the King whom they are with one consent to choose; and that the "coming" or "going up out of the land" together is based, in point of language, on the exodus from Egypt, as the great prophecy and pledge of this yet greater deliverance—he says: "With regard now to the historical reference, it must in the first place be remarked, that, whatever is here determined regarding it must be applicable to all other parallel passages also, in which a future reunion of Israel and Judah, and their common return to the promised land, are announced (such as Jer. iii. 18, 1. 4; compare also Isa. xi.; Ezek. xxxvii. 18-20)." After shewing that in the return from Babylon, there was "but a small beginning of the fulfilment," and that if this had been all, "Hosea would more resemble a dreamer and an enthusiast, than a true prophet of the living God," he proceeds as follows: "Although the whole, both of Judah and Israel had then returned, the real and final fulfilment could not be sought for in that event. It is not the renewed possession of the country, *as such*, which the prophet promises, but rather *a certain kind of possession—such a possession as that the land is completely the land of God, partaking in all the fulness of His blessings, and thus a worthy residence for the people of God, and for their children.*"

I have printed these last few lines in Italics, to mark precisely what kind of restoration I myself contend for, and what only. If the author would only abide by his own faultless definition of the restoration here intended by the prophet, I should desire nothing more. But in the very next words he slips away from it. "*One may be in Canaan*," he adds, "*and yet at the same time in Babylon or Assyria*." In *spirit*, certainly, he may; but in *fact*, not. In the sense explained by our author himself, in the immediately preceding sentence, one cannot be in Canaan anywhere but in Canaan. Already, indeed, we are "risen with Christ," if so be we have tasted that the Lord is gracious; but we do not therefore, with some early heretics, conclude that "the resurrection is past already." Already we "sit with Christ in heavenly places;" but we hope this is not all the heaven we are to have with our dear Lord. Yet this is the gist of our author's reasoning with respect to the re-possession of Canaan. But let us hear how he proceeds. "Had not the threatened punishment of God been indeed as fully executed upon those who, during the Assyrian and Babylonian captivities, wandered about the country in sorrow and misery, as upon those who were carried away?" I answer, Certainly; for I contend for no restoration to "wander about the country in sorrow and misery." "Can the circumstance that Jews are even now living in Jerusalem in the deepest misery, be adduced as a proof that the loss of the land, with which the people were threatened, had not been completely fulfilled?" Certainly not, I reply; nay, though Palestine should have every Jew now alive residing in it, in unbelief and misery, it would not prove that the promised land had not been lost to them, nor, after being lost, that it had been restored to them, or them to it. The only future possession of Canaan which I believe in is that which our author himself so well defines—the possession of it by Israel circumcised in *heart*. "It is true," he continues, "that during the times of the old covenant, there existed a certain connexion betwixt the lower and the higher kinds of possession. As soon as the people ceased to be the people of the Lord, they lost with the former, after being often warned by the decrease of it, the latter also. As soon as they obtained again the lower kind of possession, which could happen only in the case of a return to the Lord, they recovered to a certain degree—in proportion to the earnestness and sincerity of their conversion—the higher kind of possession also. A commencement of the fulfilment therefore, must be assumed in the return from the Babylonish captivity; but only a very feeble commencement. That which was in one respect the termination of the captivity, was, in another, much rather a continuation of it. *It was certainly not the true Canaan which they possessed, any more than one still possesses the beloved object while embracing only his corpse. Where the Lord is not present with His gifts and blessings, there Canaan cannot be.* IT WAS JUST AS THE LAND OF THE LORD'S PRESENCE THAT IT WAS SO DEAR AND VALUABLE TO ALL BELIEVERS." I have printed these two last sentences in an emphatic form, as expressing with great precision the essential principle of my whole argument—that while it *is* possession of Canaan which the Lord promises to the natural Israei, it is only as "the land of the Lord's presence" with the

Lord's true people. But now observe the strange inference which the author draws from this. "From what has now been said, it appears that, as regards the historical reference, we need not limit ourselves to the times of the Old Covenant, *nor dream of a return to Canaan to take place at some future time*." Why not? Or why should the expectation be termed a dream? It *may* be a dream; but how strange to argue that the fact, that the only return promised is that which our author so well defines, is a strong proof that there will be no return at all, and that the expectation is a dream! "It is not," he adds, "the form, but the essence of the divine inheritance which the prophet has in view. The form is a different one under the New Covenant, where the whole earth has become a Canaan, but the essence remains." All this is just mere affirmation, and my affirmation to the contrary is just as good. I deny not that believers under the Gospel have the *spirit* of all these promises: the only question is, Is that all that they were meant to express? Is there nothing beyond this for the natural Israel? This is a question purely of *evidence*, and I might as well argue, as already hinted, that because believers are already risen with Christ *in spirit*, therefore to expect a future *bodily* resurrection is but a dream. "To cling here," proceeds the author, "to the form would be just as absurd as if one, who for Christ's sake had forsaken all, were to upbraid Him because he had not received again, according to the letter of His promise, precisely 'an hundredfold, brothers, sisters, mothers,' &c. (Mark x. 30.)" As I have sufficiently answered this in my reply to the preceding sentences, I proceed to give our author's concluding observations on this point. "Suppose that the children of Israel were at some future time to return to Canaan, this would have nothing to do with our prophecy." This is right enough, if a return *in their present unbelieving, unconverted state* be meant; as I have already conceded. But to say that their return, in the very state and circumstances which our author himself defines to be the only return contemplated, would have nothing to do with the prophecy, is something more than unfounded—it is outrageous. "The three stations—*Egypt*, the *Wilderness*, and *Canaan* —will continue to exist for ever: but we go from one to the other only with the feet of the spirit, and not, as under the Old Covenant, with the feet of the body at the same time." This is finely conceived and expressed, and it embodies a truth which comes home to every Christian heart. Every believer may be said to have come out of Egypt, and out of Sodom too, and to be journeying through the wilderness on his way to Canaan. Bunyan, in bringing his Christian out of "the City of Destruction" and at length to "the City of Zion," meant the same thing. The historical exodus of the children of Israel, their journeyings through the wilderness of Arabia, and their arrival at length in the delightsome land, have furnished a sacred and dear and imperishable language for the history of the children of God, from the first to the last step of their salvation. No one disputes this. But the question still remains—Is all under the Gospel "spirit" only? Do "form" and "body" belong wholly to the Old Covenant? Then is the Society of Friends right in disusing the external rites of Baptism and the Lord's Supper; and then, perhaps, the heretics were right in saying, "the resurrection is past already." If it be replied, 'Nay, for the observance of those rites is expressly enjoined for all time, and the resurrection of the body is matter of explicit promise:'—I answer, So, according to my belief, is the territorial restoration of the natural Israel. I may be wrong in this, but you cannot disprove it by dwelling on the *spirituality* of the New Covenant. It *is* spiritual, but *under what limitations* must be determined solely by Scripture. I give my Scripture grounds for believing the restoration. Disprove them, and I yield the point; but I will yield to no general reasonings on the spirituality of the New Covenant, which may be found to prove more than those who advance them are prepared to accept.

I shall not regret the length of these extracts, and of my own comments on them, if I have succeeded in shewing the fallacy of a line of argument which some able students of prophecy in this country too readily fall in with, and too sweepingly follow out. To Dr. Hengstenberg we owe much, for the critical defence and exegetical illustration of the Old Testament against the learned and subtle attempts of his own countrymen to undermine it. But a certain generalising tendency, which has for many years injuriously affected his view of the Messianic Psalms, pervades his expositions of the more strictly prophetical portions of the Old Testament; while a self-confident and dogmatic air is apt to carry away the admirer of his various and ready learning.

In concluding my reply to this plausible objection, I will enunciate what I take to be the right view of those prophecies which one extreme party contends have already been all fulfilled, and another extreme party insists have not been fulfilled at all. Say the former party: "The house of Israel and the house of Judah," with which the Lord said He would make "a New Covenant," is expressly interpreted (in the 8th of Hebrews) to mean *the Gospel Church*; and, therefore, no future fulfilment of it is to be looked for. Say the latter party: "The house of Israel and the house of Judah," in that prophecy—in the proper historical sense of those terms—are, and have been for ages, out of covenant, with the exception of a small remnant; and, therefore, the whole prediction, in its strict and proper sense, must be regarded as unfulfilled. Both parties, I believe, are so far right, and the uniting principle lies between the two extremes. What is wrong in both is the exclusiveness of their principle of interpretation. The principle of the one party tends too much to *preterise* the Old Testament predictions relating to the Gospel economy; while the principle of the other tends too much to *futurise* them. But if we will attentively observe the apostolic principle (Rom. xi. 16)—

"IF THE FIRST-FRUIT BE HOLY, THE LUMP IS ALSO HOLY: AND IF THE ROOT BE HOLY, SO ARE THE BRANCHES"—

we shall find in it a *canon of interpretation* which will carry us through many a difficulty. Applied to the case in hand, it is just this, that the *catholic and comprehensive* fulfilment which these predictions have undoubtedly found in the small remnant of the natural Israel that now believe, together with as many of the Gentiles as have become "fellow-citizens with saints and of the household of God," is a sure pledge and blessed earnest of a *complemental* and *exhaustive* fulfilment of these same predictions, yet future, by the inbringing of the now rejected and disinherited mass of the Jewish nation, "beloved for the fathers' sakes:"—and so "all Israel shall be saved." These are not two *heterogeneous fulfilments* of the same prophecy, (which were a clumsy key) but *one fulfilment in two homogeneous, successive stages*—general and specific, comprehensive and complemental. Accordingly, when the prophet says of "the last days," that then "all nations shall flow to the house of the Lord, and be at peace among themselves," (Isa. ii. 2-4,) he plainly announces not only the *erection* and the *character*, but the *final results* of the Gospel Economy. So that while you may say with truth, in respect of erection and character, that this prediction is fulfilled already, it is equally true, and quite indisputable, that the final results are yet to come. In like manner, when Zechariah says, that "in that day" when "the Spirit of grace and of supplications is poured out upon the house of David, and upon the inhabitants of Jerusalem," and when, in consequence, "they look upon Him whom they have pierced, and mourn for Him as for an only son"—when he says further that "*in that day* there shall be a fountain opened for the same house of David and the inhabitants of Jerusalem, for sin and for uncleanness"—he undoubtedly announces the one opening, once for all, of that 'fountain filled with blood,' which washed and made white the robes of the then believing remnant of Israel after the flesh, and along with them the robes of as many Gentiles as, though far off, were made nigh by the blood of Christ. But that apostle who in the holiness of the "first-fruits" saw *the eventual* holiness of the entire "lump"—in the holiness of the root beheld a pledge of the holiness of the branches too—would not have rested content with this view of Zechariah's prophecy, but have seen, in the prophet's majestic and glowing words, "all Israel" gazing on their pierced Messiah, themselves pierced to the heart at the spectacle of what their own hands once did, and—unable to endure the thought—hastening to the fountain, opened in that very blood, for sin and uncleanness. Oh yes! it was opened to them ECONOMICALLY ages before, but all in vain: now they find it opened to them ACTUALLY and illustriously, as though but newly done, when "the Lord will remove the iniquity of the land in one day."

PART THIRD

THE BEARINGS OF THE QUESTION

CHAPTER I

ISRAEL'S CONVERSION AND RESTORATION IN THE LIGHT OF SCRIPTURE

In the preceding Part of this treatise I have given my reasons for thinking that the Conversion and Restoration of the Jews is a scriptural expectation, and have only now to take up the Bearings of those great events. But as these must depend a good deal upon their precise character, and in part, also, upon their accompanying circumstances, it will be necessary, in the first place, to consider the Scripture testimony upon those points.

A host of questions have been raised by the expectants of the Restoration, which it is no part of my plan to discuss; although, for the right apprehension, at least, of some of them, the reader may find materials in the foregoing part of this work. For example: If it be asked whether the Restoration of the Jews will *precede* or *follow* their Conversion, a prior question should be asked, What *is* the Restoration promised in Scripture? Is it the mere bodily repossession of Palestine by the Jewish nation, apart altogether from their moral and spiritual character? To this question I answer, with Hengstenberg, Certainly not. I have shewn[1] that the law of the Divine procedure towards the nation of Israel has ever been that *Defection* shall be eventually followed by *Dispersion*, and *Reconciliation* by *Restoration* "Son of man, when the house of Israel dwelt in their own land, *they defiled it . . . And I scattered them, . . .* and they were dispersed through the countries." But "*from all your filthiness, and from all your idols, will I cleanse you. . . . . And ye shall dwell in the land* that I gave to your fathers; and ye shall be my people, and I will be your God." (Ezek. xxxvi. 17, 19, 25, 28.) There is not, so far as I remember, one passage in which the promised Restoration is held

[1]Prop. v., pp. 135-149; and Prop. vi., pp. 150-151.

forth otherwise than as God's public token of *Reconciliation* to his ancient, and now penitent and believing people. I am not here arguing that the Jews will be converted in the countries of their dispersion, and then transported to Palestine. For aught I know, they may all be in Palestine ere they get the "new heart" promised to them. Not a few of them are there already. In a few years many more may flock thither, encouraged by colonisation-societies, or by political powers for the settlement of difficult questions of their own. Some fancy that they have Scripture warrant for expecting that the nation will not only be resettled in Palestine, with Jerusalem as of old for the metropolis of their nationality, but that they will erect a temple there, and begin to set up the ancient worship, ere they look penitentially upon Him whom their fathers pierced. I confess that I think the evidence for all this slender enough, and some things seem to look quite the opposite way. But even though it were so, *this is not the predicted Restoration.* The only light in which the eventual Restoration of Israel is held forth in Scripture is as *the Divine sequel and public seal of Reconciliation* to the now contrite and converted nation.

What will be the essential character of this change? The answer of Scripture is, *An entire change of heart, issuing in a contrite and cordial reception of Christ.*

The following is the most explicit intimation of this subject; and as it is one of the richest Messianic prophecies of the Old Testament, I request the reader's patient attention to its statements:—

"And I will pour upon the house of David, and upon the inhabitants of Jerusalem, the spirit of grace and of supplications: and they shall look upon Me whom they have pierced, and they shall mourn for him, as one mourneth for his only son, and shall be in bitterness for him, as one that is in bitterness for his first-born. In that day shall there be a great mourning in Jerusalem, as the mourning of Hadadrimmon in the valley of Megiddon. And the land shall mourn, every family apart; the family of the house of Nathan apart, and their wives apart; the family of the house of Levi apart, and their wives apart, the family of Shimei apart, and their wives apart; all the families that remain, every family apart, and their wives apart. In that day there shall be a fountain opened to the house of David and to the inhabitants of Jerusalem for sin and for uncleanness." (Zech. xii. 10—xiii. 1.)

Viewed merely in its spiritual elements, apart from all historical reference, we have in this passage the three essential stages of every sinner's salvation: a believing look to the crucified Saviour, in virtue of a gracious operation of the Spirit upon the soul; ingenuous, pungent grief, as the consequence of this; and the removal both of the guilt and the stain of that sin of deepest dye—the crucifying of the Lord of glory—through the efficacy of that very death, which proves a fountain of atoning blood, opened for the washing of those that shed it. In this general view of it, the passage is rich in evangelical encouragement alike to the chief of sinners and the most advanced of saints here below. But we must not strip such glorious passages of their historical connexions and references. What are they?

If the reader would see to what shifts the Jewish rejecters of Christ are driven, in order to get rid of the application of this prophecy to Jesus of Nazareth, let him consult Dr. M'CAUL'S *Translation of Rabbi David Kimchi's Commentary upon the Prophecies of Zechariah*: with Notes and Observations on the Passages relating to the Messiah;[2] and HENGSTENBERG'S *Christology of the Old Testament*.[3] With Hengstenberg I entirely agree in repudiating any spiritual Israel, *as distinguished from the natural seed of Abraham*, in these prophecies; and when he sees this prediction fulfilled in "that portion of Israel which welcomed and believed on the Messiah when He came, and which *received the heathen nations into its bosom, instead of merely uniting with them*, so as to form together one Church,"[4] I emphatically concur with him, as will be expected from what I laid down in the last chapter of the preceding Part. But in restraining the prophecy to this primary and, as I would call it, *economical* fulfilment of it—in not seeing, in the magnificent sweep of this prophecy, a *complemental* and *culminating* fulfilment yet to be expected, when "ALL ISRAEL SHALL BE SAVED"—that learned and penetrating interpreter of the Old Testament seems to me to fall far short of the comprehensive principle on which the great Apostle of the Gentiles read such predictions, and would teach us to read them.[5] Looking at the prediction, then, with reference to the future inbringing of the Jews, let us see what it announces.

1. *There shall be a glorious effusion of the Spirit upon the whole nation.*

By "the house of David," as distinguished from "the inhabitants of Jerusalem," I understand the official *rulers*, as distinguished from the mass of the *people*; and by "the inhabitants of Jerusalem," I understand, not those who had their ordinary abode in the metropolis, as

---

[2]Pages 151-164. London, 8vo, 1837.

[3]Second edition, vol. iv., pp. 78-86.

[4]Second edition, p. 57.

[5]Dr. HENDERSON'S *Translation of the Twelve Minor Prophets, with a Commentary*, (8vo, 1845,) is satisfactory in its exegetical criticism, and only errs by interpreting such prophecies too exclusively of the future destiny of Israel.

distinguished from those who dwelt in other parts of the country, but those who looked to Jerusalem as "the city of their solemnities," and thus *the home of their religious life*—as every Jew did. If I am right in this, then we have here *the entire nation* held forth as yet to experience this outpouring of the Spirit. And what puts this interpretation beyond doubt, is the predicted result of this effusion:—"They shall look," and, in consequence, "shall mourn." But who shall? "THE LAND *shall mourn*:"—so much in general, which is decisive. But more particularly, "The family of the house of *David* apart, and their wives apart; the family of the house of *Nathan* apart, and their wives apart." Nathan being one of David's sons, (2 Sam. v. 14; Luke iii. 31,) the families of the houses of David and Nathan mean the main line, with the subordinate branches, of the *royal* family. In like manner, "the family of the house of *Levi*"—or the main branch of the sacerdotal line—"apart, and their wives apart; the family of *Shimei*"—one of Levi's grandsons (Num. iii. 17, 18)—"apart, and their wives apart," representing the subordinate branches of the *priestly* line. The prophecy, having begun with a statement of the universality of this evangelical contrition—"*the land shall mourn*"—and then particularised the families of the civil and ecclesiastical rulers in whom the whole people stood represented, closes in the same manner, but, if possible, more explicitly: —"*all the families that remain*; every family apart, and their wives apart." If it had been the design of this bright prophecy to express emphatically and unmistakably the whole surviving nation of Israel—not the handful who, embracing Christ at the first, just sufficed to preserve the continuity of the Church of God in the family of Abraham—I say, if the intention was to express the entire surviving nation of Israel, as destined one day to experience such a glorious effusion of the Spirit as would revolutionise their whole religious character, and particularly their view of Him whom once they had nationally pierced, how could this have been done more effectually than by the terms actually employed?

Will this effusion of the Spirit, it may be asked, and the saving fruits of it here specified, take place without any *preparation*, outward or inward? Not likely; if we are to judge from the analogy of the Divine procedure. What, then, will likely be those preparations? In the present state of Europe and the East, it is easy to imagine not a few external events which, either separately or in combination, might bring the Jews as a nation into public view as one possible solution of difficult problems. This, however, unless accompanied by events of a very different nature, would tend rather to feed than humble their pride. If external circumstances at all are to contribute towards *a change of heart* upon the Jewish nation, they must be of an *afflictive* nature. But what these are likely to be, I will not venture to indicate. They may be of a very mixed and complicated nature. Some intelligent and ingenuous Jews have been first drawn towards Christianity by reflecting on the unquenchable and universal *vitality* that seems to reside in it, contrasted with the utter lifelessness of rabbinical Judiasm, and the hopelessness of any other resurrection of their national faith than what Christianity gives it. Even this, however, without a sense of *sin*, is but a partial adjustment of the inner vision for looking on Him whom they have pierced; nor will that ever be done till the predicted effusion of the Spirit shall be experienced—in connexion, we can hardly doubt, with some external pressures which shall penetrate the heart of the nation.

2. *The fruit of this effusion of the Spirit will be an entire change upon the heart of the nation.*

The Spirit is to come down upon them, says the prophecy, as a "Spirit of *grace* and of *supplications*:" begetting an ingenuous and kindly, soft and subdued, convinced and contrite frame—just the opposite of what has all along characterised the nation in its unbelieving condition—prompting them to "confess their iniquity, and the iniquity of their fathers, and that they have walked contrary to the Lord, and that He also hath walked contrary unto them, and hath brought them into the land of their enemies;" and when thus "their uncircumcised hearts are humbled, and they then *accept the punishment of their iniquity*," (Lev. xxvi. 40, 41,) "out of the depths will they cry unto God" for mercy and light. No longer will it be said of them, "The pride of Israel testifieth to his face; and they do not return to the Lord their God for all this" (Hos. vii. 10); "I will go and return to my place, *till they acknowledge their offence, and seek my face*: in their affliction they will seek me early" (Hos. v. 15). For that time having now at length come, even the set time, the call will somehow go through the nation—oh, how easily might it, in fifty supposable circumstances, go forth!—"Come, and let us return unto the Lord: for he hath torn, and he will heal us; he hath smitten, and he will bind us up. After two days will he revive us; and the third day he will raise us up, and we shall live in his sight. Then shall we know, if we follow on to know the Lord: his going forth is prepared as the morning; and he shall come unto us as the rain, as the latter and former rain unto the earth." (Hos. vi. 1-3.) The *contrition* expressed here is not more beautiful than the *ingenuousness* of it, and the calm *confidence* with which light is expected and complete recovery anticipated.

When thus the inward vision is clarified, all things are seen in a new light. For "when thine eye is single, thy whole body also is full of light; as when the bright shining of a candle doth give thee light." (Luke xi. 34, 36.) Now the spirituality of their own Scriptures is discerned, where nothing was seen before but narrow and carnal ideas, the true relief which they hold forth to the hopes of the guilty supplants the vague generalities which made up all the comfort they were able to extract from the Book of God.

This is strikingly expressed by one who seems in penning it to have had his own past experience in view: "But their understandings were hardened:[6] for until this day remaineth the same vail untaken away in the reading of the Old Testament; because it is done away in Christ.[7] But even unto this day, when Moses is read, a vail lieth upon their heart.[8] But what time it (their heart) turneth to the Lord, the vail is taken away."[9] (2 Cor. iii. 14-16.) *Christ*, says the apostle, being the key to the Old Testament Scriptures, it is impossible that a Christ-rejecting nation can understand them; for they read and hear them with a vail upon their heart: but so soon as their *heart* shall turn to the Lord, they will find the vail has disappeared, and the living oracles to be full of glory.

But the grand point is, how they now view JESUS OF NAZARETH. With their old contempt and horror, can we think, which, springing from a blinded and proudly obdurate heart, only deepened their religious infatuation, and aggravated their spiritual misery? Impossible. The renovation which has come over their whole inner man, and marvelously clarified their spiritual vision, cannot leave the glorious Object which fills all the field of that vision unaltered in its aspect. Accordingly, another feature of the change emerges in our prophecy.

3. *In Jesus of Nazareth beholding now a pierced Messiah, by their own wicked hands crucified and slain, their hearts break with bitter but generous grief.*

When He hung upon the Cross, they looked—and mocked: now, they "look and mourn." The Object is the same, but the look—O how different! That was a look of bitter derision: this is a look of bitter sorrow. To what is this inner revolution owing? To the effusion upon them, says the prophet, of the Spirit of grace and of supplications. And who that has tasted that the Lord is gracious—who that knows anything of Divine teaching, and supernatural renovation, and

---

6 *'Αλλ' ἐπωρώθη τὰ νοήματα αὐτῶν.*

7 *'Οτι* is better supported then the received reading, ὅ *τι*.

8 *Κάλυμμα ἐπὶ τὴν καρδίαν αὐτῶν κεῖται.*

9 *'Ηνίκα δ' ἂν ἐπιστρέψῃ πρὸς Κύριον, περιαιρεῖται τὸ κάλυμμα.*

a totally altered view of Christ from what he once took—can be at a loss to comprehend this predicted change upon a nation that will then feel its hands to be stained with blood-guiltiness of unparalleled dye? Very striking are the characteristics of this mourning, as here depicted.

It shall be *evangelical*: "They shall look upon Me, whom they pierced, and they shall mourn."

It shall be *generous*: "They shall mourn for HIM"—for their own sin, indeed, but chiefly in piercing *Him*.

It shall be exceeding *bitter*: "They shall mourn as for an only son, and for a first-born."

It shall be *universal*: "The land shall mourn"—"even all the families that remain."

It shall be *domestic*: "Every family apart."

It shall be *personal*: "Their wives apart."

What a mourning will that be! When first "He came unto His own, His own received Him not." But, "at the second time, Joseph shall be made known unto His brethren," amid the astonishment and the tears of those who had so cruelly entreated Him; "and the Egyptians and the house of Pharaoh shall hear the weeping."

But the most refreshing particular of this comprehensive prophecy has yet to be noticed.

4. *In the fountain of that blood, by them shed, they shall then be washed at once from the guilt and the stain of that and all their sins.*

"In that day"—of their looking on Him whom they pierced and mourning for Him—shall the fountain be opened. It was opened *economically from* the day when, after the shedding of it, the preaching of the Gospel began "with the Holy Ghost sent down from heaven;" and glorious was the result, as Israel came trooping into the infant Church, by thousands in a day—"the first-fruits unto God and to the Lamb." But, after all, the bulk of the nation "judged themselves unworthy of everlasting life." "All day long he stretched forth his hand to a disobedient and gainsaying people." So "the wrath came upon them to the uttermost," and *practically*, the fountain was shut to them. But in precisely the same sense shall it now be opened to them. What in reality was never shut—else how could there be "even at this present time a remnant according to the election of grace?"—shall be by them *found* to be open, begetting all the surprise of a new discovery. It shall be as though—when they hie them to it, with the new ideas and feelings that have sprung up in their minds and sweetly propelled them thither—it opened to them, like the gate of Peter's prison, of its own accord, or was opened expressly for them, as the Father's house for the returning prodigal. And they will find it free as opened; a *fountain* too—springing fresh and perennial. And it will be for "sin" and "uncleanness" both. The word "sin," when alone, stands usually for both the *condemning* and the *defiling* property of sin. But since here the "uncleanness" is distinguished from the "sin"—the sin of sins—the first term must be referred to its condemning, the second to its defiling character. Accordingly, *pardon* and *sanctification*, though distinguished in the New Testament, are both ascribed to the virtue of Christ's death, as sealed upon the believing heart by the Holy Ghost: "Such were some of you, but ye are *justified*, in the name of the Lord Jesus"—that is, by the virtue of His death—"and by the Spirit of our God"—by whose operation that virtue is carried home to the heart. (1 Cor. vi. 11.) So He "removes the iniquity of that land in one day." (Zech. iii. 9.) What land? The same, of course, of which it is said in our prophecy, "The *land* shall mourn."

Yes, the land and the people will now be for ever identified. "Then will I remember my covenant with Jacob, and also my covenant with Isaac, and also my covenant with Abraham will I remember; *and I will remember the land*." "Rejoice, O ye Gentiles, with his people, for . . . . he will be merciful unto his *land* and to his *people*." And in that day shall this song be sung in the land of Judah, "Lord, thou hast been favourable unto thy *land*; thou hast brought back the captivity of Jacob: thou hast forgiven the iniquity of thy *people*; thou hast covered all their sin: thou hast taken away all thy wrath; thou hast turned thyself from the fierceness of thine anger." "And in the day thou shalt say, O Lord, I will praise thee: though thou wast angry with me, thine anger is turned away, and thou hast comforted me. Behold, God is my salvation; I will trust, and not be afraid: for the Lord Jehovah is my strength and my song; he also is become my salvation." (Lev. xxvi. 42; Deut. xxxii. 43; Ps. lxxxv. 1-3; Isa. xii. 1, 2.)

"Upon the land of my people," said the prophet, "shall come up thorns and briers, ... *until the Spirit be poured upon* us from on high." But now that He hath poured upon the house of David, and upon the inhabitants of Jerusalem, the Spirit of grace and of supplications, "the wilderness has become as a fruitful field, ... and the work of righteousness is peace, and the effect of peace quietness and assurance for ever." "Neither will I hide my face any more from them: for I have poured out my Spirit upon the house of Israel, saith the Lord God." (Isa. xxxii. 13, 15, 17; Ezek. xxxix. 29.)

CHAPTER II

THE BEARINGS OF THE CONVERSION AND RESTORATION OF ISRAEL

I HAD intended to handle these in separate chapters; but this work has already reached its proposed limits, and there may be some advantage in compressing them, as I shall now do, into one chapter.

The most comprehensive and pregnant passage upon this head is the following (Rom. xi. 12, 15):—

"Now if the fall of them be the riches of the (Gentile) world, and the diminishing of them (or the reduction of the *true* Israel to so small a remnant as then believed) be the riches of the Gentiles; how much more their fulness (or full recovery)? . . . . For if the casting away of them be the reconciling of the (Gentile world, what shall the receiving of them be (to that Gentile world) but

LIFE FROM THE DEAD?"

The import of these remarkable words seems to be, (as I have expressed it at page 131,) that the reception of the whole family of Israel, scattered as they are among all nations under heaven, and the most inveterate enemies of the Lord Jesus, will be such a stupendous manifestation of the power of God upon the spirits of men, and of His glorious presence with the heralds of the Cross, as will not only kindle devout astonishment far and wide, but so change the dominant mode of thinking on all spiritual things, as to seem like a *resurrection from the dead.*) But in what respect?

I. *Men's faith in the Biblical History, and in the reality of religion, will then seem as "life from the dead."*

That even now there should exist a whole nation, lineally descended from him who four thousand years ago came out of Ur of the Chaldees, is astonishing enough; and truly, in a living Jew, seen in the light of his nation's past history, an intelligent eye may see a standing monument at once of miracle, prophecy, and retribution. "There are now Jews permanently resident at Madras"—says the late devoted Free Church missionary there, the Rev. Robert Johnston—

"and the Hindus generally know nothing about them. After our first conversions, some years ago, when the enmity of the heathen was greatly stirred up against us, and keen discussions were maintained on the rival claims of Christianity and Hinduism, two young Brahmans, hardly pushed in argument in connexion with the history of the Jews, boldly asserted that such a people never existed. It so happened that, about this time, two Jews, travelling from Bagdad to Calcutta, passed through Madras, and found their way to our Institution. This opportunity was not to be lost. We introduced the strangers to the assembled Hindus and Mohammedans, and told them that they would now have a full proof of the existence of the Jewish nation, whose sacred writings they were daily reading in the English language. The youths were all greatly excited, and every eye and ear was arrested. A *Hebrew Bible* was brought and put into the hands of one of the Jews, and he was requested to read part of the first chapter of Genesis, and to translate it; which he did into Hindustani, the language of the Mohammedans, and the only medium through which he could hold intercourse with us. A young Mohammedan then stood up beside the Jew, and turned the Jew's *Hindustani* into *English*. The assembled youths were filled with astonishment when they heard the Mohammedan give in *English* the facts with which they had been long familiar from their converse with the English Bible. The Brahmans were confounded; and the existence of the Jews was never again questioned in the Institution."[1]

Even children, to whom the Old Testament History has been faithfully taught, have it all brought up to them and almost vivified by the presence of a living Jew. Some years ago, an Israelitish minister of the Gospel of Christ was visiting an English gentleman, who carefully trained his children in Bible History. On introducing to his boy this friend of his, as "one of the children of Israel," the boy fixed his gaze upon him with unusual steadiness. "Why look you on me?" asked the Israelitish guest. "I want to ask you a question." "Do, my boy." "*I want to know how you felt when you were passing through the Red Sea*," was the astounding question. The whole story of the race that "went through the flood on foot" must have risen up in a moment before the mind's eye of that simple boy, at the sight of this Jewish stranger, whom he wanted, accordingly, to report to him the feelings of "the ransomed of the Lord" as they "passed over."

---

[1]The Conversion of the Jews; and its Bearing on the Conversion of the Gentiles. By the late Rev. Robert Johnston. With a Preface, by the Rev. John Braidwood—his equally-devoted brother missionary. Edinburgh, 1853.—The proof-sheets of this small pamphlet, the fruit of deep interest in Israel by a missionary to the Gentiles, were corrected by the lamented author on his deathbed.

Nor was this sinking of the whole intervening space of time, at the sight of this living representative of the race that did it, a mere childish conception. There is a principle in it, and I find it in the language of the prophet Hosea, as he sends back his people to the scenes of Bethel and Peniel. "By his strength he had power with God: yea, he had power over the angel, and prevailed: he wept, and made supplication unto him: He (the angel) found him (Jacob) in Bethel, and *there He spake with us*; even the Lord God of hosts; the Lord is his memorial." (Hos. xii. 3-5.) The one lonely traveller to whom the angel spake at Bethel had been dead and buried for nearly a thousand years before this was written. Yet "*there* He spake with *us*," says the prophet. In our progenitor's person at Bethel *we* lay on that stone pillow, and were cheered by the vision and animated by the promises of that night: at Peniel too we wrestled with the angel, and praying "Jacob" was transformed into prevailing "Israel." Thus would the prophet "turn the hearts of the fathers to the children," rousing in them by these ancestral recollections the slumbering spirit of their former selves. And truly, if they were not dead to generous impulses, this was the way to do it.

In their present miserable condition, the children of Jacob would seem inaccessible to such an appeal. No wonder then that the marvels of their ancient history and present existence make little impression upon the nations among whom they live and move. But how different will the effect be, if their whole religious and moral character shall be changed; if—from being the very embodiment of religions pride and self-complacency, of scornful and bitter hatred of that Name which is above every name, of a love and pursuit of this world proportioned to the misery they have endured in it—they shall become a nation of contrite and glowing followers of the Lord Jesus; if they shew a determination that *their* song to Him that loved them shall be the loudest of all, and their devotedness to Him that died for them and rose again shall be the most signal? Would not this arrest the attention and stir the heart of the most senseless that witnessed it, and would not scepticism itself be forced to exclaim, "Surely there is no enchantment against Jacob, neither is there any divination against Israel. The Lord his God is with him, and the shout of a king is among them. Let me die the death of the righteous, and let my last end be like his!"

II. *The triumphs of the Gospel thence accruing will be as "life from the dead."*

"O Jerusalem, Jerusalem, thou that killest the prophets, and stonest them that are sent unto thee, how often would I have gathered thy children together, even as a hen gathereth her chickens under her wings, and ye would not." (Matt. xxiii. 37.) Truth-hating, mercy-spurning, prophet-killing Jerusalem, how often would I have gathered even *thee!* But though they would not be gathered then, those blessed wings were yet again to be extended to Jerusalem, even after the blood of the Son of God was in its skirts; for while that darkest of all deeds was yet warm, their wounded Lord directed, ere He went up where He was before, "that repentance and remission of sins should be preached in his name among all nation, BEGINNING AT JERUSALEM." (Luke xxiv. 47.) And right faithfully was the commission executed, and thousands daily, melted by a grace which embraced its enemies, took shelter under that Wing, to their unspeakable safety and joy. But even this is not to be the most affecting exhibition to the world of mercy to the chief of sinners. When not thousands out of the murderous nation, but the nation itself, bowed down under the "bitter" discovery of their unparalleled blood-guiltiness, shall descry in the very blood which is in their skirts a fountain opened for their perfect cleansing, what a voice will this have to the Gentile world, to 'Jerusalem-sinners' all the world over, with guilt of deepest dye and hearts crushed under apprehensions of the wrath to come: 'Mercy for the chief of sinners! Come, all ye that fear God, and I will declare what he hath done for my soul! Flee, flee under that Wing, and though your sins be as scarlet, they shall be white as snow; though they be red like crimson, they shall be as wool!'

Very glorious will that voice be. Nor can we suppose that it will be the silent voice of the *facts* merely—the astounding impression which this revolution upon a nation's character and faith will make upon the world. No; even though there were no hints of such a thing given in Scripture—which there are—we could not doubt that, as when "they that were scattered abroad went everywhere preach the word," (Acts vii. 4, xi. 19, 20,) unable to keep to themselves what they knew was life to the world, so the word of the Lord will be a fire in the bones of multitudes of Israelites, on their coming forth from the fountain opened, with the joy of a new-found salvation, and a withered existence now blooming with life and beauty; and that, as they lift up their voice, with a glow of feeling peculiar to themselves, to declare what the lord hath done for their souls, it will thrill to the inmost soul of multitudes everywhere. For we have reason to believe that the same Spirit of grace and of supplications which caused Israel to look on Him whom they had pierced, and mourn for Him, will descend upon the Gentiles—to whom in turn they will now be preachers, and with the like effect—to send them to the fountain opened, and beautify them with salvation. Nothing less than this can be meant by that question, "What shall the receiving of them be but life from the dead? Even now, we observe that whenever the Spirit of God descends at once upon even a small number in any place, turning them notably from darkness unto light and from the power of Satan unto God, the impression is diffused, the work spreads, and a *revival*, more or less remarkable, is the result there. Such occurrences, on a large scale, extort the attention even of the unthinking world, and awe them into the secret conviction that earnest, vital religion is a mighty reality. We may be sure, then, that such an event as the fulfilment of Zechariah's prediction on "the whole house of Israel" will not merely arrest the world, and send a thrill of astonishment and awe through all its ranks, but carry spiritual life through the nations, diffusing joy and transport through the Church of God, and issuing in immense accessions to the ranks of living Christendom. I advert to but one more of the bearings of Israel's Conversion and Restoration.

III. *Men's confidence in the faithfulness of God will then be as "life from the dead."*

It is true that God's promises to his people are *conditional;* that is, they carry with them the supposition—expressed or understood—that they embrace those promises, repose on them, and carry them faithfully and consistently out. "We are made partakers of Christ, *if* we hold the beginning of our confidence steadfast unto the end." "The just shall live by faith; but *if* any man draw back, my soul shall have no pleasure in him." (Heb. iii. 14, x. 38.) But *these conditions are themselves secured.* "Whom he did predestinate, them he also called; and whom he called, them he also justified; and whom he justified, them he also glorified." (Rom. viii. 30.) In predestinating us to be conformed to the image of His Son in final glory, He settled all the successive steps of it.[2]

But what light will the Conversion and Restoration of Israel cast upon this truth? I answer that question by asking another:—Why does the apostle, in opening up the future destiny of his nation, say that all Israel must yet be saved? Because

"THE GIFTS AND THE CALLING OF GOD
ARE WITHOUT REPENTANCE." (Rom. xi. 29.)

Thus, the final inbringing of His ancient people will illustrate a great and glorious *law of the kingdom of God.* And, just in proportion to the depth of their past declension, the aggravated character of

[2]See "Commentary on Romans," (*ut supra,*) p. 89, and Note (1), p. 93.

their guilt, their prodigal distance from their Father's house, the virulence of their refusal to return, and the appalling length of their exclusion from the Divine favour, will be the revelation of unquenchable paternal affection in receiving them again, and rejoicing over them as the dead alive, the lost found! They will be a palpable, outstanding assurance to all the world that "God is *faithful*, by whom we are called unto the fellowship of His Son Jesus Christ our Lord," and that "neither death, nor life, nor angels, not principalities, nor powers, nor things present, nor things to come, nor height, nor depth, nor any other creature, shall be able to separate us from the love of God, which is in Christ Jesus our Lord." (1 Cor. i. 9; Rom. viii. 38, 39.)

These are but the more catholic bearings of Israel's Conversion and Restoration. But they carry others in their bosom, which it requires no great stretch of ingenuity to supply. (Suffice it here to hold up the *all-vivifying* effect of this great revolution upon the character and the faith of a whole nation—the nation, whose life of some four thousand years' duration, studded with Miracle and Prophecy, and Retribution, shall at length blaze forth with "*Mercy*, built up for ever, and *Faithfulness*, established in the very heavens!" While the spectacle cannot fail to penetrate and arouse all thinking Christendom, the active life, and quick intelligence, and ubiquitous movements of a nation proverbial for these qualities, now consecrated to higher ends, must make themselves felt everywhere, to the encouragement and the joy of all the children of God, and to the ingathering of multitudes to swell the ranks of the redeemed. And thus "the remnant of Jacob will be in the midst of many peoples (עַמִּים) as a dew from the Lord, as the showers upon the grass, which tarrieth not for man, nor waiteth for the sons of men." (Mich v. 7.)

"*O Israel, return unto the Lord thy God; for thou hast fallen by thine iniquity. Take with you words, and turn to the Lord: say unto Him, Take away all iniquity, and receive us graciously; so will we render the calves of our lips. Asshur shall not save us; we will not ride upon horses: neither will we say any more to the work of our hands, [Ye are] our gods; for in thee the fatherless findeth mercy. I will heal their backsliding, I will love them freely: for mine anger is turned away from him. I will be as the dew unto Israel: he shall grow as the lily, and strike his roots as Lebanon: his branches shall spread, and his beauty shall be as the olive tree, and his smell as Lebanon. They that dwell under his shadow shall return. They shall revive as the corn, and grow as the vine: the scent thereof shall be as the wine of Lebanon. Ephraim shall say, What have I to do any more with idols? I have heard him* (thus speak), *and observed him* (thus changed): *I am like a green fir tree,"* or *cypress*, for cool, refreshing shade:" *from me is thy fruit found. Who is wise, and he shall understand these things? prudent, and he shall know them? for the ways of the Lord are right, and the just shall walk in them; but the transgressors shall fall therein."* (Hos. xiv.)

THE END

Hal Lindsey should tell Bantam Books that he wants them to recall* The Road to Holocaust *because of its inaccurate portrayal of Christian Reconstruction and its assertions of "anti-Semitism."*

---

*Gary DeMar and Peter Leithart, *The Legacy of Hatred Continues: A Response to Hal Lindsey's The Road to Holocaust.* (Tyler, TX: Institute for Christian Economics, 1989), p. 18.

Appendix A

On the Dispensational Hermeneutic
by Steve Schlissel

The basic hermeneutical principle of the Dispensationalist (from which is derived their dogma that "Church" always and only means church, and "Israel" always and only means Israel) is, "If the plain sense makes common sense, seek no other sense." This has gotten them into no little trouble since they understand that to mean, "If there is any possible way that you can interpret something as being capable of a literal fulfillment, go for it." It has been pointed out by Berkhof (*Principles of Interpretation*, p. 85) "that in practice this becomes merely an appeal to every man's rational judgment." It has been pointed out by numerous other commentators that Dispensationalists sometimes apply this principle to ridiculous extremes, and sometimes fail to do it at all. They do not, for example, interpret Revelation 13 literally, about a literal beast rising from the sea. It is possible, is it not? Certainly as possible as the literal splitting of the Mount of Olives they anticipate, or the leveling of the earth (valleys exalted, mountains raised), and any number of other oddities.

Anthony Hoekema has pointed out what I have long regarded as the Achilles' heel, make that the whole leg, by which the Dispensational hermeneutic is clearly proved inadequate, viz., Ezekiel 40-48. "Extremely significant is the note on page 888 of the *New Scofield Bible* which suggests the following as possible interpretation of the sacrifices mentioned in these chapters of Ezekiel's prophecy: 'The reference to sacrifices is not to be taken literally, in view of the putting away of such offerings, but is rather to be regarded as a presentation of the worship of redeemed Israel, in her own land and in the millennial temple, using the terms with which the Jews were familiar in Ezekiel's day.' These words convey a far-reaching concession on the part of dispensationalists. If the sacrifices are not to be taken literally, why should we take the temple literally? It would seem that the Dispensational principle of the literal interpretation of Old Testament prophecy is here abandoned, and that a crucial foundation stone for the entire Dispensational system has here been set aside!" (*The Bible and the Future*, [Grand Rapids, MI: Eerdman's, 1979, reprinted 1984], p. 204). Bingo. I would only change the metaphor of "foundation stone" to "bottom card", for the dispensational system is actually a house of cards. So dependent is every postulate on every other, that the removal of *any one* means the downfall of the system. That is why the testimonies of what it was that led individuals out of dispensationalism (and most often, into the Reformed faith) are so diverse. One recognizes that the Church is, in fact, called Israel. Another notices that the Church was, in fact, prophesied in the Old Testament. Still another, that the Law of God, while not the basis of our justification, should not be spoken against as Dispies do. Still another cannot find a multitude of future physical resurrections taught in Scripture. At any of these or a hundred other points, the *entire system* collapses.

The crux of their hermeneutical problem, then, is this: Their bottom line, *common sense*, leaves it up to each individual's imagination, determining for himself what is to be taken literally or symbolically or metaphorically. A better hermeneutical principle, one which I believe is generally followed by Reformed folk, especially of the Puritan stock, is, *If the plain sense makes **Biblical** sense seek no other sense.* Thus the *Westminster Confession of Faith*: "The infallible rule of interpretation of Scripture is the Scripture itself: and therefore, when there is a question about the true and full sense of any Scripture..., it must be searched and known [not by the number of nations in a European confederacy; not by the number of letters in Ronald Wilson Reagan's name; not by rendering grasshoppers into helicopters in the mind's eye, but—SMS] by other places that speak more clearly." (I:ix). Again, in a Confession that is too little called upon today, *The Second Helvetic Confession* (penned by Zwingli's successor, the saintly Henry Bullinger), we find the same principle: "We hold that interpretation of Scripture to be orthodox and genuine which is gleaned from the Scriptures themselves (from the nature of the language in which they were written, likewise according to the circumstances in which they were set down, and expounded in the light of like and unlike passages and of many and clearer passages) and which agree with the rule of faith and love..." *The Second Helvetic* (i.e., Swiss) *Confession* "was adopted, or at least highly approved, by nearly all the Reformed Churches on the Continent and in England and Scotland" (Schaff) This led Charles Hodge to observe that it may "be regarded as the most authoritative symbol of the Reformed Church." It also discusses other hermeneutical principles (mostly by way of rejection of errors, however) more fully than other Reformed symbols. Of the many books which have been written demonstrating from Scripture the hermeneutical and exegetical errors of Dispensationalism, *Prophecy and the Church*, by O.T. Allis (Presbyterian and Reformed, recently reprinted) remains the best.

Appendix B

On Church and Synagogue
by Steve Schlissel

Perhaps a more intriguing question than the relation of Church and Israel is that of Church and Synagogue. The Church is the synagogue founded by Jesus Christ. Consider that in John 9 we learn that "if any man did confess that He was the Christ, he should be put out of the synagogue." This was the Jewish form of excommunication. It cut that person off from the nation of Israel, separated him from social and business intercourse, and excluded him from synagogue worship (though not the temple). Now notice that when Christ asks Peter, "Who say ye that I am?" (Matt. 16), Peter's answer, "Thou art the Messiah, the Son of the Living God," becomes the rock upon which Christ will build His church. That is, the very confession that resulted in excommunication from the unbelieving synagogue was the confession upon which admission to the church (Christ's synagogue) was predicated. "The Christian Church was thus to come in the place of the synagogue; and the privileges conferred upon St. Peter, and afterwards upon all the disciples [apostles], were those which belonged to the scribes. They were the authorized interpreters of the oral and traditionary laws which had been superinduced upon the law of Moses [the apostles revoked the former and established the latter in Christ. See 1 Peter 1:18 and Romans 3:31—SMS]; and in this capacity they were held by the Jews to possess the key of the kingdom of heaven."

The power thus exercised by the scribes was known to the Jews as that of binding and loosing...It was the mode by which they expressed their decision as to what was prohibited and what was permitted by the traditionary law of the elders (the expression occurs in this sense constantly in the Talmud). These powers are now conferred upon St. Peter: 'I will give unto the the keys of the kingdom of heaven: and whatsoever thou shalt bind on earth shall be bound in heaven; and whatsoever thou shalt loose on earth shall be loosed in heaven." The same power of binding and loosing was extended to all the apostles after the transfiguration...On this occasion, too, we find the church taking the place of the synagogue...(We read) in the Book of Leviticus (19:17), 'Thou shalt not hate thy brother in thine heart: thou shalt in any wise rebuke thy neighbor, and not suffer sin upon him.' Their rule was that any one against whom a sin had been committed must 'deliver his soul by reproving his brother;' and if he could not bring him back to the right way, he must reprove him before witnesses, so that they might testify that he against whom the sin was committed used due reproof, the witnesses also adding their friendly admonition; and if the offender hearkened not unto them, then they made proclamation concerning him in the synagogues for four Sabbaths. Jesus here directs the same procedure to be adopted, only substituting the church for the synagogue: 'If thy brother sin against thee, go and tell him his fault between thee and him alone: if he shall hear thee, thou hast gained thy brother. But if he will not hear thee, then take with thee one or two more, that in the mouth of two or three witnesses every word may be established. And if he shall neglect to hear them, tell it to the church." (G. Bickell and W.F. Skene, *The Lord's Supper and the Passover Ritual* [Edinburgh, T&T Clark, 1891], pp. 12ff).

There are other conspicuous similarities between the synagogue and the church, all contributing to the understanding of the local church as the replacement of the synagogue (e.g., synagogues could be established in communities of 120 Jews (compare Acts 1:15); there were officers to minister to the poor, and teachers in each congregation (Titus 1:5; Phil. 1:1; Acts 6:1-7—careful consideration of the last passage will show that the seven were most likely chosen to be *Elders* rather than deacons); the very order of worship in the Christian church is intimately connected with that of the synagogue. Thus, the synagogue finds its Christian fulfillment in the church while the temple finds its fulfillment in Christ in heaven (and His body indwelt by Him on earth). The only things that remain of the old economy, then, are the people and the land. There relation to each other, to the church and to God's plan form the important subjects of Dr. Brown's book.

While we're on the subject of the synagogue model for the Church, let me add that I believe we stand to benefit greatly by a study of the place and functioning of the synagogue as it is found among the Jews today. It is here we find the nerve center of the covenant community idea which *ought* to characterize the Church. Among the Jews it works something like this: Two key traditions make it imperative for Jews to live in community. They are, 1) the prohibition of travel on the Sabbath (beyond the limits of a Sabbath day's journey—see Acts 1:12), and 2) the required minimum of ten men to constitute a worship service. Add to these the requirement to corporately worship each morning, and the normativity of marriage & large families, and you can see where I'm headed. In order for

Jews to be Jews, *they must live in community*. The orthodox Jews in New York City do not move into a neighborhood in depotentized drips and drabs. They move *en masse*. And they have revitalized more than one dying neighborhood as a result. Antinomian, anti-covenantal mission has zero hope of reaching the urban centers for Christ. Instead of attempting to "fulfill" Christ's prayed-for unity (John 17) by focusing on a *universal* ecumenical expression of some watered down version of Christianity, we ought to concentrate on building confessionally *unified* communities in urban centers. I have seen the impact of the Jews, *and they don't even have a Great Commission*. I have also seen the "impact" of Christians who do. No comparison. The pastors of Zurich, seeking to urge a reluctant Calvin back to Geneva, wrote, "You know that Geneva lies on the confines of France, of Italy, and of Germany, and that there is great hope that the Gospel may spread from it to the neighboring cities, and thus enlarge the ramparts (*les boulevards*) of the kingdom of Christ.—You know that the Apostle selected metropolitan cities for his preaching centres, that the Gospel might spread throughout the surrounding towns." (cited in T.M. Lindsay, *History of the Reformation* [T&T Clark, reprinted 1951], Vol.II, p.126) This is sound mission strategy, a strategy I believe to be impossible of implementation, unless we learn a lesson or two from the synagogue.

Appendix C

Eschatology and Work
by Rousas J. Rushdoony

In 18th century colonial America, George Whitefield, while in New Jersey, dined with a number of American clergymen. We are told that,

> After dinner, in the course of an easy and pleasant conversation, Mr. Whitefield adverted to the difficulties attending the gospel ministry arising from the small success with which their labours were crowned. He greatly lamented that all their zeal-activity and fervour availed but little; said that he was weary with the burdens and fatigues of the day; declared his great consolation was that in a short time his work would be done, when he should depart and be with Christ; that the prospect of a speedy deliverance had supported his spirits, of that he should before now have sunk under his labour. He then appealed to the ministers around him, if it were not their great comfort that they should soon go to rest. They generally assented, excepting Mr. Tennent (The Rev. William Tennent, Jr.), who sat next to Mr. Whitefield in silence; and by his countenance discovered but little pleasure in the conversation. On which Mr. Whitefield, turning to him and tapping him on the knee, said, "Well! brother Tennent, you are the oldest man amongst us, do you not rejoice to think that your time is so near at hand, when you will be called home and freed from all the difficulties attending this chequered scene?" Mr. T. bluntly answered, "I have no wish about it." Mr. W. pressed him again; and Mr. T. again answered, "NO, SIR, IT IS NO PLEASURE TO ME AT ALL, AND IF YOU KNEW YOUR DUTY IT WOULD BE NONE TO YOU. I HAVE NOTHING TO DO WITH DEATH: MY BUSINESS IS TO LIVE AS LONG AS I CAN—AND TO SERVE MY LORD AND MASTER AS FAITHFULLY AS I CAN, UNTIL HE SHALL THINK PROPER TO CALL ME HOME." Mr. W. still urged for an explicit answer to his question, in case the time of death were left to his own choice. Mr. Tennent replied, "I have no choice about it; I am God's servant, and have engaged to do his business as long as he pleases to continue me therein. But no, brother, let me ask you a question. What do you think I would say if I was to send my man Tom into the field and find him lounging under a tree, and complaining, 'Master, the sun is very hot, and the ploughing hard and difficult; I am tired and weary of the work you have appointed me, and am overdone with the heat and burden of the day; do, master, let me return home and be discharged from this hard service.' WHAT WOULD I SAY? WHY, THAT HE WAS AN IDLE, LAZY FELLOW; THAT IT WAS HIS BUSINESS TO DO THE WORK THAT I HAVE APPOINTED HIM, UNTIL I,THE PROPER JUDGE, SHOULD THINK FIT TO CALL HIM HOME. Or suppose you had hired a man to serve you faithfully for a GIVEN TIME in a particular service, and he should, without any reason on your part, and before he had performed half his service, become weary of it, and upon every occasion be expressing a

> wish to be discharged or placed in other circumstances. WOULD YOU NOT CALL HIM A WICKED AND SLOTHFUL SERVANT, AND UNWORTHY OF THE PRIVILEGES OF YOUR EMPLOY? "The mild, pleasant, and Christian-like manner in which this reproof was administered, rather increased the social harmony and edifying conversation of the company, who became satisfied that it was very possible to err, even in desiring with undue earnestness to "depart and be with Christ," which in itself is "far better," than to remain in this imperfect estate; and that it is the duty of the Christian in this respect to say, "All the days of my appointed time will I wait till my change come"[1]

This was the Biblical and Puritan temper. Murray has shown the importance of this temper to the Puritan achievement, adding,

> The opportunity of honouring Christ by fulfilling our present duties is a priceless privilege and those who thus serve him will not be found waiting at his Coming. 'Blessed is that servant, whom his Lord when he cometh shall find so doing.'[2]

This belief that God has an important work for man to do, and that man must do it, was coupled with a belief that, what God has done for us, He can do for others. The present belief is increasingly a humanistic faith in the power of a scientific elite who alone can save man, if men will recognize their lack of expertise and submit to the experts. Certain races and classes are held to need this government if they are to advance. The Christian view is opposed to this, and it was manifested in the FORM OF AGREEMENT of the Baptist missionaries, Puritan in temper and faith, who met at Serampore early in their missionary advance into India and declared,

> He who raised the Scottish and brutalised Britons to sit in heavenly places in Christ Jesus, can raise these slaves of superstition, purify their hearts by faith, and make them worshippers of the one God in spirit and in truth. The promises are fully sufficient to remove our doubts, and make us anticipate that not very distant period when he will famish all the gods of India, and cause these very idolators to cast their idols to the moles and to the bats, and renounce for ever the work of their own hands.[3]

Such missionaries clearly believed that by God's grace the were superior, and it was their desire to give that same superiority of grace to all men. As their homeland, once given to savagery, had been transformed by God's grace, so every people, tribe, and tongue could and would be transformed, because God has so declared it in His word.

---

[1]Archibald Alexander, *The Log College* (London: Banner of Truth Trust, [1851] 1968), p. 25f, emphasis added.

[2]Iain Murray, *The Puritan Hope* (London: Banner of Truth Trust, 1971), p. 219.

[3]*Ibid.*, p. 153.

A.A. Hodge of Princeton, who in his early years served as a missionary in India, saw the missionary effort hamstrung by premillennialism and wrote:

> Millenarian missionaries have a style of their own. Their theory affects their word in the way of making them seek exclusively, or chiefly, to conversion of individual souls. The true and efficient missionary method is, to aim directly, indeed, at soul winning, but at the same time to plant Christian institutions in heathen lands, which will, in time, develop according to the genius of the nationalities. English missionaries can never hope to convert the world directly by units.[4]

Under the influence of the new premillennialism, "the Church was regarded as an institution without a future."[5] NOT WORK BUT WAITING was the new emphasis, waiting for the rapture, for premillennialists, and waiting grimly for the tribulation and end, for amillennialists.

Two other factors reinforced the retreat occasioned by false eschatology. FIRST, pietism saw life in essentially emotional and personal terms, and as a preparation for heaven. Work was seen as a chore, an aspect of the curse, not a way of dominion, and the goal of man was seen as an eternal vacation with the Lord. Pietism produced a shallow life, intellectually and vocationally. The test of faith was made an emotional experience, and, not surprisingly, women began to predominate in both Catholic and Protestant circles: religion became a woman's affair, and the men in it were full of pietism and low on manhood. Pietism exalted the nothing people, pious poops who reduced the faith to pious gush and, for almost two centuries, have bedeviled the godly clergy with their sinful, sanctimonious ways. The nothing people avoid open acts of sin, not because they love and fear God but because they are timid souls who love and fear people and dare not offend them. In their hands, virtue ceased to be associated with dominion and strength and came to be associated with weakness and fear.

SECOND, the doctrine of evolution strengthened the humanism of false eschatologies and pietism. Man could now make himself by controlling his own evolution. A new philosophy of work resulted, work as a means of evolving a new man, a new society, and a new world. For Scripture, work was God's ordained means of dominion in Eden. After the Fall, a curse was laid on man's work insofar as he is fallen; to the degree that redeemed man is sanctified, to that degree his work again results in godly dominion.

---

[4]*Ibid.*, p. 205.

[5]*Idem.*

The 20th Century has seen the failure of humanistic man to usher in a new paradise by means of his work, and the result is a flight from work and a lust for retirement, for vacations, and for escape from the world of work. Humanism thus has a false philosophy of work and rest. Its claims ape those of God, to renew man and the world; it is a desperate evil, though fair of face, because its hope is, that out of evil good may come. It believes that sinful man can change himself and the world and vindicate his revolution against God.

A central fallacy of premillennial and amillennial views is the common assumption that the Fall somehow frustrated God's original purpose as set forth in Eden. But God is never frustrated, nor can He be. To believe this is to be a humanist, and humanism, wherever it is, must be strangled, because it assumes that man's way can prevail over God's Way.

God's purpose was not frustrated by the Fall but was manifested therein. All things are aspects of God's predestination and purpose, and nothing can be understood in terms of itself or the moment, but only in terms of God. The salvation of man is not the ultimate purpose of God, although a part of His declared purpose, but the manifestation of His glory and purpose in and through man.

The Fall thus advanced God's purpose. Weeds (Gen. 3: 18) frustrate man, but they replenish the earth and prevent man from destroying it. The empires of old, the communists of today, the ungodly men of science, and others, all believe that they frustrate God and mock Him, but their every effort only advances God's purpose and His glory. Their wealth and achievements will be garnered by His Kingdom. In Isaiah 60:3, 5, 11 and Isaiah 66:12, as well as elsewhere, we are assured of this. Of God's Kingdom, we are told that "the kings of the earth do bring their glory and honour into it" (Rev. 21: 24). Communism is an evil; we must oppose and wage war against its presence in our midst. Humanism is an evil: we must do battle against it on all fronts. We must remember, however, that their coming and their going will only further God's purpose and enrich God's Kingdom, because NOTHING HAPPENS THAT WILL NOT FURTHER GOD'S KINGDOM AND THE GLORY ULTIMATELY OF HIS PEOPLE IN HIM AND TO HIS PURPOSE.

"Therefore, my beloved brethren, be ye steadfast, unmoveable, always abounding in the work of the Lord, forasmuch as ye know that your labour is not in vain in the Lord" (Cor. 15: 58).

The world's doctrine of rest is a flight from work. Vacationing means a restless quest for entertainment and preoccupation to avoid the claims of work. Work gives no dominion in the world of humanism, and vacationing is and attempt to escape from the fact of frustration and castration. Man without dominion, is a eunuch, and humanistic man, lacking true dominion, runs from work into a frenetic sexuality, trying to prove a false potency, because he knows in his heart he is an impotent man insofar as true dominion is concerned.

For the man of God , rest is a privilege as is work. He RESTS because he has the assurance that the infallible and omnipotent God has assured him of victory, and that his labour is never in vain in the Lord. The man of God rests in the pride and joy of dominion, in delight in the God who makes ALL things work together for good to them that love Him, to them who are the called according to His purpose (Rom. 8: 28).

Retirement is a modern principle, the secular counterpart of the idea of a rapture. It is a surrender of manhood and of life. As long as a man is able, he NEEDS to work, and he NEEDS to rest. The rapture and retirement are falsely premised and mean a surrender; they treat a retreat from dominion as a privilege rather than a tragedy or grief. Postmillennialism gives us a theology of work and rest, and an eschatology of victory.

Scene at the printing house during the Reformation.
(*The History of Protestantism* by J.A. Wylie 1:1, Page 288)

There's an old rule of politics: "You can't fight something with nothing." If you're really serious about getting answers to your questions, then you're going to have to do some reading. No; you're going to have to do a lot of reading. More reading than you ever thought you could invest in an "extra-curricular" project. You may have to work on this project for years, depending on how fast you read, how much you remember, and how detailed you want your answers.

If you aren't willing to read, and read extensively, then you're not serious about Jesus Christ. You're not serious about your responsibilities before God. You're a milk-drinking Christian (1 Corinthians 3:2)*

***Gary North, 75 *Bible Questions Your Instructors Pray You Won't Ask* (Tyler, TX: Spurgeon Press, 1984), p. 279.**

Further Study Section

Most of the following items are what could be considered some of the finest in Christian scholarship from our own and past ages. It should go without saying, but we should note, that we do not endorse everything that is stated in the following recommended items. We do believe that each and every one of the sources have made their contributions with the intent of glorifying God. But, as with our Reformation forefathers, we must "shout from the rooftops" that the inspired and infallible word of God alone *(sola Scriptura)* is our standard. Thus we reject what are merely the ideas of men. At the same time we acknowledge and recognize God's hand in providing teachers for the edification of His body, praising Him for those works which will (and have) endured the test of time and will ultimately endure the fiery test to come (1 Cor. 3:9-15).

Publisher's Note

Newsletters & Magazines

Organizations included here do not necessarily agree with all the ideas and conclusions contained in this publication. When you contact these groups, please mention that you read about them in *Hal Lindsey and the Restoration of the Jews* published by Still Waters Revival Books. Anyone wishing to submit their publication or tapes (preaching, music or video) for review and possible inclusion in future listings should send samples to the first address below.

CHRISTIAN RECONSTRUCTION TODAY & REVIVAL REVIEW
(Dept. J) 12810-126 St.
Edmonton, AB. T5L 0Y1

MESSIAH'S MANDATE
Steve Schlissel
2662 East 24th Street
Brooklyn, NY. 11235

THE TEACHING HOME
P.O. Box 20219
Portland, OR. 97220-0219

THE COUNSEL OF CHALCEDON
P.O. Box 888022
Dunwoody, GA. 30356

ANTITHESIS
4521 Campus Dr., Suite 435
Irvine, CA. 92715

THE BIBLICAL WORLDVIEW
P.O. Box 720515
Atlanta, GA. 30328

BLUMENFELD EDUCATION LETTER
P.O. Box 45161
Boise, ID. 83711

HOME LIFE, HELP: THE FAMILY LIFE TOOLBOX
P.O. Box 1250
Fenton, MO. 63026

THE TRINITY FOUNDATION
P.O. Box 169
Jefferson, MD. 21755

INSTITUTE FOR CHRISTIAN ECONOMICS
P.O. Box 8000
Tyler, TX. 75711

CHALCEDON REPORT
P.O. Box 158
Vallecito, CA. 95251

RECONSTRUCTION MAGAZINE
3032 Hacienda Ct.
Marietta, GA. 30066

BIBLICAL FOUNDATIONS
P.O. Box 297
Veradale, WA. 99037

CARIBBEAN CHRISTIAN MINISTRIES
1113 S. Cypress Rd. Suite 100
Pompano Beach, FL. 33060

THE AMERICAN REFORMATION MOVEMENT
P.O. Box 85152 MB 138
San Diego, CA. 92138

MEDIA ALLIANCE
Dr. D. James Kennedy
Coral Ridge Ministries
P.O. Box 1
Ft. Lauderdale, FL 33302-0001

RUSSIAN REFORMATION FOUNDATION
P.O. Box 17966
Boulder, CO. 80308-7966

THE CHRISTIAN OBSERVER
9400 Fairview Ave.
Manassas, VA. 22110

THE BIAS REPORT
Rt. 1 Box 57
Mott, ND. 78646

JOURNEY
1021 Federal St.
Lynchburg, VA. 24504

THE CHRISTIAN HERITAGE PARTY OF CANADA
P.O. Box 22009, St. "B"
Vancouver, B.C. V6A 3Y2

NATIONAL COVENANTING PACKET
26580 Evergreen Road
Southfield, MI. 48076

FIRE ON THE MOUNTAIN
P.O. Box 143
Cedar Bluff, VA. 24609

CERCOS
P.O. Box 5834
Pretoria 0001,
Republic of South Africa

FOUNDATION FOR CHRISTIAN RECONSTRUCTION
P.O. Box 1
Whitby, North Yorkshire YO21 1HP
England

SIGNPOSTS
P.O. Box 26148
Arcadia 0007 South Africa

Cassette Libraries

BASILEIANS
1319 Newport Gap Pike
Wilmington, DE
19804-2895

MOUNT OLIVE TAPE LIBRARY
P.O. Box 422
Mt. Olive, MS 39119

REFORMATION TAPE LIBRARY
12810-126 St.
Edmonton, AB T5L 0Y1

MESSIAH'S TAPE RACK
c/o Messiah's CRC
2662 East 24th Streeet
Brooklyn, NY 11235

SPECIALTY MEDIA SERVICES
P.O. Box 28357
Atlanta, GA 30357

COVENANT TAPE MINISTRY
24198 Ash Court
Auburn, CA 95603

Books & Cassettes

Calvinistic Soteriology

Adams, J. *Decisional Regeneration*. Canton, Georgia: Free Grace Publ., 1983.
Boettner, Loraine. *The Reformed Doctrine of Predestination*. Phillipsburg, New Jersey: The Presbyterian and Reformed Publ. Co., 1932.
Clark, Gordon. *Biblical Predestination*. Nutley, NJ: Presbyterian and Reformed, 1969.
Luther, Martin. *The Bondage of the Will*. Grand Rapids, Michigan: Baker Book House, (1525) 1976.
McFetridge, N.S. *Calvinism in History*. Edmonton, Alberta: Still Waters Revival Books, (1882) 1989.
Murray, Iain. *The Forgotten Spurgeon*. Edinburgh, Scotland: The Banner of Truth Trust, (1966) 1978.
Murray, Iain. *The Invitation System*. Edinburgh, Scotland: The Banner of Truth Trust, 1984.
Ness, Christopher. *An Antidote Against Arminianism*. Edmonton, Alberta: Still Waters Revival Books, (1700) 1988.
Owen, John. *A Display of Arminianism*. Edmonton, Alberta: Still Waters Revival Books, (1642) 1989.
Owen, John. *The Death of Death in the Death of Christ*. Edinburgh, Scotland: The Banner of Truth Trust, reprinted 1959.
Pink, Arthur, *The Sovereignty of God*. Grand Rapids, Michigan: Baker Book House, (1930) 1986.
Spurgeon, Charles. *Spurgeon's Sovereign Grace Sermons*. Edmonton, Alberta: Still Waters Revival Books, 1990.
Talbot, Ken and Crampton, Gary. *Calvinism, Hyper-Calvinism and Arminianism*. Edmonton, Alberta: Still Waters Revival Books, March 1990.

Covenant Theology

Campbell, Roderick. *Israel and the New Covenant*. Philadelphia, Pennsylvania: The Westminster Press, 1954.
Fisher, Edward (with Thomas Boston's notes), *The Marrow of Modern Divinity*. Edmonton, Alberta: Still Waters Revival Books, (1853) forthcoming.
Murray, John. *The Covenant of Grace*. Phillipsburg, NJ: Presbyterian and Reformed Publ. Co., (1953) 1988.
Neilands, David. *Studies in the Covenant of Grace*. Phillipsburg, NJ: Presbyterian and Reformed Publ. Co., (1980).
Robertson, O. Palmer. *The Christ of the Covenants*. Grand Rapids, Michigan: Baker Book House, 1980.
Spencer, Duane. *Holy Baptism: Word Keys Which Unlock the Covenant*. Tyler, TX: Geneva Ministries, 1984.
Sutton, Ray. *That You May Prosper: Dominion By Covenant*. Tyler, TX: Institute for Christian Economics, 1987.

Presuppositional Apologetics

Bahnsen vs. Sproul — *Apologetics Debate* on cassette (2 cassette set).
Clark, Gordon, *Three Types of Religious Philosophy*. Jefferson, Maryland: The Trinity Foundation, 1989.
Clark-Hoover *Debate on Apologetics* (2 cassette set).
Morecraft, Joseph. *Biblical Presuppositionalism* (Basileian cassette lectures).
North, Gary, ed. *Foundations of Christian Scholarship*. Vallecito, CA: Ross House Books, 1979.

Pratt, Richard. *Every Thought Captive*. Phillipsburg. NJ: Presbyterian and Reformed Publ. Co., 1979.
Rushdoony, R. J. *By What Standard?* Tyler, TX: Thoburn Press, 1983.
Talbot, Ken and Gary Crampton. *For This Reason: An Introduction to Biblical Apologetics*. Edmonton, Alberta: Still Waters Revival Books, forthcoming.
Talbot, Ken. *An Introduction to Biblical Philosophy*. (7 cassette set—Reformation Tape Library).
Van Til, Cornelius. *The Defense of the Faith*. Phillipsburg, NJ: Presbyterian and Reformed Publ. Co., 1955.
Van Til, Cornelius. *Modern Theology*. (6 cassette set).

Postmillennialism

Allis, Oswald T. *Prophecy and the Church*. Phillipsburg, NJ: Presbyterian and Reformed Publ. Co., 1945.
Bahnsen, Greg. *Exegesis of the Book of Revelation* on cassettes.
Boettner, Loraine. *The Millennium*. Phillipsburg, NJ: Presbyterian and Reformed Publ. Co., (1957) 1986.
Brown, David. *Christ's Second Coming: Will it be Premillennial?* Edmonton, AB: Still Waters Revival Books, (1882, 7th edition) 1990.
Canfield, Joseph. *The Incredible Scofield and His Book*. Vallecito, CA: Ross House Books, 1988.
Chilton, David. *The Days of Vengeance: An Exposition of the Book of Revelation*. Ft. Worth, TX: Dominion Press, 1987.
Chilton, David. *Paradise Restored*. Tyler, TX: Reconstruction Press, 1984.
Crenshaw, Curtis and Grover Gunn. *Dispensationalism Today, Yesterday and Tomorrow*. Memphis, TN: Footstool Publications, 1985.
Davis, John. *Christ's Victorious Kingdom: Postmillennialism Reconsidered*. Grand Rapids, MI: Baker Book House, 1986.
DeMar, Gary. *The Legacy of Hatred Continues: A Response to Hal Lindsey's The Road to Holocaust*. Tyler, TX: Institute for Christian Economics, 1989.
Gentry, Ken. *The Beast of Revelation*. Tyler, TX: Institute for Christian Economics, 1989.
Gentry, Ken. *Before Jerusalem Fell: Dating the Book of Revelation*. Tyler, TX: Institute for Christian Economics, 1989.
Gentry, Ken. *Eschatology* (Basileian cassette lectures—5 cassette set).
Hodge, A.A. *Evangelical Theology*. Edinburgh, Scotland: The Banner of Truth Trust, 1976, Chapter 12-14.
Hulse, Erroll. *The Restoration of Israel*. Worthing, Sussex: Henry E. Walter Ltd. 1968.
Kik, Marcellus. *An Eschatology of Victory*. Phillipsburg, NJ: Presbyterian and Reformed Publ. Co., 1971.
Lee, Francis Nigel. *Eschatology of Victory*. (Mt. Olive Tape Library).
Morecraft, Joseph. *The Evangelization of the World*. (Mt. Olive Tape Library).
Moore, T.V. *A Commentary on Haggai, Zechariah and Malachi*. Edinburgh, Scotland: The Banner of Truth Trust, 1960.
Murray, Iain. *The Puritan Hope: Revival and the Interpretation of Prophecy*. Edinburgh, Scotland: The Banner of Truth Trust, 1971.
North, Gary, ed. *The Journal of Christian Reconstruction: Symposium on the Millennium*. Vallecito, CA: Chalcedon, Winter, 1976-77, Vol. III, No. 2.
Rushdoony, R. J. *The Meaning of Post Millennialism: God's Plan for Victory*. Fairfax, VA: Thoburn Press, 1980.

Commentaries explaining Romans 11 include those by David Brown, John Murray, Charles Hodge, W.G.T. Shedd and Robert Haldane.

Theonomic Ethics

Bahnsen, Greg L. *By This Standard: The Authority of God's Law Today*. Tyler, TX: Institute for Christian Economics, 1985.

Bahnsen, Greg L. *Theonomy in Christian Ethics*. Phillipsburg, NJ: Presbyterian and Reformed Publ. Co., (1977) 1984.

Bahnsen, Greg L. *Theonomy and its Critics*. (6 cassettes—Covenant Tape Min.).

Bahnsen, Greg L. *Theonomic Approach to Ethics*. (6 cassettes—CTM).

Bahnsen, Greg L. *Theonomic Thesis Presented to Dispensational Pluralists*. (6 cassettes—Covenant Tape Ministry).

Bolton, Samuel. *The True Bounds of Christian Freedom*. Edinburgh, Scotland: The Banner of Truth Trust, (1645) 1978.

Brutus, Junius. *A Defense of Liberty Against Tyrants*. Edmonton, AB: Still Waters Revival Books, (1689) 1989.

Kickasola, Joseph. *Law and Society: A Basic Course in Theonomy*. (Mt. Olive).

North, Gary, ed. *The Journal of Christian Reconstruction: Symposium on Biblical Law*. Vallecito, CA: Chalcedon Foundation, Winter, 1975-76, Vol. II, No. 2.

North, Gary. *Tools of Dominion: The Case Laws of Exodus*. Tyler, TX: Institute for Christian Economics, 1990.

Rushdoony, R. J. *The Institutes of Biblical Law*. Nutley, NJ: Craig Press, 1973.

Rushdoony, R. J. *Law and Society (Volume 2 of the Institutes of Biblical Law)*. Vallecito, California: Ross House Books 1982.

The Westminster Confession of Faith & Creeds

Clark, Gordon. *What Do Presbyterians Believe?* Phillipsburg, NJ: Presbyterian and Reformed Publ. Co., (1956) 1989.

Gentry, Ken, *The Usefulness of Creeds*. Maudlin, SC: Good Birth Publ., 1980.

Hodge, A.A. *The Confession of Faith*. Edinburgh, Scotland: Banner of Truth, (1869) 1983.

Numerous Authors. *Westminster Confession of Faith*. Glasgow, Scotland: Free Presbyterian Publications, (1646) 1983.

Rushdoony, R. J. *The Foundations of Social Order: Studies in the Creeds and Councils of the Early Church*. Fairfax, Virginia: Thoburn Press, 1978.

Shaw, Robert. *An Exposition of the Confession of Faith*. Lochcarron, Ross-shire: Christian Focus Publications, (1845) 1980.

Smith, Egbert W. *The Creed of the Presbyterians*. Toronto, Ontario: Poole-Stewart Ltd., 1901.

Smith, William. *What is Calvinism? or the Confession of Faith in Harmony with the Bible and Common Sense*. Edmonton, Alberta: Still Waters Revival Books, (1908) forthcoming.

Vincent, Thomas. *The Shorter Catechism Explained from Scripture*. Edinburgh, Scotland: The Banner of Truth Trust, (1674) 1984.

Williamson, G.I. *The Shorter Catechism: For Study Classes*. Phillipsburg, NJ: Presbyterian and Reformed Publ. Co., 1970.

Williamson, G.I. *The Westminster Confession of Faith: For Study Classes*. Phillipsburg, NJ: Presbyterian and Reformed Publ. Co., 1964.

General (Reformed/Reconstructionist)

Bahnsen, Greg and Ken Gentry. *House Divided: The Breakup of Dispensational Theology*. Tyler, TX: Institute for Christian Economics, 1989.

Beza, Theodore, among others (translation and notes). *The Geneva Bible: The Annotated New Testament*. New York, NY: The Pilgrim Press, (1602) 1989.

Bogue, Carl. *The Scriptural Law of Worship*. Dallas, TX: Presbyterian Heritage Publications, 1988.

Brown, David. *The Four Gospels*. Edinburgh, Scotland: The Banner of Truth Trust, (1864) 1976.
Calvin, John. *Institutes of the Christian Religion*. Philadelphia, Pennsylvania: The Westminster Press, (1559) 1960.
Clark, Gordon. *God's Hammer: The Bible and Its Critics*. Jefferson, Maryland: The Trinity Foundation, 1982.
Clark, Gordon. *Religion, Reason and Revelation*. Jefferson, Maryland: The Trinity Foundation, 1986.
Crampton, Gary. *The Bible: God's Word*. Lynchburg, VA: Journey Publications.
Cunningham, William. *Historical Theology*. Edinburgh, Scotland: Banner of Truth, (1862) 1979.
Dabney, Robert L. *Lectures in Systematic Theology*. Edinburgh, Scotland: Banner of Truth, (1878) 1988.
DeMar, Gary. *The Debate Over Christian Reconstruction*. Fort Worth, Texas: Dominion Press, 1988.
DeMar, Gary. *God and Government*. Atlanta, GA: American Vision Press, 1984.
DeMar, Gary and Peter Leithart. *The Reduction of Christianity: A Biblical Response to Dave Hunt*. Ft. Worth, TX: Dominion Press, 1988.
DeMar, Gary. *Ruler of the Nations: Biblical Principles for Government*. Ft. Worth, TX: Dominion Press, 1987.
Duncan, Mark, *The Five Points of Christian Reconstruction from the Lips of Our Lord*. Edmonton, AB: Still Waters Revival Books, 1990.
Gentry, Ken. *Light for the World: Studies in Reformed Thought*. Edmonton, Alberta: Still Waters Revival Books, forthcoming.
Grant, George. *The Changing of the Guard: Biblical Principles for Political Action*. Ft. Worth, TX: Dominion Press, 1987.
Grant, George. *In the Shadow of Plenty: Biblical Principles of Welfare and Poverty*. Ft. Worth, TX: Dominion Press, 1986.
Grant, George. Basileian lectures on *Cultural Involvement* (5 cassette set).
Groothuis, Douglas. *Unmasking the New Age*. Intervarsity Press, 1968.
Kuyper, A. *Lectures on Calvinism*. Grand Rapids, MI: Eerdmans, (1898) 1987.
Lachman, David. *The Marrow Controversy 1718-1723: An Historical and Theological Analysis*. Edinburgh, Scotland: Rutherford House Books, 1988.
M'Crie, Thomas. *The Statement of the Difference* (on Church & State, Liberty of Conscience etc.). Edinburgh, Scotland: C.F. Lyon, 1871.
M'Crie, Thomas. *The Unity of the Church*. Dallas, TX: Presbyterian Heritage Publications, (1821) 1989.
Merle d'Aubigne, J.H. *The Reformation in England*. Edinburgh, Scotland: Banner of Truth, (1853) 1977.
North, Gary. *Backward Christian Soldiers: An Action Manual for Christian Reconstruction*. Tyler, TX: Institute for Christian Economics, 1984.
North, Gary. *Dominion & Common Grace: The Biblical Basis of Progress*. Ft. Worth, TX: Dominion Press, 1987.
North, Gary. *Political Polytheism: The Myth of Pluralism*. Tyler, TX: Institute for Christian Economics, 1989.
North, Gary, ed. *Tactics of Christian Resistance* (Christianity & Civilization 3). Tyler, TX: Geneva Divinity School Press, 1983.
North, Gary, ed. *The Theology of Christian Resistance* (Christianity & Civilization 2). Tyler, TX: Geneva Divinity School Press, 1983.
North, Gary. *75 Bible Questions Your Instructors Pray You Won't Ask*. Tyler, Texas: Spurgeon Press, 1984.
Otis, John. *The Distinctives of Biblical Presbyterianism*. no publisher listed, 1985.
Reed, Kevin. *Biblical Church Government*. Dallas, TX: Presbyterian Heritage Publications, 1983.

Reformation Covenant Church. *Christian Reconstruction: A Call for Reformation and Revival.* Beaverton, OR: RCC, 1988.
Rushdoony, R. J. *Christianity and the State.* Vallecito, CA: Ross House, 1986.
Rushdoony, R. J. *The Flight From Humanity: A Study of the Effect of Neoplatonism on Christianity.* Fairfax, VA: Thoburn Press, 1978.
Rushdoony, R. J. *Politics of Guilt and Pity.* Fairfax, VA: Thoburn Press, 1978.
Rutherford, Samuel. *Lex, Rex, or The Law and the Prince.* Harrisonburg, Virginia: Sprinkle Publications, (1644) 1982.
Schlissel, Steve. *Television and Dominion.* Edmonton, Alberta: Still Waters Revival Books, forthcoming.
Schlossberg, Herbert. *Idols for Destruction: Christian Faith and its Confrontation with American Society.* Nashville, TN: Thomas Nelson, 1983.
Smith, Gary, ed. *God and Politics: Four Views on the Reformation of Civil Government.* Phillipsburg, NJ: Presbyterian and Reformed Publ. Co., 1989.
Symington, William. *Messiah the Prince or The Mediatorial Dominion of Jesus Christ.* Edmonton, Alberta: Still Waters Revival Books, (1884 edition) 1990.
Terry, Milton. *Biblical Hermeneutics.* Grand Rapids. MI: Zondervan, n.d.
Van Til, Henry. *The Calvinistic Concept of Culture.* Phillipsburg, NJ: Presbyterian and Reformed Publ. Co., 1959.
Walker, James. *The Theology and Theologians of Scotland 1560-1750.* Edinburgh, Scotland: Knox Press, (1888) 1982.
Wilkins, Steve. *America: The First 350 Years.*(16 cassette set—from Covenant Publications, 224 Auburn Avenue, Monroe, LA 71201).
Wylie, James Aitken. *The History of Protestantism.* Co. Down, N. Ireland: Mourne Missionary Trust, (1878) 1990.

Schooling and Education

Clarke, Gordon. *A Christian Philosophy of Education.* Jefferson, Maryland: Trinity Foundation, (1946) 1988.
Clark, Suzanne. *Blackboard Blackmail.* Memphis, TN: Footstool Publ., 1988.
Gamble, David. *Christian Education vs. Secular Education.* (Mt. Olive Tapes).
Gentry, Ken. *The Case for Christian Schooling.* Maudlin, SC: Good Birth Publications, 1980.
Harris, Greg. *The Christian Home School.* Brentwood, TN: Wolgemuth & Hyatt, Publishers, Inc., 1988.
North, Gary, ed. *The Journal of Christian Reconstruction: Symposium on Education.* Vallecito, CA: Chalcedon , Summer, 1977, Vol. IV, No. 1.
Otis, John. *The Necessity for the Christian School.* no publisher listed, 1984.
Rushdoony, R.J. *The Messianic Character of American Education.* Phillipsburg, NJ: Presbyterian and Reformed Publ. Co., 1963.
Talbot, Ken and Gary Crampton. *The Education of a Covenant Child.* Edmonton, Alberta: Still Waters Revival Books, forthcoming.
Thoburn, Robert. *The Children Trap—Biblical Principles for Education.* Ft. Worth, Texas: Dominion Press, 1986.

The Family

DiLella, Fred. *The Family: A Biblical View.* Edmonton, Alberta: Still Waters Revival Books, forthcoming.
Dobson, James. *A Winnable War: Fighting Pornography.* (2 cassette set).
Grant, George. *Trial and Error: The American Civil Liberties Union and Its Impact on Your Family.* Brentwood, TN: Wolgemuth & Hyatt, 1989.
Grant, George. *Grand Illusions: The Legacy of Planned Parenthood.* Brentwood, TN: Wolgemuth & Hyatt.

Lockman, Vic. *The Catechism for Young Children with Cartoons*. P.O. Box 1916, Ramona, CA. 92065.
Lockman, Vic. *The Family: A Biblical Catechism* (tract), see above.
Merle d'Aubigne, J.H. *Family Worship: Motives and Directions for Domestic Piety*. Dallas, TX: Presbyterian Heritage Publications, (1827) 1989.
Palmer, B.M. and J.W. Alexander. *The Family*. Harrisonburg, VA: Sprinkle Publications, (1876, 1847) 1981.
Pride, Mary. *All the Way Home: Power for your Family to be its Best.* Westchester, IL: Crossway Books, 1989.
Pride, Mary. *The New Big Book of Home Learning*. Westchester, IL: Crossway Books, 1988.
Pride, Mary. *The Way Home: Beyond Feminism Back to Reality*. Westchester, IL: Crossway Books, 1985.
Provan, C. *The Bible and Birth Control.* Monogahela, PA: Zimmer Printing, 1989.
Ray, Bruce. *Withhold Not Correction*. Phillipsburg, NJ: Presbyterian and Reformed Publ. Co., 1978.
Ryle J.C. *The Duties of Parents*. Choteau, MT: Chr. Heritage Publ. (1888) 1983.
Sutton, Ray. *Who Owns the Family?—God or the State?* Fort Worth, Texas: Dominion Press, 1986.

MUSIC

Rogers, Judy. *Go to the Ant*. (write: P.O. Box 888442 Atlanta, GA 30338).
Rogers, Judy & Craig Pitman. *Pilgrim's Praise*.
Rogers, Judy. *Walkin' Wise*.
Rogers, Judy. *Why Can't I see God.*
RPCNA Board of Education and Publication. *The Book of Psalms for Singing*. Pittsburgh, Pennsylvania: Crown and Covenant Publications, 1973.
Morecraft, Becky. *Amazing Grace & Hymns of the Church Victorious.* (write: 4488 Mountain Creek Dr., Roswell, GA 30075).

VIDEO

Grant, George. *Charity that Works: Any Church Can*. (Fort Worth, Texas: Dominion Press).
Grant, George with Gary North. *Planned Parenthood: Your Tax Dollars at Work.* (Fort Worth, Texas: Dominion Press).
Hunt, Dave & Tommy Ice vs. Gary North & Gary DeMar (Debate). *Christian Reconstruction: A Deviant Theology?* (Fort Worth, Texas: Dominion Press).
Schlossberg, Herbert. *Idolatry in America*. (Fort Worth, Texas: Dominion Press).
Talbot, Kenneth. *Christian and Home Education Conference*. (contact Still Waters Revival Books for more information).
Thoburn, Robert with Gary North. *No Limits to Dominion: Practical Christianity in Action*. (Fort Worth, Texas: Dominion Press).
Rushdoony, R. J. with the Chalcedon Scholars. A 16 video series ranging from *Education* to *Eschatology* (contact Chalcedon Report from newsletter section).

Those interested in supporting a pioneering work in the area of educational video and a video seminary should contact Whitefield Theological Seminary (ROJ) at P.O. Box 6321, Lakeland, FL 33807.

Turn off the Godless television and movies and pursue peace and righteousness... this further study section is a good place to start.

"...and the gates of hell shall not prevail..."

Send a self addressed stamped envelope to:

Still Waters Revival Books
12810-126 St. (Suite B)
Edmonton, AB Canada
T5L 0Y1

We will send you a set of free sample newsletters and a current list of our publications.

For if thou wert cut out of the olive tree which is wild by nature, and wert grafted contrary to nature into a good olive tree: how much more shall these, which be the natural branches, be grafted into their own olive tree? For I would not, brethren, that ye should be ignorant of this mystery, lest ye should be wise in your own conceits; that blindness in part is happened to Israel, until the fulness of the Gentiles be come in. And so all Israel shall be saved: as it is written, There shall come out of Sion the Deliverer, and shall turn away ungodliness from Jacob: For this is my covenant unto them, when I shall take away their sins.

(Romans 11:24-27)